Maximizing the
VALUE *of*
CONSULTING

Maximizing the
VALUE *of*
CONSULTING

A GUIDE for **INTERNAL** and **EXTERNAL CONSULTANTS**

JACK J. PHILLIPS

WILLIAM D. TROTTER

PATRICIA PULLIAM PHILLIPS

WILEY

Published by John Wiley & Sons, Inc., Hoboken, New Jersey
Published simultaneously in Canada

For general information about our other products and services, please contact our Customer Care Department within the United States at (800) 762-2974, outside the United States at (317) 572-3993 or fax (317) 572-4002.

Wiley publishes in a variety of print and electronic formats and by print-on-demand. Some material included with standard print versions of this book may not be included in e-books or in print-on-demand. If this book refers to media such as a CD or DVD that is not included in the version you purchased, you may download this material at http://booksupport.wiley.com. For more information about Wiley products, visit www.wiley.com.

Library of Congress Cataloging-in-Publication Data

Phillips, Jack J., 1945-
  Maximizing the value of consulting : a guide for internal and external consultants / Jack J. Phillips, William Trotter, and Patricia Pulliam Phillips.
     pages cm
  Includes index.
   ISBN 978-1-118-92340-5 (hardback)
  1. Consultants. 2. Consulting firms—Management. I. Trotter, William Dow. II. Phillips, Patricia Pulliam. III. Title.
   HD69.C6P4695 2015
   001—dc23

                                                                    2015008310

Printed in the United States of America

10 9 8 7 6 5 4 3 2 1

From Jack and Patti:

To all the great consultants we have met, who are adding value to their clients

From Bill:

To the great network of internal and external consultants in the Association of Internal Management Consultants (AIMC)

Contents

About the Authors

Jack J. Phillips, PhD

Jack J. Phillips, PhD, is a world-renowned expert on accountability, measurement, and evaluation. Phillips provides consulting services for Fortune 500 companies and major global organizations. The author or editor of more than 75 books, he conducts workshops and presents at conferences throughout the world.

Phillips has received several awards for his books and work. On three occasions, *Meeting News* named him one of the 25 Most Powerful People in the Meetings and Events Industry, based on his work on ROI. The Society for Human Resource Management presented him an award for one of his books and honored a Phillips ROI study with its highest award for creativity. The American Society for Training & Development gave him its highest award, Distinguished Contribution to Workplace Learning and Development for his work on ROI. His work has been featured in the *Wall Street Journal*, *BusinessWeek*, and *Fortune* magazine. He has been interviewed by several television programs, including CNN. Phillips served as president of the International Society for Performance Improvement from 2012 to 2013.

His expertise in measurement and evaluation is based on more than 27 years of corporate experience in the aerospace, textile, metals, construction materials, and banking industries. Phillips has served as training and development manager at two Fortune 500 firms, as senior human resource officer at two firms, as president of a regional bank, and as management professor at a major state university.

This background led Phillips to develop the ROI Methodology—a revolutionary process that provides bottom-line figures and accountability for all types of learning, performance improvement, human resources, technology, and public policy programs.

Phillips regularly consults with clients in manufacturing, service, and government organizations in 60 countries in North and South America, Europe, Africa, Australia, and Asia.

Phillips has undergraduate degrees in electrical engineering, physics, and mathematics; a master's degree in decision sciences from Georgia State University; and a PhD in human resource management from the University of Alabama. He has served on the boards of several private businesses—including two NASDAQ companies—and several nonprofits and associations, including the American Society for Training & Development and the National Management Association. He is chairman of the ROI Institute, and can be reached at 205-678-8101, or by e-mail at jack@roiinstitute.net.

Patti P. Phillips, PhD

Patti Phillips, PhD, is president and CEO of the ROI Institute, the leading source of ROI competency building, implementation support, networking, and research. A renowned expert in measurement and evaluation, she helps organizations implement the ROI methodology in 60 countries around the world.

Since 1997, following a 13-year career in the electric utility industry, Phillips has embraced the ROI methodology by committing herself to ongoing research and practice. To this end, she has implemented ROI in private sector, public sector organizations, and nongovernmental organizations. She has authored or edited more than 30 books.

Phillips teaches others to implement the ROI methodology through the ROI certification process, as a facilitator for ATD's Measuring ROI and Evaluating Learning Workshops, and as professor of practice for The University of Southern Mississippi Gulf Coast Campus PhD in Human Capital Development program. She also serves as adjunct faculty for the UN System Staff College in Turin, Italy, where she teaches the ROI methodology through their Evaluation and Impact Assessment Workshop and Measurement for Results-Based Management. Phillips serves on the board of the Center for Talent Reporting and as principal research fellow for The Conference Board's Human Capital Analytics Practice. She serves on numerous doctoral dissertation committees, assisting students as they develop their own research on measurement, evaluation, and ROI.

Phillips's academic accomplishments include a PhD in international development and a master's degree in public and private management. She is certified in ROI evaluation and has been awarded the designations of Certified Professional in Learning and Performance and Certified Performance Technologist. She can be reached at patti@roiinstitute.net.

William D. Trotter, PhD

William Dow Trotter, PhD, is an internationally recognized expert in the areas of strategic planning, process and organizational transformation, and creating high-impact internal consulting capabilities.

His career has spanned more than 40 years, including holding executive positions in major corporations and a leading management consulting firm. Key areas of focus included strategy development and execution, enterprise process reengineering, and cross-organizational performance measurement and management.

Dr. Trotter has also taught postgraduate programs at leading universities and conducted seminars on related subjects around the world. His academic endeavors also involved serving as the Director of the Institute for Global Business Strategy, which included a worldwide network of thought leaders in academic institutions and research organizations.

He is currently managing director of the Association of Internal Management Consultants (AIMC) and president of Trotter Consulting International.

The AIMC consists of a powerful network of consulting professionals and provides linkages to leading businesses and public sector organizations. The association has developed an extensive knowledge base of methodologies and best practices to help realize success in the internal consulting field—and also provides training to increase skills and achieve professional certification. Its membership also includes external consultants who work closely with internals on a partnering basis.

Dr. Trotter has also led joint benchmarking studies with other associations to study the increasing need for internal consulting capabilities in a variety of functional areas, including human resources and quality management—with new initiatives in other areas in progress.

He has also authored numerous books, articles, and research papers in the areas of strategic planning, process reengineering, performance measurement, and global business development—including his most recent book, *Internal Consulting Excellence*, which was a predecessor of this book and included the results of a global survey of more than 1,000 organizations on current practices and key success factors.

Finally, Dr. Trotter is currently providing consulting services to both private and public sector organizations seeking to either establish or further develop and enhance their internal consulting capabilities.

Acknowledgments

We want to thank the many organizations who have allowed us to provide consulting services. Consulting is a principal activity in the ROI Institute, and we are fortunate to provide our services to some of the most admired and most impressive organizations in the world. From the business side, we have been fortunate to work with over half of the Fortune 500 List of Companies. We work with 25 different national governments, hundreds of nongovernmental organizations, including the United Nations, countless nonprofit organizations, colleges and universities, charitable trusts and foundations, and health-care organizations, providing a rich background of experiences for this book.

We are fortunate to have contact with literally thousands of individuals as we provide consulting services. These clients have allowed us to assist them and, in many cases, we learned with them. So the dedication of this book is to those clients who have embraced our processes, added to our experience base, and helped to generate hundreds of published case studies.

We are very pleased to work with Bill Trotter on this important work. Bill has an outstanding reputation and keen insight into the internal consulting world. As executive director of AIMC, Bill knows this field, and knows the value that consulting can deliver. We are pleased and honored to be connected with him and this important contribution to consulting, both internal and external.

Closer to home, we want to thank the ROI Institute team for their efforts as they support us in our publishing endeavors. We particularly appreciate Hope Nicholas, director of publications, who provided editorial coordination and management support for this book. Hope is an important and valuable member of our organization, as she has done an outstanding job of editing, coordinating, and delivering this manuscript. We appreciate her efforts and we enjoy working with her.

—Jack and Patti Phillips

I would like to thank the many members of the Association of Internal Management Consultants (AIMC) for their contribution in helping to develop the extensive body of knowledge on internal consulting best practices and their partnering arrangements with the numerous external consultants with whom they work.

Over the past 40 years, this association has led the way in developing operational models, competency frameworks, performance measurement programs and other methodologies, tools and techniques to establish and enhance professional-level internal groups and maximize the effectiveness of their total consulting spend.

The AIMC's continual knowledge sharing process through its international network of local chapters, periodic Affinity Group calls, annual conference and various publications has provided great input into both this publication and its predecessor, *Internal Consulting Excellence*,[1] which included a benchmarking study of more than 1,000 organizations.

In addition, our joint benchmarking studies with other associations on the emerging need for internal consulting skills in a variety of functional areas across the enterprise has also contributed to our continuing research. This includes collaboration on research regarding the need for internal consulting skills for the future quality professional and on the evolving business partner role in human resources.

Considerable input has also been gathered from the AIMC's board of directors and executive advisory board.

Finally, I have been fortunate to learn a lot from the numerous clients for whom I have provided consulting services to help them establish or further develop their internal consulting practices across a broad spectrum of industries and consulting practice areas.

—Bill Trotter

Preface

The Dilemma

The consulting field is facing a dilemma. It is one of the most attractive occupations in the professional jobs category. Internal consultants have high levels of engagement and acceptance in their companies. External consultants have the pleasure of seeing the value-add of their services in all types of organizations. However, according to a recent benchmarking survey, internals don't think they have enough training in key areas. Also, externals are often viewed as outsiders, and their projects seem poorly implemented due to a lack of ownership transfer to their clients. It does not have to be this way. This mutual frustration is sometimes associated with consulting not delivering the promised value. This is easily corrected. This book addresses the issue of maximizing the value of the consulting investment, which is achieved in four major ways. First, this book ensures that consulting is initiated, managed, and delivered with value in mind always—early, often, and as part of the follow-up. Second, it focuses on managing the consulting investment, ensuring that consulting is an efficient process and delivers high ROI. Third, this book shows you how to monitor and report the success of consulting as an entire function, or as an entire organization for external consulting. Finally, it shows you how to deliver value in a project, showing how any consulting project can be measured all the way through to the impact and the financial ROI. This relentless focus on value is the major advantage of this book.

The Foundation

This publication represents a follow-on work to Dr. Trotter's previous book, *Internal Consulting Excellence*[1], which provided an overview of the research and learnings from his collaboration with the Association of Internal Management Consultants (AIMC). One of the key learnings during his affiliation with this network of internal consulting leaders around the world was the importance of clearly demonstrating their value to the enterprise. This led to discussions with Dr. Jack Phillips and Dr. Patti Phillips of the ROI Institute on incorporating their comprehensive methodology into a jointly authored book focusing on enhancing the value of internal consulting through the development and deployment of a comprehensive performance measurement system.

For two decades the ROI Institute has provided consulting services, now in over 60 countries through 41 partners. In addition, the ROI Institute teaches consultants, both external and internal, methods of delivering business value and measuring success. As part of this, they have built their own consulting network with the ROI Institute and have developed several publications to support consulting, including a best seller from McGraw-Hill, *How to Build a Successful Consulting Practice.*[2]

William Trotter brings many years of consulting experience, primarily focused on internal consulting. Bill is the managing director of the Association of Internal Management Consultants. He brings a wealth of experience on how to make consulting successful, effective, and efficient. Through AIMC, Bill works with internal consultants (and numerous external consultants with whom they partner) all over the world to help them become more effective at what they do. This new book combines the best thinking of the ROI Institute and AIMC.

This book is not about how to start a consulting business, market consulting services, or address the legal issues of consulting—many other books do that already. This book is about delivering value from consulting and maximizing the value for the client. But delivering value is more than just measuring the outcomes and ROI, it is about organizing your consulting practice internally and/or externally to deliver value. Projects should begin with the end in mind with clear business connections. Individuals involved in the project must focus on business contribution throughout the process. And yes, at the end, there should be a clear connection between consulting and a business contribution up to and including the financial ROI.

The Flow

The book starts off with early chapters describing the opportunity for consulting, how the field has evolved, how it has grown, some of the key challenges, and issues. This clearly shows the importance of consulting as an integral and permanent part of organizational landscapes. Next, the book begins the journey of maximizing the value, by focusing on how the value is delivered through-out the process—from the beginning of the project to the end. The book explores how the function of consulting and the external consulting practice is managed with value in mind, with value expressed as efficient, effective, and even the financial ROI. The book then moves into capturing the value of the entire function, representing the macro view of the consulting process. This shows how to report results to senior executives, so they can see collectively how well consulting is working, the value it is adding to the organization, and how it connects to critical issues and business outcomes. Finally, a major part of the book shows how to measure the impact and ROI of consulting projects. Using the ROI methodology, the most used and documented evaluation system in the world, this book takes those who are ready step-by-step through the process and shows how to make it work, how to produce the results, and use the results. Finally, this book caps off with a chapter focusing on how to report results to the proper audience and use that data to drive improvement in the future.

For those providing consulting services within their company or public sector organization and external consultants who want to work effectively with clients, this book provides highly practical insights into how to maximize the value of their work and capitalize on future opportunities. All of the material provided here is based on proven best practices from both internal and external consulting organizations.

The Role and Importance of Internal and External Consulting

The beginning point of the journey described in this book is to reflect on the role and importance of consulting, from both the internal and external perspectives. At the same time, it is helpful to review the practices, changing expectations, and new requirements for these important areas. Finally, a snapshot into emerging trends and key success factors make this chapter a fitting introduction to this new book.

Trends in Internal and External Consulting

Both internal and external consulting have grown recently, and their importance continues to emerge. There is a natural evolution that makes consulting a logical solution for many situations. Also, there are a number of forces that have come together to make consulting a great choice for organizations and also as an occupation. While the drivers for growth in internal and external consulting have much overlap, some unique issues are emerging.

Emergence of Internal Consulting

The rapid rate of change coupled with heightened competition on a global basis is increasing the need for companies and public sector organizations to develop effective internal consulting capabilities. The development of this capability helps to better control overall consulting expenditures and obtain greater value for this investment. Internal consulting groups can support the development of key capabilities across the organization essential for future success in areas, such as strategic planning, project management, change leadership, and process improvement.

There are various areas across the organization that are realizing the importance of increasing their internal consulting skills to effectively provide services to their internal clients and developing more of a "business partner" role:

- One overall observation is that there is a new business model evolving regarding the emergence of more formalized and structured internal consulting service and their relationship with the external consulting resources with which the organization engages.

- The need to unlock the value potential of the total cadre of advisory resources spread across the organization is another key driver in the development of more formalized internal consulting capabilities. For example, most functions in an organization have a few internal consultants.

- Organizations are attempting to reduce staffing levels to keep their total employee count very low. This is driven by the desire to be efficient, and the employees on the payroll represent a fixed cost that can be very significant. Reduced staffing leads to opportunities for internal consultants to provide specialized assistance.

- Organizations and the work accomplished within are becoming more complex. This means that managers need help with a variety of work-related issues and processes.

- The continuing growth of globalization and fast pace of change requires specialized assistance with rules, regulations, culture, and change issues, creating opportunities for internal consultants.

- Outsourcing and shifting of transactional activities have created more opportunities for internal consultants. For example, in the human resources function, many of the activities are transactional (e.g., benefits administration, payroll administration) and they have been shifted to other functions such as finance and accounting. Other functions have been outsourced (e.g., help desks, training delivery). This leaves the HR function with a few generalists, often labeled HR advisors or consultants.

It is clear that internal consulting is not only a critical occupation in an organization, but one that is growing and adding tremendous value. From all indications, internal consulting will continue to grow and flourish and add value in all types of organizations.

The Growth of External Consulting

Consulting clearly is a growing occupation, at least among small consulting businesses. The following trends underscore its tremendous growth:

- In the United States, baby boomers are moving into their early retirement years. Many of them are seeking new challenges away from the bureaucratic structure of traditional organizations. Wanting to use their expertise and experience in a profitable way, they see consulting as a rewarding and natural next career.

- Shareholders of organizations increasingly demand more efficiency, profitability, and growth from organizations. This trend requires management to examine processes and work flow to ensure that organizations are the best that they can be. This, in turn, creates opportunities for external consultants who can assist in this important goal.

- Demanding customers are changing the dynamics of customer service. Organizations are constantly under pressure to provide the fastest, most reliable, and friendliest customer service. Consultants provide assistance in this vital area.

- Executives often require external validation of particular processes, products, performance areas, and outputs. External validation leads to the need for external consultants.

- Globally, there are many opportunities for consultancies as emerging nations eagerly seek to become more modern, up-to-date, and efficient in their processes.

- Demographic shifts in all countries are creating changes in market demands, creating opportunities for those who understand these issues and can help organizations meet these particular needs.

- The constant flow of fads in and out of organizations creates opportunities for consultants to help organizations address these trends and attempt to make them work in their organization. Some executives constantly seek the newest methods and employ consultants to help implement them.

- Executives sometimes prefer to use outsiders rather than rely on the input and advice of their own staff. They feel that the independence of the external viewpoint is important.

- In an attempt to become streamlined and efficient, some organizations outsource major parts of their work, creating opportunities for consultants. Often, these consultants come from the ranks of their previous employees.

- Executives and managers often have unpleasant tasks, processes, and issues to address. They prefer to use external consultants who are viewed as dispensable and can be quickly removed after the dirty work has been done.

- Finally, organizations, desperate to survive, seek all types of assistance and support to improve their situations. This creates many opportunities for consultants.

These trends and others create growth for the consulting industry. Depending on which estimates are used, the figures range from a growth of 15 to 25 percent per year for this profession. At the same time, the actual growth of large consulting practices is not as strong.

Opportunities for Collaboration

A key consideration for external consultants to develop their business in the long term is to explore ways to effectively partner with internal consulting groups and other internal support areas growing into that role. An increasing number of external consultants, from large organizations to sole proprietorships, are realizing significant opportunities to expand their business by working with internal consulting groups and other internals in that role. These partnering opportunities consist of various arrangements, including the following:

- Training on key skills and emerging methodologies
- Supplementing their expertise and research capabilities
- Providing additional resources for joint project activity
- Taking on projects for which the internals don't have the capacity or expertise

The important issue is that internal and external consultants are vital to an organization. Both groups are growing, and they must collaborate, as they can learn from each other.

Key Benefits of Building an Internal Consulting Practice

There are numerous benefits to the organization for developing internal consulting groups. Internal consultants perform a key role in identifying, prioritizing, and aligning strategic initiatives by participating in client planning sessions across the organization and helping to identify projects that will have maximum impact on overall performance going forward.

Internal consultants play a major role in facilitating proper implementation and continuous improvement by working with client teams throughout the project, helping to transfer ownership, and transferring needed skills for ongoing execution. Additionally, internals play an important role in building overall organizational capabilities by training and coaching clients participating in key initiatives and maintaining associated networks of expertise.

Effectively managing total consulting spend involves both controlling the overall cost of these services and helping to ensure the maximum benefit for that investment. This includes ensuring the necessary transfer of technology and methodologies to properly train the organization going forward.

Changing Role of Internal Support Functions

Internal support functions in a variety of areas of the organization are increasingly realizing the need to enhance their consulting skills in order to ensure their long-term viability and better service their clients. In a number of these areas, a new organizational structure is evolving to help improve the focus on the need to work more closely with clients and better understand their requirements. In this new structure, one area of the group is often organized to perform the basic operations of the function, sometimes referred to as functional Centers of Excellence (CoEs), while the other area is organized around the major business areas being served as liaison groups to gear services to their needs and act in an advisory type of role. For example, in a human resources department, this would mean that one subgroup in this functional area would be devoted to each of their key operational services, such as benefits, compensation, and staffing, while the other would be aligned with key client groups to work jointly with them in areas such as human capital planning, meeting their specific current and future HR support needs, and addressing issues that might arise in a liaison-type role.

Another example of the many support areas that are in a similar position is information technology (IT). Here, in addition to a number of subgroups providing operational systems development and data processing services, there is an increasing emphasis on developing client interface groups, focusing on providing consulting services to various areas of the organization to help their needs in the areas of technology planning, business case development, process redesign, and project portfolio management. These client interface groups require the same internal consulting skills, as the core internal consulting group. In addition, in many cases, members of the internal consulting group partner with their IT representatives to conduct needs analysis, redesign work processes before new systems requirements are developed, and form/facilitate associated work teams. A best practice approach in this situation is for the internal consulting professional from the core group to mentor their IT counterpart(s) in these areas and have them assume increasing responsibility for the work and deliverables as they gain experience.

Key Practice Areas and Projects

Many consulting groups have found that the development of a broad portfolio of service offerings helps to improve their overall effectiveness by enabling them to become involved in more key projects/initiatives across the organization and play a larger role in these projects. In addition, consultants are increasingly becoming involved in providing external research and benchmarking services to keep with industry trends and increase their knowledge of best practice approaches on a cross-industry basis. This capability helps them to be more proactive in identifying emerging issues and improvement opportunities. The development of a formalized best practice benchmarking project and associated knowledge base helps the internal consultants drive a greater external focus across the organization.

Internal consulting groups generally provide the same portfolio of services as those provided by external consulting practices. The six broad areas of practice are common:

1. Strategic/business planning
2. Process and operational improvement
3. Change management

4. Organization effectiveness

5. Compliance and risk management

6. Performance measurement and management

Strategic/Business Planning

The strategic/business planning area involves working with leadership in various areas of the organization to help develop and implement their strategic plans and major initiatives. This often includes utilizing methodologies such as the following:

- Visioning workshops
- Business model reframing
- Strength, weakness, opportunity, and threat (SWOT) analysis
- Brainstorming (including critical thinking and creativity exercises)

There has also been a renewed emphasis on team-based planning initiatives where internal and external consultants can add great value in helping to structure and facilitate the project to more fully engage the organization and create a broader buy-in to future plans.

Process and Operational Improvement

The process and operational improvement area involves working with various segments of the organization to redesign and streamline both core and support processes; eliminate waste, delay, and redundancy; and improve the effectiveness of product and service delivery. This often includes such methodologies as the following:

- Business process improvement
- Responsibility charting
- Network reengineering (including external vendor and partner linkages)
- Lean Six Sigma analyses
- Project management practices
- Activity-based costing

In this area, the internal consultants can add considerable value in addition to their expertise by engaging client groups in opportunity analysis and transferring key skills to help ensure more effective implementation.

Change Management

The change management area involves developing and facilitating projects to modify the organizational structure and associated management processes as external conditions and internal priorities change—in addition to increasing the capability of the organization to effectively deal with these changes. This often includes methodologies such as the following:

- Organization change
- Overcoming resistance and building resilience
- Implementation management
- Innovation management
- Culture change

By developing these change management capabilities in the client groups with which they relate, consultants are helping the overall organization function more effectively.

Organizational Effectiveness

Many organizations have an organizational effectiveness function designed to make the organization more efficient and effective, usually from a total organizational viewpoint. The organizational effectiveness group could be located in operations, engineering, IT, or human resources. Sometimes there is a business redesign process attempting to redesign processes to meet shifting customer patterns, technological advances, and evolving regulatory environments, for example. Sometimes even the term *organizational architecture* is used as these consultants design new divisions, departments, or entire companies from the ground up, considering all of the different elements to make a very successful and profitable business. This may also involve the analytics groups that have been created recently with particular emphasis in marketing, logistics, operations, and IT. Recently, this has moved to the human capital area as well. This includes the projects aimed at reinvention for organization or improvement; reinventing so that it can change, adjust, adapt, grow, and become more efficient and effective. Finally, transformational projects that aim at transforming an organization may be housed in this group. This has become an important component where some internal consultants operate and external consultants are engaged.

Compliance and Risk Management

Being out of compliance and having too much risk exposure can be disastrous for an organization. With this in mind, organizations constantly focus on projects and activities aimed at keeping the organization in compliance to ensure that preventive measures are in place so that out-of-compliance situations do not evolve. Also, this involves interpretation of regulations to ensure that the organization can comply with regulations. Consultants provide input to adjust, adopt, and adapt regulations to the organization, perhaps even serve as a force in changing regulations in the future.

This may include risk management, that is, clearly understanding the risks involved and taking steps to mitigate those risks or protect against them. This issue is particularly critical for high-risk organizations, because unexpected events or catastrophes can have a disastrous effect on operations. Some projects would involve scenario planning, in which the organization examines different scenarios to adjust to future changes of regulations, environment, political landscape, and other factors where risks are involved. From an operations perspective, this sometimes involves business interruption processes and contingency planning for disasters of all types. This is a very active, growing area for consulting and consultants.

Performance Measurement and Management

This growing area of internal consulting, particularly in the municipal sector, involves developing and administering the performance measurement system across the organization, in addition to identifying projects to improve overall performance. This includes coordinating the overall performance measurement system, working with executives to identify areas for improvement, and helping lead initiatives to realize better results. Comprehensive performance measurement systems often include the following key components:

- A corporate-level performance scorecard, linked to the overall business model containing key metrics in the financial, operations, customer, and employee areas
- A cascade of operational level dashboards from the business unit down to the individual contributors
- Specification of key performance levels or targets that are aligned vertically, in addition to local operations measurements

Unfortunately, the performance management system in most organizations is not working. It is either disliked by managers or employees, or both, and its connection to the performance of the organization is weak.

Other Areas

Other areas where the internal consulting function is developing include mergers and acquisitions; human capital planning; operations, facilities, and sustainability planning; technology management; and external affairs. In addition, project management, leadership, and facilitation pervades all of these areas of practice.

Shifting Expectations for the Consulting Role (Both Internally and Externally)

Organizations across both the private and public sectors, and client groups within them are creating higher expectations for the consulting services needed to help improve their performance. Key aspects of this trend involve the following:

- Creating a more results-based orientation
- Delivering more value to the client
- Providing increased implementation support
- Creating improved capabilities in the organization for learning and continuous improvement
- Focusing more attention on sustainability

The increased emphasis on a results-based orientation is borne out of frustration about projects in which deliverables too often do not have measurable performance improvement as an outcome. The "activity orientation" often results in improvement recommendations that are not tied to a clear path for realizing benefits. The pressure for results has led to the proliferation of "rapid results" projects that focus on mapping out a series of expected results during the project life cycle.

Tied very closely to the above trend is the need to deliver more value to the client. This means that the measures of success have changed to include a variety of measures both qualitative and quantitative, and sometimes the financial ROI. More important, the set of data collected profiles success during the consulting project and allows for adjustments along the way. This is a way for project value to be maximized and goes beyond merely focusing on results, instead providing a dynamic way to *enhance* results.

The need for increased implementation support comes from client experiences of numerous implementation issues and poor acceptance because of a lack of careful planning and coordination of this phase of important projects and programs. Internal consultants are in a unique position to help ensure effective implementation of projects by working closely with their clients to develop effective implementation plans and help onboard and train those who are involved with execution on an ongoing basis.

There is also an increasing realization of the importance of creating improved capabilities for learning and continuous improvement throughout the organization. This involves including a program to transfer key skills to project team members and to process owners who will be responsible for continuing management of the operation going forward. Internal consultants are in a unique position to help ensure effective implementation of projects by working closely with their clients to develop proper implementation plans and help onboard and train those involved with execution on an ongoing basis. Internal consulting groups are strongly positioned to meet these shifting expectations, both utilizing their own resources and partnering with externals to provide additional capabilities.

Finally, an important trend is the focus on sustainability. When a process is improved, initiated, or completed by consultants the issue is, "Can it be sustained?" "Will it still be viable in the years to come?" Consultants are required and expected to make sure that their improvements can be sustained. This eliminates the narcotic effect, in which the consultant is called back again and again to keep the projects going. Instead, sustainability ensures a lasting value, or at least a longer-lasting value, for the consulting project. Also, the focus on sustainability of all types of processes, systems, and technologies can create a need for consultants to teach how to sustain processes and keep methods evolving for long periods of time.

Key Success Factors

For consultants working within major private and public sector organizations, the following areas are among their most important success factors.

Adequate Planning—Early and Often

The obvious starting point for the first success factor is adequate planning in the beginning with routine adjustments along the way. This means that a compelling business plan is the beginning of the planning process. Planning is so important that it is covered in more detail in Chapter 2. In addition, there are often annual plans made and all the planning processes are subject to constant change, review, and revision. An ill-planned consulting project is doomed for failure. Proper planning helps to make your consulting project succeed.

Developing Client Partnerships

A second success factor, building strong client partnerships and credibility, is viewed as being critical in obtaining the needed level of sponsorship to help sustain their practice areas and develop new business opportunities. This includes the ability to work with clients and other stakeholders during their planning process to identify opportunities for improvement. The cultivation of interpersonal skills in the consulting group is an important aspect of building these relationships including team building, overcoming resistance, coaching, and communications planning and management.

Delivering Value

A third success factor is the ability to make a positive impact and continually demonstrate value. This involves developing a strong performance measurement system and tracking return on investment and other benefit measures on both individual projects and the overall internal consulting group investment. It also involves helping to realize successful implementation of the various initiatives in which they are involved.

An additional aspect of maximizing the impact of internal consulting is to focus on transferring key skills throughout the organization. This includes both practice area skills, such as process improvement and lean management, and core skills, such as change leadership and project management. One highly useful technique is to build networks of expertise across the organization to help with project implementation and continuous improvement and to help identify new opportunities.

Address the Financial Issues

A fourth success factor is to focus on the financial aspect of consulting. No topic is more important than the finances of a consulting practice, internal or external. Most consultants typically do not have financial and accounting expertise. If this is the case, it will be necessary to arrange for that expertise. Financial issues are vital and must be addressed often and thoroughly to ensure that the business or practice remains fiscally sound. The initial funding or budget often is the first step in developing the practice. The need for an adequate budget to keep the business going should be part of the original plan, and having the appropriate budgeting process to take the organization through its early startup is critical. Appropriate, fair, and equitable fees or transfer pricing must be established for externals and internals with a charge-back policy, and financial reporting must be in place, so the operational results will be known.

Later, several issues may surface, such as managing the spend, which will be explored later.

Manage the Consulting Practice Effectively

A fifth success factor is to manage the business effectively. For some consultants, the most unpleasant and distasteful aspect of consulting is managing the business itself. Because most consultants are not good managers, one classic reason for failure is that they neglect this important issue. Even a one-person practice involves some management issues.

As the practice grows, you may need to employ a business manager, operations manager, or administrative manager. One of the key issues here is not only finding the appropriate person but also being willing to let go of operational control of the organization. An effective business manager can maintain the operations, implement appropriate controls, and build the team. The support staff needs direction and someone available to make day-to-day decisions. A business manager may be the answer for most consulting practices.

Develop a Unique Approach

A sixth success factor is having a unique approach. Every consultant uses a process that clearly defines the practice—usually an expertise developed over several years. The process may include accepted principles with defined and articulated techniques, models, and methods.

That process usually determines the niche opportunity and enhances the uniqueness of the practice.

The consulting practice may be connected to an existing, well-known model or methodology, such as Business Process Improvement or Lean Six Sigma. In this case, the consulting process must be standardized with procedures and practices that are documented and spelled out, ensuring that the expressed method is available, adhered to, and consistent from one project to another. As other consultants use that process, the same standards and procedures must apply. The documentation of the process may include an underlying philosophy as well.

Create Effective Proposals or Consulting Contracts and Reports

A seventh success factor is to create effective proposals. A well-written proposal can make the difference between attracting and losing a new client, either internally or externally. Some consultants prefer to document as little as possible in a proposal, attempting to describe the project in conversations and to bind the consultation commitment with a handshake. This informal approach inevitably creates problems later. Written proposals avert misunderstandings and miscommunications. More important, a well-crafted document represents an opportunity to showcase the organization and sell the consulting practice.

A winning proposal begins with clearly defined objectives. The main points in a proposal can vary considerably but should include the following eight elements:

1. **Background and situation.** This is a detailed understanding of the problem and the current situation. It is presented so that the client and consultant agree on the current situation and the statement of the problem that will be addressed.

2. **Objectives of the project.** These objectives define what will be accomplished and the ultimate outcome of the project.

3. **Assumptions.** Various assumptions important to the project are developed and listed.

4. **Methodology.** The consulting process is outlined and includes steps, techniques, models, and approaches that are clearly established. This is the heart of the consulting practice and provides the beat by which the consulting project will move forward.

5. **Deliverables.** Include a list of exactly what will be delivered at the end of the project.

6. **Specific steps.** In addition to the methodology, the specific steps that will be needed as the deliverables are developed and presented are detailed.

7. **Project costs** (for externals and internals with a charge-back policy). A detailed listing of costs is presented. Sometimes there is concern about detailing too many costs; however, it's better to show the client the detailed costs in advance than to have added costs at the end of the project. This approach

builds credibility and respect for the consultant and the practice.

8. **Satisfaction guarantee.** A statement of a guarantee is essential.

When accepted, the proposal provides a reference point throughout the project, spelling out exactly what is to be delivered, when, how, and at what cost. It should be reviewed often—and not allowed to collect dust until the end of the project.

Operate in an Ethical Way

An eighth success factor is to operate ethically. Operating Ethical standards, defined as the value system of the owner/consultant, typically are developed as the consulting practice is structured. These standards often are a reflection of personal convictions and define how the consultant will operate in given situations.

Ethical issues surface in many ways. In the external sphere, the consultant may be asked to deliver results completely different from those that were planned. In the internal sphere, the client may require that the work be completed on an unrealistic, perhaps impossible schedule. In either situation, the relationship with a client may be difficult and demanding. There could be organizational issues where the culture and dysfunctional practice of the organization interfere with the completion of the project.

Whatever the ethical issues, when they arise they must be addressed quickly. Ethical issues materialize from the perspective of both the consultant and the client. The consultant must establish appropriate ethical standards and communicate them clearly so that the consultant her- or himself does not become the ethical issue.

Measure Success and Communicate Routinely

The ninth success skill is to measure and communicate. The success of individual consulting projects is directly linked to the overall success of the organization. But, of course, success is measured in different ways.

For external consultants, positive financial results are usually the first definition of success: profits or the reduction of losses extending over an initial time period. It may also include other financial goals, such as the profit per assignment, office expense, revenue per consultant, and so forth. Without financial success, at least in the long term, the consulting practice will not survive.

But in reality, client success must come before the consultant's success. After all, if clients are dissatisfied, the consulting practice probably will fail ultimately. Not only will there not be repeat business with that client, but there likely will be a loss of engagements with other clients as well. Routine client satisfaction data must be collected to keep tabs on this critical dynamic.

And then there is the personal success one experiences in delivering consulting services. Consulting is a rewarding process when it operates correctly—when the consultant provides counsel that assists the client in measurable ways. Personal success is a powerful motivator in maintaining the discipline and determination necessary to make the practice work.

When measuring the success of a given consulting project, seven types of outcome measures are necessary: satisfaction, learning, implementation, impact, costs, return on investment (ROI), and intangibles. This approach reflects a balanced set of measures by which data are collected in different categories and at different timeframes, often from different individuals. It is very credible, as the process always includes some method to isolate the effects of the consulting. Because of its importance, several chapters further on in the book are devoted to this topic.

Communication is an important issue. Routine communication throughout the project is critical. Reporting results through a variety of changes is necessary to reach the stakeholders. Subsequent chapters address these measurement and communication issues.

Improve Your Skills

The tenth success factor is improving skills. Consulting requires a specific set of skills that may be different from those demanded in other types of work. Although almost everyone performs some consulting duties no matter what his or her profession or job description may be, a full-time consulting effort demands distinct skills. While other skills can be helpful in the consulting task, the following are among the most important skills needed for the successful consulting practitioner.

Communication Skills. Perhaps the most important skills for the full-time consultant are communication skills, both written and oral. Consultants must be able to communicate effectively with potential clients— listening, understanding their needs, articulating the solution, proposing projects, and reporting results.

During the project, the consultant must routinely communicate with the client in an open and honest fashion, and when the project is complete, the consultant will generate a report. Writing skills are crucial. What the consultant documents essentially reflects his or her work and reputation. Oral communication skills are also crucial when the project is completed so that the process and results are understood and the recommendations for action are based on a compelling case.

Feedback Skills.   During the consulting project, the consultant must observe, listen, and be aware of the different inputs, positions, balances, and misunderstandings. The consultant must be a careful listener and be able to provide information to the client and other stakeholders to ensure that both groups understand the consultant's observations and analysis. Sometimes feedback is informal and sometimes it's structured, but in any case, it is almost always routine during a project.

Problem Solving and Analytical Skills.   At the heart of most consulting projects is the ability to help the client solve a problem, grapple with an issue that seems insurmountable, or explore an area that may be new territory. The consultant must be able to sort through the issues, uncover potential causes of problems, and allow the interaction between the factors to lead to solutions—solutions that are incremental and practical. Some projects will require significant data analysis using a variety of systems and routines. The consultant must be familiar with these techniques or at least find someone who can provide these services. At a minimum, the consultant must understand the analysis and be able to reach conclusions.

Organizational Skills. Successful consultants must be highly organized. They must work through checklists, to-do lists, and other planning tools. They must adhere to schedules and project management tasks, using a range of templates and tools to keep themselves and the project on track—avoiding sloppiness, procrastination, and tardiness. Otherwise, clients and others will justifiably be upset.

Build Relationships

The eleventh success factor is to build relationships with individuals and teams. Three relationships are important. First, the relationship with the client is crucial for project success. Second, the relationship with key executives must be productive to gain their respect. Third, the relationship with the project team must be respectful and engaging. When working with a group, the consultant must make sure that each person is engaged and that the group functions as a productive team.

Assessment with Success Factors

It may be helpful to have a consulting practice team access their current success status on these ten dimensions of success. Table 1.1 provides a handy place for this self-assessment along three dimensions. A number 1 rating is not successful at the present time. Number 2 is already considered successful now. A number 3 rating is very successful now. In addition to overall assessment, this provides a quick gap analysis indicating which areas might need attention. For example, if a success factor is rated 1, but the team would like to see a score of 3, this is an obvious area for focus and attention.

Table 1.1   Success Factor Assessment

Success Factor	Not Successful 1	Successful Now 2	Very Successful 3
1. Adequate Planning—Early and Often			
2. Developing Client Partnerships			
3. Delivering Value			
4. Address the Financial Issues			
5. Manage the Consulting Practice Effectively			
6. Develop a Unique Approach*			
7. Create Effective Proposals and Reports			
8. Operate in an Ethical Way			
9. Measure Success and Communicate Routinely			
10. Improve Your Skills			
11. Build Relationships			
Totals			

*More important for externals.

The interpretation of the score in a very rough way is presented as follows:

- Less than 15—Needs Improvement Now
- 15–19—A Struggling Practice
- 20–24—A Good Solid Practice
- Over 24—Best Practice

This is presented as a beginning point for a quick assessment. More details regarding opportunities, processes, and assessments are provided at different points in the book.

Increasing the Value of Internal Consulting to the Enterprise

Looking ahead, in order for internal consulting groups to sustain and further expand their impact on the enterprise, they need to continue to explore approaches to increase their value and help the overall enterprise "manage to value." The following four sections provide a summary of some key approaches to help achieve this goal.

1. Building Centers of Excellence (CoEs) in key practice areas and aligning consulting capabilities across the enterprise

   Consulting-related CoEs, also often termed Communities of Practice, provide a vehicle to develop and align expertise related to the service offerings of the internal consulting group across the enterprise.

Some examples of such CoEs include the following:

- Process Improvement and Continuous Improvement
- Lean Six Sigma and Complexity Reduction
- Organization Effectiveness and Development
- Change Management
- Performance Measurement and Management

These networks of common interest and expertise form, as a result of projects which they have conducted with client team members and others involved, and share learnings on an ongoing basis, both from continuing work within the organization and tapping information sources outside the company.

These complementary resources can both be utilized on other projects in their respective business areas and can also provide future staffing for the internal consulting group on rotational assignments. External consultants who work closely with these internals can also participate, thereby adding a valued external perspective.

A related program to effectively leverage internal consulting involves aligning these capabilities across the enterprise. This consists of first identifying all of those groups providing these types of advisory services, whether they are formally designated as internal consultants or simply perform in this type of role. A useful technique to help identify those acting in this role is to look for client interface or liaison activities as part of the charter of various functional areas. Then, the various approaches and methodologies used by these groups in areas such as change management, process improvement, or project management are compared, and current best practices in each area are identified. This results in the development of a plan to transition over time to a more consistent approach that will be spread across the entire organization.

2. Coordinating external research and analysis, including best practice benchmarking

Some internal consulting groups coordinate the external research for the entire enterprise, while others focus on key areas of intelligence that will assist in further developing their consulting practice. This often includes areas such as industry trends, emerging technologies, positioning of current and future competitors, changing business models, and best practice approaches on a cross-industry basis.

This approach is becoming even more important due to the increasing rate of change and uncertainty in the external environment. It also not only provides a valuable service to the overall organization but also better positions the internal consulting group to identify key initiatives that need to be undertaken.

In addition, a comprehensive benchmarking program, as described in the book *Internal Consulting Excellence*,[1] can help to provide a structured approach to gathering, analyzing, and acting on the intelligence gathered. External consultants can also play a valuable role in the process.

3. Administering a framework for improved alliance integration and strategic partnering arrangements

As internal consulting groups are becoming more involved with strategic initiatives of the enterprise, two areas of involvement will become increasingly more prevalent.

The first involves bringing a more structured and rigorous approach to help effectively align and integrate alliance parties, including mergers and acquisitions and joint ventures arrangements. This includes alliance planning and due diligence, evaluation of intellectual property and other assets (including human capital), and implementation planning and coordination assistance.

Second, with strategic partnering with external suppliers and customers across the value chain, internal consultants can also help to increase the probability of long-term success through participation in the planning and effective integration of key interface processes.

4. Developing a systematic approach to realizing an effective program for innovation across the enterprise

Stimulated by increasingly dramatic shifts in competitive frameworks, consumer positioning, regulatory environment, and technology developments, companies are increasingly focusing on continual innovation as a key factor for sustained viability and growth.

Internal consulting groups can help to bring a systematic approach to realize the maximum impact of corporate innovation initiatives, including skill-building interventions in the areas of creativity and problem solving.

A comprehensive approach to managing innovation developed from leading programs is detailed in the Innovation Management Framework section of the book, *Internal Consulting Excellence*.[2]

This starts with coordinating the Planning Phase, including the following areas:

- External research
- Key opportunity areas identified in the strategic plan(s)
- Idea mining process through the organization

The Analysis Phase then involves the following:

- Creating opportunity maps
- Conducting a gap analysis
- Prioritizing

Finally, the Execution Phase is undertaken:

- Selecting the portfolio of innovation initiatives to be executed over the next planning period
- Developing and executing the associated project plans
- Monitoring progress and helping to resolve issues

This approach provides the ability to effectively coordinate both the ongoing process of continual improvement type of innovation from sources, tapping sources across the enterprise with the major innovation imperatives driven by the strategic plan and allocating resources appropriately.

Internal consulting groups play a key role in both helping to structure the overall innovation program to accelerate results on a sustainable basis and to introduce supporting methodologies, including business model level innovation, process-level redesign, and creative thinking and problem solving techniques.

Final Thoughts

This introductory chapter focuses on the important trends in consulting for both internal consulting and external consultants. The good news is that there is a tremendous need for consultants, both internal and external and the two groups often work together quite well. In fact, many internal consultants use external consultants, and sometimes internal consultants replace the work of external consultants. In other cases, the external consultants replace the work of internal consultants. So to a certain extent, they are interchangeable and often work together in a "strategic partnering" role. The important point is that the field is growing, the role of consultant is important, and the applications are varied. In addition, there are many success factors involved in how organizations make the most out of consulting, making the process successful from both an internal and external perspective.

Organizing the Consulting Practice to Deliver Value

A structured approach to organizing consulting services is important for success. The most important step is to create a strategic or business plan tied to key needs, developing your methodology, managing the project, structuring the consulting processes, planning for skill and resource requirements, creating a high-performance culture, establishing and integrating areas of practice, and orchestrating an effective performance measurement and management system.

The business plan section of this chapter applies primarily to external consulting, some areas of which may also apply to internals. However, the Planning Process section of Chapter 4, which details the components of the internal consulting strategic plan, is the recommended approach for internal consulting groups because it is more focused on their unique environment.

Creating a Business Plan

A key component to properly positioning the consulting team to maximize their value to the organization is to develop a rigorous business plan that is approved by both leadership and client groups. Although some individuals regard this as an unnecessary step, a properly used business plan can make a critical difference in the ongoing success of the organization. To achieve this, the plan must be developed following specific guidelines and with the right spirit and process in each step.

Importance of the Business Plan

To understand the purpose of the business plan, you must first understand the need for the business plan. Is it being developed as a management tool or to secure funding? Is it being developed to achieve certain objectives or specific milestones? Is it being developed to impress various stakeholders? Whatever the reasons, the plan itself is critical. By definition, the business plan is the framework, strategy, resources, and the means necessary to develop a successful consulting practice, internally or externally. This definition begins to position the importance of the plan.

Is it necessary? This is an important question to raise. After all, there might well be resistance to developing a document that averages 20 to 40 pages. In fact, just the process of developing the plan encourages the consultants and other staff members to think strategically about the business. It also requires examination of all important aspects of the business and anticipating challenges and obstacles, and can be used as a tool to collect input and stimulate ideas from various stakeholders—particularly those who will be most involved in the consulting practice.

The result is a living document that clearly addresses the strengths and weaknesses of the consulting practice while communicating the visions and expectations for the future. If investors or loans are needed, for external consultants, this document provides the information necessary for the investment or lending decision. The business plan also serves as a tool for measuring the progress as important milestones are achieved, and through its revision, becomes a historical document highlighting how things have evolved and changed from the beginning to the present.

A business plan is not just for new consulting practices; it also should be in place for existing practices. While it is essential for a start-up business—because the plan shows how the practice will thrive and grow—it shows how the existing practice will be sustained, grow, and become even more successful in the future. Thus, it should be a living document for all types of consulting practices in any stage of maturity.

Audience for the Plan

It is helpful to identify the stakeholders. Table 2.1 shows the major stakeholders who would be interested or involved in the development of the business plan.

Perhaps the most critical stakeholders are the top executives. The business plan provides them with a tool

Table 2.1   The Role of Stakeholders in the Business Plan

Stakeholders	Develop the Plan	Review the Plan	Approve the Plan	Receive a Copy of the Plan
Top Executives and Sponsors		✓	✓	✓
Consultants	✓	✓	✓	✓
Support Staff	✓	✓		✓
Partners/Alliances				✓
Key Clients				✓
Other VIPs				✓

to develop and manage the business and help it grow. It also is an excellent tool for consultants and the support staff to provide input and help to develop the plan. The support staff includes all employees other than the consultants. For a small consulting practice, this may be a very small group. For a one-person consulting practice, there are no staff members, but there may be in the future. In the one-person situation, the "staff" could include those providing important outsourced services such as office support functions.

Various partnerships and alliances that are created in the business may be another important type of stakeholder, as long as the information in the plan is not sensitive. This may include IT, finance, accounting, and other consulting teams. Most partners need to know how your business is growing; what is planned; and the key issues, challenges, and opportunities. In some cases, certain customers may be a key audience. This is particularly important for consulting practices that have just a few large customers—customers so important to the practice that it's helpful for them to see how your business is being developed and how it will evolve. If the financial portions are sensitive, they can be omitted for those stakeholders.

Finally, there may be other VIPs who could be clients in the future, or professional colleagues and others who are interested perhaps from a mentoring or coaching standpoint. The business plan provides an excellent vehicle to show these parties how the practice ideally would evolve.

While the content of the document is very important, its effective use is paramount. It must include input from others and undergo regular reviews and adjustments. In effect, it becomes a living document that evolves as the business does, and it should stay in step with the current state of the practice.

An outline of the typical business plan follows. It covers all of the major topics and issues that must be addressed for the plan to be effective, efficient, and usable. It may be necessary to add more detail for larger, more involved consulting practices, while it may be shortened and abbreviated for smaller operations, such as a one-person shop.

Outline of a Typical Business Plan

Title Page

Table of Contents

Executive Summary

1. Purpose and Approach
   a. Mission
   b. Vision
   c. Values
2. Market Analysis
   a. Target Market
   b. Size of Market
   c. Client Description
   d. Competition

3. Niche Products and Services
   a. Niche
   b. Services
4. Client Development
   a. Acquiring Customers
   b. Retaining Customers
5. Operations
   a. Facilities
   b. Equipment
   c. Technology
   d. Resources
6. Management
   a. Key Individuals
   b. Job Description
   c. Staffing Philosophy
   d. Professional Support
7. Financial Plan
   a. Revenue Projections
   b. Cost Projections
   c. Capital Requirements, if necessary
   d. Cash Flow Statement, if necessary
8. Goals and Milestones
   a. Revenue or Business Volume
   b. Clients
   c. Profits
   d. Staffing

    e. Facilities

    f. Technology

    g. Alliances and Partnerships

  9. Risks and Opportunities

Purpose and Approach

Fundamental to any practice is its purpose and approach. These usually involve mission, vision, and value statements and are developed with considerable thought and effort with input from key stakeholders.

Mission. Every organization, whatever its size—even if it consists of a single individual—needs a mission statement to show the purpose of the consulting practice or individual consultant. This is an enduring statement, a purpose for an organization, identifying the scope of its operation in product and market terms and reflecting its values and priorities. A mission statement will help a company or function make consistent decisions, motivate, build an organization entity, integrate short-term objectives with longer-term goals, and enhance communications.

Essentially, the mission statement should have 50 words or less, describe what the consulting practice should provide, define its customers, and differentiate the practice from other consulting practices. The following lists some examples of consulting mission statements:

- Provide operating functions with top-quality consulting services, helping them understand and meet their compliance responsibilities, and applying regulations and laws with integrity and fairness to all.

- Our primary goal is to help the clients we serve become the beneficiaries of advanced technology by providing consulting services to help them meet their organizational goals.

- To exceed the expectations of our clients through the delivery of superior service and continuous quality improvement that rewards our employees and enhances the value of our shareholder's investment.

- We provide outstanding advice in change management and a valuable consulting experience to top executives.

- We provide consulting services on risk management for all types of projects, programs, and solutions.

Vision.   The vision differs from the mission statement. It is a concise word picture of the organization at some future time, and as such, sets the overall direction of the organization. It is what the consulting practice strives to be in the minds of the key stakeholders and clients. Further, a vision is something to be pursued, while a mission is something to be accomplished. For example, in the last example in the previous list, the vision is to be recognized as experts in risk management.

Value Statements.   The values stated represent the collective principles and ideals that guide the thoughts and actions of the consulting practice's owners and managers.

Values often define the character of the organization and its beliefs, essentially describing what the organization stands for as it pursues its business. The feature suggests possible value statements for a consulting practice.

Value Statements for a Consulting Practice

1. Provide complete customer satisfaction, including full refunds or no invoices to dissatisfied customers.
2. Provide quick responses to customer inquiries and requests, at least within one business day.
3. Enhance the loyalty to customers by providing them outstanding services that are competitively priced (for externals and internals with charge-back arrangements).
4. Treat employees with respect and dignity at all times.
5. Foster a creative spirit among employees, recognizing accomplishments, improvements, and project completions.
6. Build loyalty among employees to enhance retention and commitment.
7. Offer above-market pay for qualified, productive staff members (market pay targets may be different for externals and internals).

(Continued)

(*Continued*)

8. Link employee rewards to key performance goals.

9. Operate efficiently with cost control in mind at all times.

10. Operate with integrity and trust, following precise ethical guidelines.

Market Analysis

Whether internal or external, it's critical to understand the market that is being served by the consulting practice. It begins by clearly defining the market. Is the target audience a particular type of organization (or a part of it)? Is it a function, a subfunction, a department, or even individuals? A precise definition helps consultants and would-be consultants fully understand the potential.

Sometimes it would be helpful to know the size of the market. The size will be an estimate. More accurate figures may be available later. Some estimates may be based on a variety of expert input or the best guesses possible.

Another important issue is to define the actual client, the individual(s) responsible for requesting or purchasing the consulting services. This may be a particular job title, or a series of job titles within an organization, or it could be individuals in a particular function area.

Finally, an important area to consider in describing the market demand is defining the competition. The extent of current and future competition is an important variable to understand, and to quantify, if possible. This will require defining who the competition is as accurately as it can be provided, and describing how it differs from your consulting practice. It may require scanning the market, discussing the competition with perspective clients, and perhaps making contacts with competitors.

Defining Your Niche

One of the most important considerations in the early stages of a consulting practice is defining a particular niche. A consulting practice should be based on an opportunity created because of a particular competitive advantage. This could be something the consultants can do that others cannot do, or that they can do much better (with less time) than others. The niche must be selected based on one or more of these three issues: more expertise, improved quality of service, or lower cost.

The narrower the niche, the less competition there will be, but then, the market will be smaller. The wider the niche, the larger the market, and consequently, the greater the numbers of competitors. This niche may have to be selected in the context of examining the market and the competition discussed above. Smaller niches make the market much smaller, but the key driver must be the expertise and reputation for the consultant or consulting practice.

After the niche is clearly identified, the exact services are detailed. For example, the assessment services, design services, and implementation services are defined. This may also include software, which is in the form of a product, and it also may involve providing workshops to explain the process or teaching others to do so if part of the philosophy is to transfer skills to the organization. As the service or product is designed, determined, or defined, any special features or benefits should be detailed, showing how this service might stand out from others. In short, a good niche has these features:

- Consultants have extensive experience and skills.
- There is a substantial market.
- Consultants have significant competitive advantage.
- There is less competition, or at least it's not overly competitive.

Client Development

Specific techniques, methods, and marketing tactics to acquire new customers should be outlined. Also, specific ways in which customers are retained to build customer loyalty should be highlighted. This exercise provides an opportunity to address the overall marketing, promotion, advertising, and public relations strategies—all in the name of developing and retaining key clients. Essentially, this part of the plan becomes the marketing plan.

Operations

The operations section of the plan is substantial for an ongoing operation with dozens of employees, but it would be minor for a small consulting practice with just one consultant. The operations section identifies the way in which the business is actually operated. It will define specific processes or systems that are important to success and how they are utilized, whether automated or manual. It describes the equipment currently in use or planned for purchase and how it will be utilized. The section would include statements on the use of technology. For many consulting practices, technology will be an important and perhaps even critical part of the delivery, and should be defined in terms of scope, use, and cost.

The operations section will also define office space requirements and specific facility needs. This could range from a consultant working at home, to having multiple offices for consultants. The various resources needed to make the organization function, such as significant outsourcing arrangements, subcontractors, or suppliers would also be identified.

Management

A critical part of the business plan details how the consulting practice will be managed. This section should describe the job scope or descriptions of key management staff. For a small consulting practice, the manager is the consultant. For larger practices, managers in the organization are the key management staff. This section should also define the staffing philosophy in terms of outsourcing or employing additional staff, and the additional professional support that might be needed as part of the delivery of services. Finally, the section provides an opportunity to describe management philosophies, management control systems, and other issues important to understanding how the practice is governed.

Financial Plan

For some stakeholders, this is the most critical part of the business plan. In describing the financial aspects of the business, it presents revenue projections, usually for a three- to five-year time frame. For internal consulting, revenue may be the transfer pricing or other mechanisms to fund consulting if they utilize a charge-back type approach. Significant cost items are also projected. For external consultants, these can be combined in the form of an income statement showing revenue, expenses, and profits. The financial plan would detail the capital requirements, if necessary, and how they will be funded; show cash flow anticipated for the three- to five-year period; and present balance sheets for that time frame.

Goals and Milestones

At the heart of a business plan are the specific goals and milestones. These provide the focus for the key stakeholders, particularly the owners and the employees who must meet specific targets, and include goals for monthly, quarterly, and revenue or transfer pricing. The number of clients might also be included here. Client growth is important, and the different types of clients may be underscored. If appropriate, rollout of new products and services would be included in the timetables.

Profit, revenue, and/or business volume goals also are included, if appropriate. If it is a start-up consulting practice, profits may not be generated for several months or even a couple of years. The goal is to minimize losses and bring the practice to profitability as soon as possible. Staffing targets may be established as additional staff members are recruited and new consultants are added, according to specific timetables. Growth of offices or facilities is included as well. New equipment and technology are detailed, with time frames for purchase and implementation. Alliances or partnerships are included.

This part of the plan should be reviewed routinely by the management and staff so that adjustments can be made. The goals it details often reflect the performance expectations of key staff members.

Risks and Opportunities

The business plan also should include any potential risks. These risks may involve technology developments that would threaten consulting opportunities, the emergence of large consulting practices that could dominate the market, or the potential loss of business through outsourcing or offshoring of work. Risk assessments require a good understanding of the market and how it may evolve in the future, based upon developing trends.

This section would also address significant opportunities, representing the upside potential and detailing how things may change or develop that could benefit the practice in the future. For some practices this exercise may involve scenario planning, where a small number of possible scenarios is described, both good and bad. For each one, the impact on the business is examined, along with the reaction to it.

Developing Your Methodology

There are two issues connected to having a unique methodology. The first is the expertise you bring to the project. This is often the rationale for starting the consulting practice and growing it into a successful business. Your methodology must be used and protected throughout the process. The second issue is the approach to consulting—showing that there is a systematic way in which the project is to be conducted and delivered. The systematic process ensures consistency and replication, and shows the client exactly what will be done and what steps will be taken to ensure success. All of this is contained in the proposal process, and now must be delivered according to the proposal's terms.

Systematic Process

Apart from the unique advantage offered by a consulting process and the expertise of the consultant(s) is the method in which the consulting is delivered. A systematic, step-by-step process should be developed that defines the approach outlined in the proposal. Figure 2.1 shows one approach, a five-phase consulting model offered by Mooney.[1]

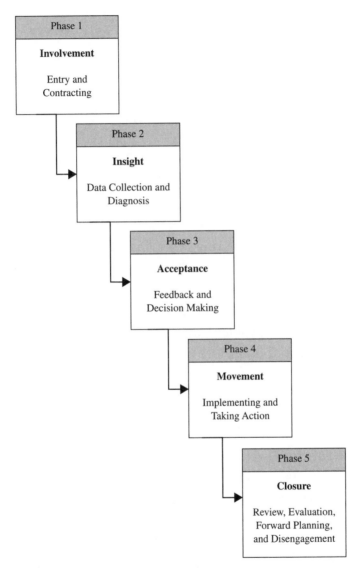

FIGURE 2.1   The Five-Phase Consulting Model
Source: Adapted from Paul Mooney, *The Effective Consultant: How to Develop the High Performance* Organisation (Dublin: Oak Tree Press).

The first phase of the process is the initial involvement that leads to firming up the objectives. As indicated in Chapter 7, the project objectives are broad and the solution objectives may be developed in more detail after the initial project has begun. This is an output of phase 1. In phase 2, data collection begins, along with the diagnosis of the situation. This is the heart of the consulting process. In phase 3, this involves communicating the data to the appropriate individuals to secure acceptance and to drive the decision making for the consulting solution. In phase 4, this is the implementation of the consulting solution. Finally, phase 5 includes the evaluation described later, along with recommendations and communication of the data described in this chapter.

The important issue is to have a systematic approach to solving the problem or pursuing the project. This approach may be separate from the unique methodology and know-how provided.

Protecting the Methodology

Sometimes it's necessary to protect the unique methodology, expertise, or know-how that is brought to the consulting process. This may include specific analytical tools, the structure of the entire project as it relates to how the data are collected, or how decisions are made and conclusions are drawn. Whatever the specific methodology, it is important to ensure that it is protected from unauthorized use.

The first decision to be made is based on the public use of the methodology. Some consultants prefer their approach to be proprietary with little discussion or disclosure of the process in the consulting reports. They may require the client to sign a confidentiality agreement with a commitment not to disclose proprietary methods. While this may work for some consultants, it can create frustration and anxiety for clients—leaving them with the impression that the consultant does not trust them to be discreet. Other consultants are very open with their process and will make presentations about it, write about it, discuss it, and display it on their websites. This is a personal decision.

The recommended approach is to be as open as possible about the process, while protecting any unauthorized use through obtaining a trademark, sales mark, copyright, or, in some cases, a patent. Part of the protection is to ensure that materials are presented with the appropriate notations and markings. Attempts to protect the methodology should be based in common sense. Copyrights, trademarks, and sales marks can be overused. It should be mentioned early in the report that the process is protected by law, but mentioning it in every instance or on every page is unnecessary. Being aware of what competitors are using and writing about will let you know if others are using the process.

Managing the Project

To ensure the success of the project and client satisfaction, everything must be delivered on a timely basis according to the initial proposal. Keeping the project on track and the client happy will require excellent project management skills.

Creating a Service Agreement

Some consultants avoid disappointments and surprises by developing a service agreement. This agreement details expectations throughout the project. It builds on the concept of guaranteed results described later and provides details about how the project will be accomplished, as well as the expected outcomes. It complements the proposal process as it addresses the major items in the proposal but often provides more details. The following list shows the topics contained in a typical service agreement.

Typical Topics in a Service Agreement

- Precisely what you will do for the client
- Precisely what benefits the client can expect from your work
- When you will start to work for the client
- When you will stop working for the client
- How much time in aggregate you will spend on the client's behalf
- How much money you will be charging as expenses*
- The basis for a cost qualifying as a rechargeable expense*
- When you will be sending invoices*
- The amount of the invoice*

---

* More important for external consultants

- When you expect your invoices to be paid*
- When the client can expect a written report
- The length of the report
- Other deliverables the client might expect
- Any other key issues relating to your work for the client
- The resources the client needs to make available to you, including access to people, systems, and premises
- How success will be measured

While this may appear to be excessive detail for proposals and guaranteed results, some consultants think the detailing is absolutely essential to avoid surprises and keep the client informed throughout the process. Service quality agreements and service level agreements are typical in many service organizations; maybe they should be a necessary part of all major consulting projects.

Project Plan

As discussed earlier, a project plan is a valuable tool to show how and when the data will be collected, along with the sequencing of events and particular decisions. There are many types of project management software available that can be used to keep a consulting project on track. One of the most popular is offered by Microsoft under the name of Microsoft Project. The important point is to have a systematic way to keep the project on schedule and ensure timely reports to the client. This leads to the next issue.

Project Communications

Several chapters in this book are focused on the importance of maintaining communication between the consultant and the client. This is particularly critical during delivery of the service. Routine feedback and debriefings are necessary to show the progress of the project as well as the issues that are being confronted. These debriefings not only keep the client aware of what is occurring, but facilitates client involvement in the process. This is discussed in more detail later in the chapter.

Deliverables

The consulting project proposal and promised deliverables must be developed and delivered on time and with the appropriate quality. Tracking the progress of the deliverables, ensuring that they are in place and approved when promised, is absolutely critical to the integrity of project management and the ultimate success of the project.

Communicating Results

With data in hand, what's next? Should the data be used to modify the consulting project, show the contribution, justify new projects, gain additional support, or build goodwill? How should the data be presented? Who should present the data? When should the data be communicated? The worst course of action is to do nothing. Communicating results is as important as achieving them.

There are at least five key reasons for being concerned about communicating results:

1. Measurement and evaluation mean nothing without communication.
2. Communication is necessary to make improvements.
3. Communication is necessary for explaining contributions.
4. Communication is a sensitive issue.
5. A variety of target audiences need different information.

Several methods, both oral and written, are available to communicate consulting success to the various audiences. The skills required to communicate results effectively are almost as delicate and sophisticated as those needed to obtain results. The style is as important as the substance. Regardless of the message, audience, or medium, a few general principles apply and are presented in Chapter 6. These principles provide guidance for effective, timely communication and offer a checklist for communicating results.

Structuring Consulting Processes

Research has indicated that the development of consistent consulting processes aligned with best practice approaches is important to consulting success. Key areas include opportunity analysis, contracting, and project/program portfolio management.

Opportunity Analysis

Opportunity analysis often involves a business case approach including an overall description of the prospective project, impact assessment (including cost and expected benefits), risk analysis, a high-level timeline, milestones, and resource requirements. In smaller projects/initiatives a more streamlined approach, often termed a "case for action" is often utilized, with a similar structure. The key here is to provide a consistent and comprehensive analytical construct to help assess the potential benefit and doability of projects up front that helps management to make better decisions about which ones to execute. The categories used in this analysis can be used to develop an overall project/initiative assessment framework where ranking across projects can occur allowing resources to be most effectively allocated. Some of the more sophisticated approaches in this area employ a rigorous decision analysis methodology to help examine alternative approaches to address the issue or opportunity helping to ensure the most effective approach.

Contracting

A next step in the consulting process is then to develop an explicit contract between the consultants and the client to execute the project. This typically includes the following key categories:

- Overview/Purpose/Scope
- Resource Requirements, Roles and Responsibilities

- Time line and Key Milestones
- Specific Objectives, Deliverables, and Measurements of Success
- Issue Resolution Process

This needs to be established at the beginning of the project, agreed to by all involved parties, and periodically revisited during execution to make necessary adjustments. A good contracting process helps to avoid "scope creep" during the project life cycle. Project/program portfolio management represents a systematic approach for prioritizing, selecting, and monitoring the group of major projects and other initiatives across the organization. The consulting group can provide a valuable service by establishing and coordinating a systematic approach to this activity, including the following:

- Engaging a top-level sponsor or leadership team to own the process, make prioritization decisions, and resolve issues
- Structuring a consistent approach
- Working with executives in various areas of the organization to help identify key initiatives tied to their business plan and develop their project plans
- Facilitating the process of selecting projects, allocating resources, providing feedback, and helping to ensure effective implementation

For those companies with a separate project or program management organization (PMO), alignment or integration with the consultants can help position their activities to deal with more strategic projects and improve the linkage to the strategic planning function.

Strategic Portfolio Management

A key approach in helping consultants become involved in more strategic projects and add more value to the organization is to promote the use of an overall strategic portfolio management process to better identify and manage the most important initiatives. This also provides a greater opportunity to help structure these from the beginning instead of just becoming involved later in the project lifecycle. Figure 2.2 presents a Strategic Portfolio Management Model that has been developed from best practice approaches in this area.

Here, the internal consulting group (ICG), identified as the Enterprise Portfolio Management Group, coordinates the overall process working with both corporate planning and the individual business units to develop streamlined business plans, termed "cases for action," including the following key components:

- Linkage to strategic plan
- Projected financial impact
- Intangible benefits
- Doability (level of risk)
- Resource requirements
- Impact on customer and competitive positioning
- Time to benefits realization

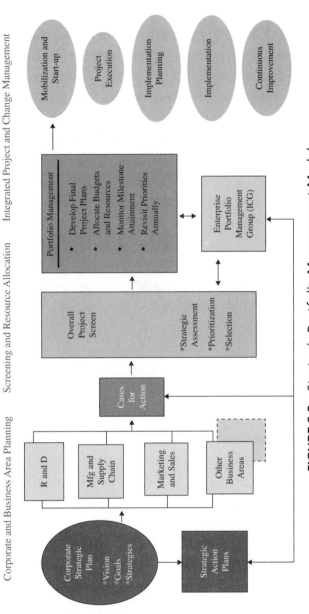

FIGURE 2.2 Strategic Portfolio Management Model

These are then put through a screening process with prioritization and selection made by a top-level executive committee. Table 2.2 provides a sample framework for the ranking of the various projects submitted, which links to the key categories in the "cases for action" submitted.

The role of the internal consulting group then extends into the project management phase, including mobilization and start-up, project execution, implementation planning, implementation, and continuous improvement. The recommended methodology to be used, integrated project and change management, is described in Chapter 3.

When properly positioned and supported, the Strategic Portfolio Management Process covers a wide variety of major projects across the enterprise. Some examples of the types of projects frequently included are as follows:

- Large new information technology development investments and implementation projects
- Key new product/services research and development
- Significant new business/market development initiatives, including alliances and acquisitions
- Major capital programs in areas such as new facilities and production capabilities
- Comprehensive supply chain reconfiguration

The internal consulting group, in their portfolio management role, then coordinates and supports the ongoing management of these projects and periodic

Table 2.2 Initiative/Project Prioritization Template (Rate from 10 [Highest] to 1 [Lowest] as Described in Case for Action)

Categories	Initiative 1	Initiative 2	Initiative 3	Initiative 4	Initiative 5	Initiative 6	Initiative 7, etc.
Linkage to Strategic Plan							
Financial Impact (ROI)							
Intangible Benefits							
Feasibility (Lack of Risk)							
Customer/Competitive Position Impact							
Resource Requirements (less is higher)							
Time to Benefits Realization (less is higher)							

monitoring of progress. The role of key stakeholders is as follows:

- Internal consulting group
  - Coordinate the overall strategic portfolio management (SPM) process
  - Train process participants on methodology
  - Provide expertise and support
- Business areas and corporate planning staff
  - Designate contacts to prepare cases for action
  - Link projects to corporate and area plan priorities
  - Learn about and participate in the SPM process
- Executive review team
  - Participate in project screening activity
  - Make final prioritization decisions
  - Proactively support the strategic portfolio management process

In order for this project to work effectively there needs to be strong top-level sponsorship, training and coaching of users on the process, and periodic progress reviews. Some of the potential pitfalls to look out for include the following:

- Poor linkage to the corporate and business area planning process
- Keeping major projects and expenditures out of the process

- A lack of objectivity in the review and evaluation
- Avoiding hard decisions about what projects to defer or stop

Planning for Skill and Resource Requirements

It is important for internal consulting groups to provide the same level of professional consulting services as their external counterparts. They also need to develop the capability to provide an integrated suite of services with associated resources to meet variations in demand and the development of new areas of opportunity. Several approaches have been used to help them prepare to achieve those goals.

Target Competency Frameworks

Target competency frameworks consist of the following key components:

- Listing of current positions and those planned in the near future
- Specification of both core and practice area competencies for each position—along with expected proficiency levels

Then, consultants are positioned in the framework and skill gaps identified. This is followed by a development planning and training project to help close those gaps with current staff. The overall curriculum should consist of several key components. Consulting process training should include the following:

- Opportunity analysis and contracting
- Team building and facilitation
- Client relationship building
- Engagement execution and implementation
- Cross business unit collaboration

Core skill training topics usually involve these areas:

- Leading through influence
- Business acumen
- Change leadership
- Consultative communications
- Critical thinking and collaborative problem solving

Potential practice area skills to be covered, depending on the scope of service offerings, such as these:

- Business process optimization and rapid results
- Strategic business planning and execution
- Change management/OE/OD at both the project and organization levels
- Performance measurement and management
- Innovation planning and operationalization

A complementary action learning project should be developed to incorporate a "learning by doing" approach with associated mentoring and coaching by experienced consultants with expertise in that area.

Recruiting Strategies

Recruiting strategies are formulated to fill the gaps and position the consultants for future business development. This is often done through a combination of external hires and internal movement within the overall organization. Internal movement often involves rotational assignments where people are brought in from various areas across the organization to learn and practice consulting skills while bringing their expertise, knowledge, and connections with a key area of the business. Internal consultants involved in a rotation project often maintain a more permanent core of experienced consultants to manage and mentor their rotational cadre.

External recruiting projects often target key competency areas that need to be filled with experienced consultants. Another approach is to utilize the internal consultant as the first assignment for high-potential hires before going out to another business area. This provides the recruits with a great overview of the organization while learning key skills. Then, after going on to their future assignments, these alumni serve as advocates throughout the organization.

Partnering

Another approach to filling resource needs involves developing partnering arrangements with externals. Internal consultants are usually involved in such an approach because of the need to be able to adjust to varying levels of demand and to bring in specialized skills in developing areas of their business. These arrangements range from bringing in selected individual contributors to contracting with external practices to provide and help manage a significant resource cadre to help staff large projects on a global basis. This external partnering model is often referred to as a "capacity-free model," in that internal consultants are not limited in the projects taken by its internal resource capacity. A successful partnering model requires explicit contracting arrangements and quality control to help ensure high-quality deliverables.

Creating a High-Performance Culture

Even though they are part of the same overall organization as their clients, internal consulting groups need to establish a culture that helps provide the skill sets and degree of objectivity critical for their long-term success. Specific aspects include the following:

- A distinctive competency model
- Supportive performance measurement system
- An emphasis on maintaining an objective and independent point of view
- A program of continuous learning

It is important to develop a distinctive competency model for internal consultants. The overall competency model for the organization is usually not geared for the type of work they perform. This is why the AIMC developed a competency model focused on the skills required for success in this area, focusing on both key core and practice area competencies. One reason for this difference is that internal consultants must develop support and lead teams without any formal authority through reporting relationships. This requires a great emphasis on what is often termed the "soft skills" such as leading through influence, constructive negotiation, overcoming resistance, and team building. It is also important to have a supportive performance measurement system that sets stretch objectives in key areas of financial performance customer feedback, consulting operations effectiveness, consultant alignment, and innovation. This represents a particular challenge for these consultants because their results can only be accomplished through effective collaboration with their clients and other stakeholders.

Another key element of a successful culture positioning for the consultants is maintaining an objective and independent point of view. This is a challenge for internal consulting groups because they are viewed as part of the organization and individual members might have allegiances with various areas of the business. One concept that has been used by some consultants to help reinforce the need for objectivity is that they are a "firm within a firm." This helps to emphasize the need for an arms-length relationship with others across the organization and not to be influenced by previous affiliations or future career plans.

Internal consultants need to adopt a personal project of continuous learning as part of their culture. This is important not only to maintain the necessary level of professionalism in their field, but also to be perceived as a thought leader by their clients. Key areas include core consulting skills, practice area expertise, and business acumen including industry trend and related emerging technology awareness.

Establishing and Integrating Areas of Practice

One of the important considerations in establishing and developing a practice involves deciding exactly what their suite of service offerings will be and how to resource them, including the following:

- Degree of focus in major practice areas
- Plan to leverage other internal and external resources
- Realization of synergies by integrating other capabilities throughout the organization

Regarding the degree of focus in major practice areas, many internal consulting groups start out providing consulting services in one of the major areas often covered, including process improvement/Lean Six Sigma, strategy execution, change leadership, and project/program management. Then, many consulting leaders have quickly realized that by adding other practice areas to their scope, they can both expand their business and provide more complete solutions to current initiatives.

Associated with this structuring of their portfolio of service offerings is the plan to leverage other internal and external resources. When leveraging other internal resources in the organization, a popular approach is to ask that a client lead on a particular project be mentored/ trained in both core consulting skills and the relevant practice area methodology, so they can assume a greater role in future projects and also identify additional opportunities for future engagements by the consultants. Relationships should also be developed with external consultants with skills in both current areas of focus and those planned for future business development to provide additional capacity for project demand.

The third key aspect of this effort is the realization of synergies by integrating other capabilities throughout the organization. This involves identifying other groups throughout the organization providing a variety of advisory type services and meeting with them to discuss opportunities for aligning their capabilities with the core consultants. This helps to identify key consulting skill sets and current methodologies used in these groups, which can result in a sharing of skilled resources and better alignment/consistency in the tools and techniques employed. In a number of instances, this discovery process has resulted in the integration of several of these groups into a more effective organization to serve the overall company.

Orchestrating an Effective Performance

Measurement and Management System

A key component of organizing the consulting function to deliver value is the establishment of an effective performance measurement and management system, for both the projects/initiatives undertaken and the consulting operations as a whole, including the following aspects:

- Project-specific measurements
- Overall consulting measurement system
- Linkages to planning and organization performance management

Project-specific measurements need to be built into the planning for each initiative and be approached consistently across the entire portfolio being managed. This will not only greatly contribute to meeting project expectations, but a consistent measurement approach at the project level facilitates a roll-up to an overall scorecard for the consulting group. These measurements often include the following:

- Financial impact metrics, such as return on investment
- Customer/client satisfaction metrics, such as customer feedback
- Operational improvement metrics, such as product/service quality and cycle time reduction

The overall consulting group measurement system often comprises a balanced or comprehensive approach including financial, customer/client, operational effectiveness, employee alignment/development, and innovation metrics. The overall consulting scorecard should be aligned with the individual project metrics for ease of rolling them up to assess overall performance. Details regarding these measurements are provided in Chapter 5.

For the consultant performance measurement system to be most effective, it should have strong linkages to planning and organization performance management. This starts with the consulting group's business plan, including measurable objectives, and linkages to their performance measurement system. Also, the consulting plan should be aligned with key objectives of their client's top-level business plans. Then, the consulting measurement system should also be aligned with the performance measurement system of the overall organization. For those companies and public sector organizations with a balanced scorecard type of performance measurement system, this means that the organization level scorecard is cascaded down throughout the organization with their own "measurement scorecard," which is linked to the upper level, to which the consulting team's measurements are also aligned.

Additionally, the consulting team can provide a valuable contribution by coordinating the development and management of the organization performance measurement system. Often utilized in the context of an overall "strategic alignment system" by top management, this approach can provide a valuable framework for focusing and prioritizing activities through various levels of the organization and across the organization. A rapidly growing number of consulting teams are developing this as a significant area of practice and utilizing it to help identify major project opportunities and cultivate relationships with senior management.

Final Thoughts

The Model of Internal Consulting, described in detail in William D. Trotter's book, *Internal Consulting Excellence*,[2] further explains how to operationalize each of the component areas this chapter covers relative to internal consulting in addition to overall success factors in developing and managing consulting operations. This book also provides details on the internal consulting competency model and performance measurement scorecard approach.

External consultants play an important role in organizing the consulting function to deliver value. First, they can lend their expertise in developing an effective business plan for the internal consulting function and linking it to a broader pool of expertise for supplemental resource requirements. External consultants can help to structure and formalize key consulting processes from contracting to project management drawing on their experience and successful applications. Another area where external consultants can add value is in the area of consulting competency development. This includes the following:

- Helping to structure the overall competency framework for both leadership and individual contributors
- Delivering specific training modules in the curriculum. Here, these will likely be a larger role in those organizations in the early stage of formalizing their internal consulting role and capability.

Additional information on the role of external consulting is depicted in detail in the book *How to Build a Successful Consulting Practice* by Jack J. Phillips.[3]

Managing the Consulting Practice to Deliver Value

Providers of consulting services are facing increasing demand to demonstrate their value to the organization and provide maximum impact. This is a more challenging task for internals than externals because of their ongoing role in implementation and continuous improvement. Key factors in demonstrating recognizable value include maintaining a professional management system (including cultivating sponsorship), positioning the business partner role, executing effective marketing and business development, and managing for results.

Maintaining a Professional Management System

In Chapter 1, the success factors for consultants are presented with an emphasis on external consultants. A best practice consulting model for internal consultants, which has been tested and refined, involves several key components in relationships, processes, competencies, culture, and performance.

Effective Relationship Management

Relationship management must be a key area of focus and systematically executed to help ensure longer-term success. It requires a proactive project to engage and cultivate relationships with key sponsors, clients, and other stakeholders. Then these relationships need to be continually monitored to help identify unmet needs, meet expectations, and build trust. Effective relationship management also involves an understanding of how to position the consulting organization for maximum influence and impact on the organization.

These relationships are often developed and cultivated by gaining access to the planning activities of top-level teams in various units of the organization and creating a partnering type of relationship in identifying opportunities, addressing key issues, and helping to improve their performance. Stakeholder mapping templates are often employed to help track the strength of these relationships and maintain a systematic approach to improving and maintaining these affiliations.

Developing emotional intelligence and empathy is a key aspect of establishing strong relationships with client organizations. This involves not only effectively utilizing core consulting skills, such as leading through influence, active listening, overcoming resistance, and team building, but also being motivated to understand the client's situation and challenges.

Internal consultants with strong technical backgrounds and skills in areas such as process improvement, Lean Six Sigma, project management, business planning, information systems, or decision analysis often view these skills as not being an important area of emphasis. This perspective can significantly decrease their effectiveness and help to isolate them from clients and restrict their ability to further develop their consulting practice.

Consistent Consulting Processes

Next, consistent consulting processes provide the mechanism to help ensure a professional-level of consulting services. An explicit contracting process at the front-end of projects is important to properly scope and resource the project. It is critical to help ensure that expectations are met and that changes in the original charter are identified and properly addressed. Consistent service delivery is also an important area of emphasis and involves the adoption of and training in consulting approaches and methodologies. Consulting project portfolio management employs a systematic approach for selecting, staffing, and managing the range of projects, initiatives, and programs.

A strong implementation and continuous improvement focus is another key success factor for the internal consulting group. It reinforces their unique role of seeing projects all the way through and enabling the impacted organization(s) to recognize and implement future improvement opportunities. It starts by including a strong implementation planning component in project plans to improve execution and help ensure a good transition to client ownership.

Client ownership development and knowledge transfer are related areas where change management techniques are utilized to effectively engage clients in buying into recommendations. The knowledge transfer aspect involves training clients in the methodologies utilized in the project so that they can assume a more proactive role in current and future initiatives.

Finally, formalized performance feedback both during and after projects helps to both facilitate needed mid-course corrections and also provide input to improve the approach on future initiatives. This often involves a structured communications program during projects and after action review (AAR) sessions at their completion.

Enhancing Consulting Capabilities

Core consulting skills provide the foundation for internal and external consultants to effectively work with their clients regardless of their area of focus or particular project. These involve developing the basic capabilities to engage clients and provide a leadership role in any project or initiative in which they are involved. Key skills typically included are as follows:

- Leading through influence and becoming a trusted advisor
- Team building and management
- Overcoming resistance and building resilience
- Active listening and probing
- Communications planning and feedback
- Meeting management and facilitation
- Project planning and management
- Opportunity/issue diagnosis and analysis
- Client relationship management
- Leading change
- Coaching and mentoring
- Decision making

Practice area skills enable the consultants to provide the methodologies to deliver a professional level of services in each of their major areas of focus. The five most frequent practice areas employed are (1) strategic planning and execution, (2) process and operations improvement (including Lean Six Sigma), (3) organizational effectiveness development and change management, (4) performance measurement and management, and (5) project/program portfolio management.

Many consulting groups have found that by including multiple practice areas into their range of services they can both provide a higher quality to clients and also become involved in a greater share of important initiatives. In addition, project management spans all of these areas and change management has become an integral part of nearly all successful initiatives. Consulting process guidelines and frameworks must also be managed effectively to help ensure a consistent and professional approach.

Action learning is utilized to train internal consultants through experience on actual projects where they develop expertise through doing and gradually assume an increased level of responsibility. This is frequently supported by an active coaching and mentoring project by senior consultants and leadership to guide development while ensuring high-quality deliverables.

Providing Integrated Project and Change Management

More and more internal consulting groups have been utilizing both strategic portfolio planning and integrated project and change management methodologies to increase the value of project/program management to the organization.

This methodology is most effective when used as part of an overall organization portfolio management process—which looks across all major projects, prioritizes them using a consistent set of criteria, and selects those which promise to have the maximum potential impact.

Then an integrated decision and risk analysis should be used before beginning an individual project to ensure that the right approach has been selected to address the problem or opportunity to be addressed. This also will help to understand the risks involved in the undertaking.

With these first two steps as a prelude and when the project has been selected for execution, the utilization of integrated project and change management has proven to significantly improve the likelihood of successful completion and implementation.

The integrated Project and Change Management Methodology developed by the AIMC arose from the recognition by several member companies of the pervasive role of change management in successful implementation and the need to integrate this technique into the project planning and management approach. This is because key change management techniques important to successful client buy-in, participation, and ongoing ownership of results are built into the project management methodology.

The first major phase, project planning and start-up, helps to ensure that the project is properly positioned with key client groups and that the project team has the needed direction and methodologies to properly support the initiative. The five key components are as follows:

1. **Sponsorship Positioning.** This involves the following key activities: developing a case for action,

cultivating an executive sponsor, identifying key stakeholders, appointing a skilled project manager, and establishing a systematic issue resolution process.

2. **Change Strategy Initiation.** This area includes developing an explicit change strategy, clearly delineating the scope and impact of the desired change, formulating a systematic change plan/program to properly execute the strategy, completing a change readiness assessment for all affected areas of the organization, and identifying potential areas of resistance and associated interventions.

3. **Stakeholder Engagement.** This involves developing a detailed communications plan with assigned resources, formulating a stakeholder management project, and structuring a systematic feedback project.

4. **Team Enablement.** This stage addresses project team training in both project and change management techniques, specifying change and project management team responsibilities, and developing a proactive project of inquiry and reinforcement.

5. **Project Planning and Launch.** The final component consists of formulating a project charter with expected benefits and risks, developing a comprehensive project plan with defined scope and resource requirements, laying out an explicit issue resolution approach, and providing an agreed-upon measurement and monitoring process.

The second major phase, project completion and implementation, provides for effective management of the project throughout its life cycle in addition to proper implementation planning of ownership transfer. The five key components are as follows:

1. **Ongoing Sponsorship Management.** This involves monitoring and updating the original "case for action," continually positioning the executive sponsor as a visible champion, actively managing key stakeholders to promote continued buy-in, ensuring project managers have effectively utilized change skills in both leading the project team and with their clients, and following up to be sure that project-related issues have been effectively addressed and resolved.

2. **Change Management Execution.** This component focuses on coordinating an effective change program throughout the project. This involves periodically revisiting the change strategy to be sure that it has been systematically implemented, effectively identifying and managing pockets of resistance, tracking milestones in the change plan, monitoring changes in project scope, clearly identifying the change management responsibilities and training needs for those who will be involved in the implementation, and continuous improvement.

3. **Engagement Monitoring.** This involves maintaining a comprehensive communications plan, continually coordinating a systematic stakeholder management program, ensuring the effective utilization of change skills by project management, and monitoring to ensure that project-related issues have been effectively addressed.

4. **Organizational Enablement.** This consists of monitoring the demonstration of a mastery of project and change management techniques by the project team, effective positioning of the project throughout the affected organization(s), tracking that project team members have been actively engaged in with stakeholders.

5. **Project Operationalization and Implementation.** This component focuses on maintaining an effective project through the latter stages of the project life cycle including ensuring milestones are met with timely project reviews and key issues effectively resolved, monitoring that project team resources effectively perform their tasks and acquire the necessary skills to fulfill their roles, monitoring "performance to plan" and making needed adjustments, and developing a detailed implementation plan with specific responsibilities for execution.

Becoming Thought Leaders and Leading Change

As internal and external consulting groups have gained the trust of top leadership, many are becoming involved in more strategic projects and orchestrating organization-level change projects. This involves five key activity areas.

1. The change leadership role is a very important one for internal consultants in order to maximize their impact on the overall organization. This involves going beyond just facilitating change and proactively positioning the need for an organization-wide change project to enable the organization to both

anticipate the need for change early on and develop the competencies needed to effectively manage it. Assuming this role requires the consultants to earn the trust of leadership and embed a change strategy and skill-building techniques into their overall program and specific projects.

2. Consultants have also become increasingly involved in executive coaching to help them more effectively deal with the increasing rate of change and build those capabilities in their management cadre. This includes enhancing their capabilities in areas such as team-based strategic planning, scenario and contingency planning, developing organization measurement and alignment programs, and creating a more visible sponsorship role for key initiatives. One technique consultants often use to help cultivate this role is to become involved in business planning facilitation. This provides an initial entry into working with leaders on developing key plans for the organization and positions them to increasingly add value as the relationship develops. The approach includes bringing a structured approach to the planning process with clear role definition, deliverables, and metrics.

3. A key competency in leading change involves overcoming resistance and building resilience. This starts with understanding that resistance is a natural component of change that needs to be dealt with constructively. Then, key interventions must be positioned to help overcome the resistance and reinforce positive behaviors, including listening to

concerns and developing an understanding of root causes, providing tools and techniques to mitigate the problem, involving the resisting parties in the change effort, and encouraging a supportive atmosphere.

4. A parallel effort to build resilience helps the organization to engage change in a positive manner, including developing a comfort level in dealing with ambiguity, being positive regarding new opportunities resulting from change, and developing a systematic approach to dealing with uncertainty.

5. Finally, developing the capability for monitoring industry trends and implications can help to position a thought leadership role by bringing key new developments and industry shifts/trends to leadership for their consideration before they are generally recognized. In order to enhance this capability, some have created linkages with external research services to monitor external developments and insights from industry experts. An enhanced positioning in this regard has been achieved by a number of these groups by coordinating the external research function for the organization. This provides access to key research services and selected experts, which can then be used to help position future projects.

Positioning Business Partner Role

A key success factor in fulfilling the consulting value proposition is being perceived in a partnership role with clients. This applies not only to formalized internal consulting groups but also to external consultants and support functions such as HR and IT as they provide effective advisory services.

A key aspect of this role is becoming a trusted advisor to key client groups. Numerous support functions are focusing on this area by dividing their organizations into two main components—(1) Centers of Excellence (CoE) or traditional transactional type of services and (2) business partner or client interface roles. This includes a wide range of functions, including human resources, information technology, quality management, and auditing and other financial services.

This is stimulated by the recognition by these organizations of the growing importance of the critical role of providing internal advisory services to their future positioning in the organization. Many of these groups are seeking to provide internal consulting services without recognizing that role or developing the expertise and processes to do so most effectively. These are termed internal consultants by role but not by title or formal designation. These groups represent the population that can most benefit from developing a more professional consulting approach.

Next, promoting involvement is important to proper positioning of the internal consulting role in order to develop the critical linkages with client and potential client groups. This includes helping to facilitate key client meetings and issue resolution activities and providing supplemental resources to address key issues. A vital message here is for consultants to develop a more proactive approach to understanding how they can assist business leaders in meeting their goals and dealing with key issues which might arise.

Then, a continuing program of gaining business knowledge is very important for the internal and external consultants. One of the areas of expertise that clients value in an advisory or consultative role is a knowledge of the industry and key trends affecting their business. This has translated into continuing education programs by members of many groups. Some internal consulting groups have established a policy that a portion of their staff be rotational positions from the business units they serve—thus helping to utilize their knowledge of various parts of the business in addition to their relationships with these organizations.

Another way to begin to develop a business partner role with various areas of the organization is to offer facilitation services to help better manage their meetings and resolve issues—particularly those involving future planning activities. This serves as an entry strategy that is of immediate use to client groups and also provides the opportunity to learn more about key issues and help to address them. It also can be used to transfer basic meeting management, team building, and issue resolution skills to clients and help them appreciate their value.

Executing Effective Marketing and Business Development

Client Development Assessment

Marketing and client development is critical for internal and external consultants alike. With so many opportunities to develop clients, the challenge is to select the correct approach. Because the marketing of consulting is much different from the marketing of retail products, the approach to client development is much different. Because client development is incremental, given the gradual development of clients, many of the strategies suggested take time and often become more complex as they grow. Consequently, it presents what might be called the building blocks of a consulting practice. Let's examine a few issues.

Marketing versus Selling

Perhaps the most important distinction is the definition of marketing versus selling. Selling is the actual transaction—closing the sale, when a customer actually buys a product or service. For many products, the sale is at the end of the cycle, but for consultants, it is often the beginning of the cycle. Marketing is a process of presenting information about a product or service, creating an image about the product and service, and providing all the information necessary to make a purchase decision. Marketing is about awareness and brand building as much as enticing people to sign the purchase order.

As it relates to consulting, marketing has six basic principles:

1. **Exposure and recognition are critical.** Prospective clients must understand that the consulting practice exists and know the consultant(s) who deliver the service.

2. **Targeting a focused client base is essential.** The consulting practice is usually narrowly focused

because of the uniqueness of the service and the niche it is attempting to develop. Consequently, marketing must be focused on a very specific target audience.

3. **Marketing must build the appropriate image.** Much of consulting is based on cost and perceived value—two areas that cannot come from an advertisement or exhibit. It must come from a clear understanding of what can be provided and who is providing the service.

4. **Cost effectiveness is an important consideration.** If marketing is not focused correctly or is not achieving the desired responses, it may be too expensive. Thus, the cost of marketing activities must be carefully weighed against the responses obtained from them.

5. **The effectiveness of various approaches should be measured to reflect their effectiveness.** Some channels, processes, and approaches produce more results than others—both long- and short-term. It is important to collect and understand this information.

6. **Consistency is critical.** A brand needs to be developed, supported, and sustained. There must be a consistent message and image throughout the process.

The most effective consulting marketing approaches are more indirect, passive, and personal in their connection to the client or prospective client—and there are dozens of approaches in this category. Fortunately, they often require low time commitments and little expense.

The outcome of a successful consulting project often hinges on the relationship between the client and consultant. Because of this, the personal approach to prospecting, selling, and client development is critical. A consultant must become familiar enough with the client's needs to be sufficiently involved, and to provide the personal touch that is needed throughout the process.

Creating a Client Development Process

Client development is the lifeblood of the consulting practice. A systemized, step-by-step process is needed; it cannot be left to chance or random events. Take the time to design a plan and stick with it. This will ensure a consistent process that can be adjusted or modified to make it better. The beginning point for creating a system is to determine the best marketing strategies. Different techniques can be worked systematically. While there may be many processes involved in building name recognition, creating exposure, obtaining referrals, and ultimately developing a brand, the goal is to obtain a face-to-face meeting with the client and turn that meeting into a future prospect.

Figure 3.1 shows the new client development system is designed to build on an inquiry. As the figure shows, the initial response will include an article or information that draws attention to the consulting practice as well as a request for a phone call. The phone call, though brief, is designed to glean information to revise the database and ensure that this is a valid prospect. If it appears that this contact does not qualify as a future prospect, the name is moved to inactive status. If a meeting is scheduled, the

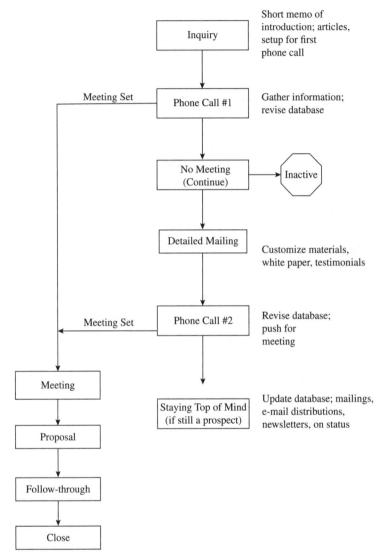

FIGURE 3.1   New Client Development Flowchart

objective of this phase—the sales cycle—is complete. If no meeting is scheduled, but there is still some interest (or no lack of interest), the process continues.

An additional communication where testimonials and a white paper are sent, or conveying more information of value to the client, would be appropriate. This is then followed up with a phone call that would push for a meeting. Phone calls are recommended over e-mails because of the ability to answer questions, discuss options, and have a give-and-take that might otherwise require a dozen e-mails. At this point, three options are available: 1) a meeting is set and the process continues; 2) there is no meeting, but the contact remains a prospect; or 3) the prospect is no longer viable and is removed from the database.

If no meeting is scheduled, but the individual or organization is still a prospect, the prospective client should be included in future mailings/communications, e-mail distributions, newsletters on current status and activities, and so forth. In essence, they become a prospect for updates and contacts only. If something develops in the future, additional mailings are in order. A judgment call has to be made on how much personal follow-up is needed to arrive at a face-to-face meeting.

Whatever the method, it is important to have a logical, rational, step-by-step approach to develop new clients. It does not have to be documented in every step, as indicated in Figure 3.1, but it must involve follow-up with every major direct contact. Obviously, there is a great deal of indirect processes, such as writing articles, giving speeches, and using clients, all of which are discussed in more detail later. These are working in the background to generate new prospects. When a prospect presents itself, the new client development system kicks in.

Using the Internet

It is hard to imagine a consulting practice without heavy use of the Internet. Imagine trying to run a practice without a phone. Some perceive the value of the Internet in the same way—it must be one of the most important communication tools and an important part of the marketing approach.

Website. Whether internal or external, the website for the practice is the key connection to the business through the Internet. To be an effective marketing tool, it must be well organized, helpful, full of easy-to-read content, and easily accessible. Website design is described in other books and sources. Also, as the technology evolves, internal consultants are increasingly utilizing their company's Intranet to market their services. This often contains not only an overview of their services, capabilities, and activities but also provides a library of tools and techniques that clients can use in their projects and to inform their team.

Blogs and Social Media. With so many blogs available on almost every conceivable topic, it is helpful to pay attention to the bloggers. Bloggers can help you, ignore you, or hurt you. They can bring what you do into the blog, and you can assist the process by getting clients to make comments, by adding comments yourself, and following the current discussion issues. Bloggers can also ignore you. This would be a call to action to ensure that you are involved. In some cases online discussions can hurt you, particularly when some individuals are criticizing your consulting practice, methodology, unique advantage, or any articles or books you have written. Ideally, any negative discussion needs to be confronted by neutral individuals.

Social media is another useful tool to get others involved in your consulting issues and practices. Ideally, the consulting practice should have a presence on LinkedIn, Facebook, and Twitter. Sharing what you're doing and adding your comments, advice, suggestions, and thoughts about particular issues can create name recognition and provide additional needed exposure.

A word of caution on both blogs and social media: They can become time consuming, particularly social media. Trying to stay in touch with discussions and activities may not be worth the effort. Also, many consultants have found that the people who are involved in detailed social media discussions are not clients but potential competitors or curious bystanders. If the clients are not reading the discussion, it may make little difference in your practice. Social media activities should be acknowledged in some way. If the discussion is adverse, the negativity should be corrected; otherwise, be careful.

Newsletter Publishing.   E-publishing makes newsletters affordable and practical. Some consulting practices create a newsletter with useful, helpful, and value-added information, and make this available to the clients at no cost. This approach is feasible for internal and external consulting practices. This information must be perceived as valuable; otherwise it becomes marketing propaganda, or spam for some potential clients. A newsletter requiring much effort may not be cost effective unless there are many current or prospective clients and the newsletter is a principal way of keeping in contact with them. If so, this is an excellent way to update them on changes and improvements, and needed services and additions, as well as to provide useful tips, trends, research, and other related innovations.

Communicating with Potential Clients.   E-mail can be a very cost effective way to provide new clients with much needed information. E-mail can be sent to prospects to announce services, provide updates, or offer more information about the consulting practice. It is helpful to distinguish this type of e-mail from what may be considered spam. Start with an eye-catching heading and get right to the point. The less they have to read, the sooner your potential clients will get the message. In some cases the e-mail may just bring up an issue and provide a website link. The key is to have a very small, focused mailing list and provide useful information for the reader.

Building Related Tools and Products

One of the most important client development activities is to build products and services related to the consulting practice. These not only enhance and support consulting but can drive significant business volume, revenue, or transfer pricing, whether internal or external. Related tools provide a steady stream of revenue when consultants are not delivering work for the consulting practice. This is more important for smaller practices because if consultants are not driving revenue, there is no revenue stream. In addition, related products and services complement consulting and may be the decisive advantage for securing a consulting contract. The related products and services can vary but usually are grouped into five categories.

Workshops. The most logical supporting process is workshops that offer the consultant's methodology. These workshops should be available to both clients and prospective clients. For some consultants, this is the principal lead-generating process—getting individuals to attend the workshop to learn what the consultant does. The risk is that a participant may learn enough about the methodology to apply it without the help of the consultant, but this is usually a minimal risk, if you have a defined niche. They can also build expertise and recognition for the consultant. Public workshops can provide all the marketing advantages of any type of promotional or advertising medium.

Software. When the consulting solution needs to be automated, software is sometimes required or essential. Many consultants recommend a commercial software package they have found helpful, or they contract with a software provider in a reseller arrangement. Some consultants develop their own software and sell it along with the consulting process. Still others use a variety of existing software and offer consulting to show how the software can be used.

Books and Articles. Books can be complementary to consulting processes and often represent one of the most effective ways to sell the consulting. Most well-known consultants will author a book about their methodology and use it as an important lead-generation tool as well as a revenue generator. A variety of articles or article series can also be effective.

Benchmarking. In some situations, benchmarking involves collecting data from organizations addressing a particular topic or issue at hand and presenting this to clients in terms of best practices. This service can be provided for a fee (or transfer price) and represents an important or significant revenue-generating process while supporting the consulting services.

Research Reports. Similar to benchmarking, research reports show how others are using various processes and tools offered by the consultant. These reports can show the success made and the challenges involved in implementing the processes offered by the consultant. For example, a research report might show the ways in which practices are utilizing the consulting solution, the successes of the solution, or the barriers to its implementation.

The AIMC also offers numerous research reports for its internal and external consulting members, including these:

- Best Practices Benchmarking Survey of more than 1,000 organizations worldwide
- Joint surveys with other associations on the emerging needs for consulting skills in various support functions, including quality management and human resources

- Profiles of the programs of leading internal consulting organizations as presented at their annual conferences and newsletters
- Summaries of Affinity Group webinars on key areas of interest

Making Related Products Part of the Process.   The   pie chart in Figure 3.2 shows the breakdown of other products and services offered by the ROI Institute, a global consulting practice. While the largest source of revenues is consulting, there is a significant amount of revenue generated with workshops that support the trademark process, software that supports consulting, books that explain the process, and research and benchmarking that also complement the process. For a new consulting practice, this may appear to be a daunting task and initially may involve only one additional related product. For a

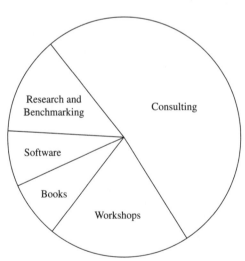

FIGURE 3.2   Sample Breakdown of All Products and Services

small independent consultant, this is absolutely essential. These other services generate revenue when consulting is not being delivered. The advantage of using related products is underscored when considering the complementary aspects of the services described. For example, a consultant who develops books and other publications will use these materials as references or texts for a workshop. The basis of the books and the workshop leads to the sale of the software that supports what is being taught in the workshop and is being described in the books. All of these generate leads for new consulting opportunities, and the consulting opportunities generate more experience to be included in more books and publications or revised editions of them. It becomes an important cycle, where one process feeds another, making the related products and services an integral part of a flourishing consulting practice.

Managing for Results

It is very important for internal and external consultants to manage for results and value. This approach often involves going beyond the initial request for a specific project and helping the client think through the best results and how to measure its accomplishment. Key elements include shifting paradigms, focusing on the proper solution, setting objectives at multiple levels, transferring ownership and knowledge, and performance management.

Shifting Paradigms

Consulting paradigms are shifting for both consultants and clients. Processes are being developed to focus directly on accountability. For years, consulting processes and consulting progress have been activity or input-focused, with success being derived by the inputs into the process rather than the outcomes. The situation is changing, though, as consulting projects and processes are now results-based. Table 3.1 shows the shift from activity-based consulting to results-based consulting, an important paradigm shift for the consulting profession.

As shown, results-based consulting includes the following characteristics:

- Consulting projects begin with the end in mind, linked to specific business needs represented by business impact measures that matter.

Table 3.1 Paradigm Shift in Consulting Accountability

Activity-Based Consulting	Results-Based Consulting
Characterized by:	*Characterized by:*
No business need for the consulting project	Project linked to specific business needs
No assessment of performance issues related to project	Assessment of performance issues related to project
No specific, measurable objectives for application and business impact	Specific objectives for application and business impact
No effort to prepare stakeholders/participants to achieve results	Results/expectations communicated to stakeholders/participants
No effort to prepare the work environment to support implementation	Environment prepared to support implementation
No efforts to build partnerships with key managers	Partnerships established with key managers and clients
No measurement of results or cost-benefit analysis	Measurement of results including cost-benefit analysis
Planning and reporting on consulting projects are input-focused	Planning and reporting on consulting projects are output-focused

- A detailed assessment of performance issues and performance effectiveness to determine the specific causes or inhibitors to the improvement of business needs

- Specific objectives developed at multiple levels, including application and business impact objectives

- Expectations of results communicated through a variety of individuals, particularly for those stakeholders and participants directly involved in the consulting project. This helps keep the end in mind in very specific, measurable terms.

- Full exploration and preparation of the work environment to support the implementation of the consulting solution

- Partnerships with key managers and clients to build their support for the process and solution, helping to ensure that they will provide the resources and commitment to make the project a success

- Measurement of results, including a cost-benefit analysis showing the payoff for major consulting projects

- Output-focused planning and reporting on consulting projects, indicating the successes obtained through the project rather than listing the resources deployed

This represents a shift in reporting as organizations report data along the six measures outlined in this book. This paradigm shift is long overdue. Fortunately, many consulting practices have adopted the results-based philosophy and are delivering results, meeting the expectations of the client. Unfortunately, not enough are basing their approach on results. Clearly, there is more talk than action on this issue.

Ensuring That Consulting Generates the Right Solution

A critical issue in terms of delivering value is to ensure that the consulting process or solution that is explored is right for the client. Although this is usually not a problem, sometimes a consultant will implement his or her favorite solution to solve a problem even though it is not the most optimum approach. This is covered in Chapter 8 regarding aligning projects to business, but it is a critical issue in making sure that value is delivered and managing the process to make sure this takes place, using the V Model described in Chapter 8.

Setting Objectives at Multiple Levels

Objectives provide guidance and direction for those involved in the consulting process. Everyone involved needs to know where the project is going and the impact it will achieve. This is accomplished by setting objectives at multiple levels beginning with reaction to the project and moving to learning what is necessary to make the project successful, applying and implementing the process successfully, and the impact that it will have in the organization. These multiple levels of objectives, which are discussed later, become very critical to define the expected value along these different levels of results.

Transferring Ownership

It is important to have a detailed and agreed-upon implementation plan in order to help ensure successful transferring of ownership from the consulting project team to the organization(s) responsible for implementation and continuous improvement. This prevents the narcotic effect of consultants: "You have to keep engaging them." Some clients want to do it themselves. The internal consultant has a distinct advantage versus his or her external counterpart in helping to ensure effective implementation and ownership transfer to clients.

In addition to transferring ownership, consultants should transfer knowledge to clients and other stakeholders throughout the organization. This is accomplished in several ways. The implementation planning activity for projects should include tasks to onboard and train both the implementation team and process owners/users. This aspect of project management is often not given enough attention, causing problems in the implementation and continuous improvement phase. Any process or organizational redesign project needs to include specific reskilling and training activities for the leaders and users. In addition, the implementation team needs to acquire many of the skills taught in the original project team training and action learning.

Project team training should begin with the onboarding process at the beginning and continue throughout the project lifecycle on a just-in-time basis. This should also include action learning and mentoring along the way. Internal consulting groups and their designated project team participant(s) frequently fulfill the project team training role, and some groups are affiliated with the corporate training organization. In this case, project team training is often provided as an integral part of the overall training curriculum and management development program.

Consulting groups are also involved in creating internal expertise networks. The training and skill building provided during project execution and implementation is of maximum value to the organization when it leads to the cultivation of an ongoing network of knowledge sharing around a particular methodology.

Often termed Centers of Excellence (CoEs), these networks continue to develop and increase their knowledge due to an ongoing interest in a particular area/methodology. Some examples of the most frequently developed CoEs are process improvement/LSS; strategy execution; project/portfolio management; change management/OE/OD; and performance measurement.

Consultants are often involved in coordinating the activities of these networks of expertise. In addition, many consultants use this pool of expertise in their projects in their area of the organization and frequently identify their members as candidates to join the internal consulting group.

Performance Measurement

Performance measurement is another important component in managing for results. Here, a variety of measurements are tracked for each project and for the internal consulting group overall. On the project level, financial, customer, operational and employee metrics should be employed to provide a complete indication of performance. Financial measures include savings or revenue generation and return on investment. Customer measures track client satisfaction and broader stakeholder impacts. Operational measures indicate such areas as timeliness of completion and other aspects of performance to plan. Employee measures calibrate project team member engagement and skill building accomplishments both for project team and affected client group(s). These areas are explored in more detail in the measurement chapters in this book.

Final Thoughts

As highlighted in this chapter, there are a number of factors involved in managing the internal consulting capability to provide a maximum level of value for the organization. The Internal Consulting Maturity Continuum provides an overarching framework to help assess the status of the development of internal consulting operations in relation to 35 criteria. This was developed from data gathered from a large number of groups in various points in their development or maturity. This data was then analyzed and grouped into the following three broad stages as shown in Table 3.2. This framework and associated criteria is further described in *Internal Consulting Excellence*[1].

External consultants can fulfill a valuable role as strategic partners with internals to help bring a high level

Table 3.2 Maturity Continuum

Stages	Overall Characteristics
Beginning	In the process of forming the group and establishing initial consulting processes and practice areas
Developing	Currently formalizing plans, processes, and training development programs
Mature	Established infrastructure and client relationships with future development path understood

of professionalism to the internal group by providing expertise in key practice areas to help staff important projects and train the internals in associated skills. They can also utilize their expertise in helping to manage effective consulting processes by working with internal consulting leaders to help improve their business development, client engagement, and project management approaches. Externals can utilize their experience in orchestrating a professional-level management system including maintaining effective client relationships and fostering a results-oriented culture. They can also play a valuable role in helping to coach relatively inexperienced internal consultants with who they might be teamed in delivering key projects.

In summary, this chapter is about managing the practice to deliver results, addressing some of the critical issues that are necessary. It described how a professionally managed system should be devised to ensure that processes are working properly and the value is being delivered. This chapter also focused on how to position the consultant as a business partner so that they may become a sought-after, important, and valued colleague. Next, the chapter explored marketing and client development, which is often not addressed so well with internal consulting, but is equally applied to both internal and external consulting. And as the chapter ended, it provided tips on managing for results, and how to ensure that the process delivers the value desired and needed for the client and the organization.

Controlling Costs and Enhancing Value

The full benefit of developing consulting capabilities is realized when it is used to not only provide internal services, but also to help maximize the value of the organization's overall consulting investment—by controlling costs and helping to ensure high-quality consulting services. Key factors in achieving success in this area are the planning and budgeting process, monitoring and controlling costs, managing suppliers for value, and pursuing avenues to achieve the "maximum value state" for internal consulting.

The Planning and Budgeting Process

The Planning Process

First, one of the key factors in the proper positioning and long-term sustainability of internal consulting groups is the development of an effective strategic planning process for their organization—and to properly align it with the enterprise planning process.

This starts with developing an explicit strategic plan that is linked with and positioned to support and enable the overall strategic direction and goals.

As further detailed in the book, *Internal Consulting Excellence*,[1] key components of the strategic plan include the following four major components:

- **Situation Analysis**

    This summarizes the internal consulting group's positioning within the enterprise and relative to external trends.

119

The internal situation assessment reviews the current positioning of the group with sponsors and client groups, state of its consulting processes, and consultant capabilities.

The external analysis reviews both current activities of external consultants within the enterprise and developments in the consulting industry. This includes keeping up with best practices in internal consulting.

A SWOT (strengths, weaknesses, opportunities, and threats) analysis is then often used to represent the findings citing key internal strengths and weaknesses and potential opportunities and threats.

- **Overall Direction Setting**

  This section positions the vision, mission, and projected role that the internal consulting group needs to play over the planning period.

  The vision provides a summary of the desired or aspirational future state of the internal consulting practice at full maturity.

  The mission statement then articulates the purpose of the internal consulting function and areas of practice.

  This is often complemented by a description of the role of the internal consulting practice in supporting its client organizations and adding value to the enterprise.

- **Goals, Strategies, and Objectives**

  Here, the desired direction is made actionable, starting with establishing key goals for the group in the areas of business development and financial performance, customer relationship management, consulting process improvement, and consultant performance.

The goal setting process often includes the articulation of key strategies, which will be employed to help reach those goals. These are comprised of overall approaches the group plans to employ to help reach these goals.

These broad goals are then translated into specific objectives with associated performance measurements and time frames, which are then aligned with the performance metrics in the internal consulting scorecard described in Chapter 5.

Supporting Action Plans

Next, specific action plans are developed to operationalize the objectives providing explicit tasks, deliverables, and responsibility assignments. Figure 4.1 is a sample Action Plan template.

This planning document can then provide great assistance in proactively positioning the consulting group with their upper management, current and potential sponsors, and target client groups. In addition, the process of reviewing the preliminary strategic plan with management and clients also helps obtain their feedback and prompt discussion about new opportunity areas for providing needed support. The annual budget is then developed to align with and help operationalize the consulting plan.

Action Plan Name:
Objective Supported:
Sponsors and Clients:
Main Tasks and Milestones:
Key Deliverables:
Responsibility Assignments (both consultant and clients):

FIGURE 4.1 Action Plan Template

The Budgeting Process

Regarding the budgeting process, as organizations recognize the importance and necessity for consulting, annual budgets continue to increase by organization, industry, and country. Consequently, the process to develop a budget for a consulting practice is becoming more structured and scrutinized.

A formal budgeting process, aligned with the business strategy, is considered one of the most important management tools for efficient and effective operation. Budgets are developed with other major functions and entities, using the same budgeting guidelines and processes. For internal consultants, the budgeting process usually begins with delivery of a package containing specific guidelines, forms, procedures, and special instructions for developing the budget. It also contains the approval process, philosophy, concerns, and other issues often communicated along with budget packages. The good news is that consulting is considered an important activity in the organization—subject to the same control and budgeting requirements as other practices. The process has become more formal, organized, and accurate. The bad news is that the budget by itself can be constraining, take time, and may be inflexible in its administration.

The budget has become the most widely used tool of control for managers. Budgets enable the consulting practice to know where it stands, spot various trends, and control resources during the fiscal year. When the budget is approved, it should communicate three things:

1. The consulting plan for providing consulting services must meet specific operational and strategic business goals.

2. Each consulting project should add value to the organization in some way, often captured as increased revenue or a reduction of costs. In essence, almost all projects should increase productivity, improve quality, save time, reduce costs directly, or improve satisfaction for customers and employees.

3. Each consulting practice will have a specific unit cost associated with its project work. The total cost of all projects and services are included in the budget while the cost per project and per participant involved is included in the detail.

These three major statements characterize an ideal budget, a situation sought by the consulting practice as the budget is developed each year. Unfortunately, some budgets fall short of providing the detail or connections of all three.

Collecting Information

In addition to information about specific needs, several types of information should be collected when the budget is being developed. For internal consultants, the following list provides a sampling of reports that might be needed for budget preparation. These items can supply information that may help provide direction for implementation of the budget. New projects should be tied to specific business needs, which are addressed later. Several items in this list represent a wealth of opportunities to explore projects for the next year's budget.

Sampling of Documents Needed for Budget Development

- Operating plans of the organization
- Strategic plans or multi-year operating plan
- Capital expenditure budget
- Operating performance of the organization

- Financial performance of the organization
- Major operating issues and concerns
- Special audit and investigative reports that address concerns or problem areas
- Customer satisfaction and loyalty data
- Engagement and job satisfaction
- Performance management process reports
- Talent management reports
- Specific projects in process

A variety of business plans clearly indicate the direction of the organization, identifying some of the major issues and problems, which often translate directly into consulting opportunities. This plan often alerts the consulting practice to strategic shifts that will occur in the business. Special audits and investigative reports uncover problems and issues, which represent a great source for project possibilities. Business issues, such as customer complaints, time to market, and delays of new products, are all business issues that can translate into consulting opportunities. Using these strategic business issues as a platform for developing organizational solutions is the responsibility of an effective consulting practice.

Types of Budgets

Although there can be many different types of budgets unique to an organization, three major categories often appear and are briefly presented here. The specific application of these types can vary with the organization and culture.

Fixed and Variable Budgets. The fixed budget represents those costs that will not directly vary with the amount of work that is to be conducted. Facilities for the consultants, technology support, and overhead support staff fit into this category. The variable budget represents costs directly related to specific output, such as the number of projects or participants involved in projects. Materials, travel expenses, and facilitators are examples of variable costs. Some organizations use a charge-back or transfer pricing model to manage consulting budgets—users of consultants in the business areas are charged to cover costs. Other companies use an allocation model where budgets are "allocated" based on a flat fee per headcount in a division or corporate area, or by some other method. External consultants use a P&L model and are managed as business entities. All of these models have appropriate application based on a business or organizational model.

Planning, Programming, and Budgeting System. Initially launched by the federal government and now used by many organizations, this system is where the budget is developed for specific projects. There are five basic steps to follow with this approach:

1. Specify and analyze basic objectives in each major area of activity.
2. Analyze the output of planned projects as defined by specific objectives.
3. Measure total cost of the projects for several years as a projection.

4. Analyze alternatives to the projects.

5. Make the approach an integral part of the budget.

Zero-Based Budgeting.   Some organizations are using a system where the budget is developed from the ground up, with no holdover from the previous year. With this approach, every project or service is justified in the budgeting process. Zero-based budgets remove the temptation to add to the previous year's budget or develop a budget based on what was accomplished in the previous year. When starting from zero, a careful analysis of the costs, as well as the value of various priorities, is required. With this approach, activities, projects, or services are developed into decision packages. Various services or projects are evaluated with resources allocated to those with the highest priority. A realistic approach to budgeting could be a blend of all three of these types or a subset of one of these types.

Using the Budget

Developing a consulting budget is an essential part of managing any function, activity, or process in an organization. The trend toward more formal budgets is based, in part, on the legitimate role of consulting. Budgets are a welcome tool for the consulting practice because they make it possible to link consulting to the business. Budgets can also act as a signaling device to take corrective action. When used properly, the budget can help the staff learn from past experiences. It also improves the allocation of resources within the practice and helps communicate priorities.

In some cases, budget performance can be an important element of the performance management process.

On the other side, budgets can become very complex, confusing, and time consuming. If the budget is not flexible, it may cause individuals to stick to the "numbers," regardless of what needs exist. Also, budgets can allow individuals to manipulate the funding, anticipating budget cuts and spending all of the money, whether it is needed or not.

Monitoring and Controlling Costs

The cost of providing consulting is increasing. As consulting practices scramble to fund their budgets, they must know how and why money is spent. Today there is more pressure than ever before to report all costs of consulting, referred to as a fully loaded cost profile. This goes beyond the direct cost and includes the time that participants are involved in consulting projects. Individual cost components are used to manage resources, develop standards, measure efficiencies, and examine alternative processes.

The Concern for Cost Control

Many influences have caused the increased attention to monitoring and controlling consulting costs accurately and thoroughly. Some of the more important ones are listed here. Every consulting practice must know how much is invested in consulting. Most consulting practices calculate this expenditure and make comparisons with other organizations. Some calculate consulting costs as a percentage of revenue, develop consulting costs on a per-employee basis, or use a per-project basis. Total expenditures go beyond the overall budget and include additional costs such as participants' salaries, travel expenses, replacement costs, facilities expense, and general overhead. A few consultants calculate and report this value.

Monitoring costs by project allows the consulting practice to evaluate the relative contribution of a project and determine how these costs are changing. If a project's cost has risen when compared to previous, similar projects, it might be time to reevaluate its impact and overall success. It may be useful to compare specific components of costs to other projects or organizations. For example, the cost of the initial needs analysis could be compared to the analysis cost for a similar type of project. Significant differences may signal a problem.

Also, costs associated with design, development, or implementation could be compared to other projects within the organization and used to develop cost standards. Competitive pressures are causing increased attention on efficiencies. Most consulting practices have monthly budgets that project costs by various accounts and, in some cases, by project or project component. Cost reports are excellent tools for spotting problem areas and taking corrective action. From a practical and classical management sense, the accumulation of cost data is a necessity.

Also, current costs are needed to predict future project costs, and historical costs provide the basis for predicting future costs. Sophisticated cost models provide the capability to estimate or predict costs with reasonable accuracy. When a cost-benefit analysis is needed for a specific project, costs must be developed. Perhaps the most significant driver to collect costs is to prepare data for use in a benefits-versus-costs comparison. In this respect, cost data is as important as the project's economic benefits.

Cost data are needed for the human capital management system. A consulting practice needs to collect cost data so that these data can be integrated into existing databases for other human resource functions such as compensation, benefits, and recruiting. Including consulting cost information in these databases provides information about the consulting contribution to human resources costs. Some human capital systems monitor costs automatically.

Detailed costs are needed to plan and budget for future operations. The operating budget usually includes all of the expenditures within consulting and may also include other costs such as participants' salaries and their associated travel expenses. In recent years, the budgeting process has come under closer scrutiny, and a percentage increase to the previous year's budget is no longer acceptable for most organizations. More organizations have adopted zero-based budgets, in which each activity must be justified and no expenses are carried over from the previous year. An accurate accounting of expenditures enables the consulting practice to defend proposed ideas and projects in a line-item review with management.

Cost Classification Systems

Capturing costs is challenging because they must be accurate, reliable, and realistic. Costs can be classified in two basic ways. One is by a description of the expenditure such as labor, materials, supplies, travel, and so forth. These are expense account classifications. The other is by categories in the consulting process or function such as analysis, project development, implementation, and evaluation. An effective system will do both: monitor costs by account categories and include a method for accumulating costs by the process/functional category. While the first grouping is sufficient to present the total cost of the project, it does not allow for a useful comparison with other projects or indicate areas where costs might be excessive by relative comparisons. Therefore, two basic classifications are recommended to develop a complete costing system.

Process/Functional Classifications

Table 4.1 shows the process/functional categories for costs in four different ways. In Column A there are only two categories: consulting operating costs and consulting support costs. Operating costs include all expenses involved in conducting the consulting project; support costs include all administrative, overhead or time involved in projects, or any other expenditure not directly related to conducting the project. While it is simple to separate the two, it does not provide enough detail to analyze costs on a functional basis. Column B adds a

Table 4.1 Process/Functional Categories for Cost

A	B
Consulting Support Costs	Operating Costs
Consulting Operating Costs	Administrative Costs
	Participant Costs

C	D
Project Development Costs	Assessment Costs
Administrative Costs	Development Costs
Operating Costs	Participant Costs
Participant Costs	Implementation Costs
	Evaluation Costs
	Administrative Costs

third category and provides more detail on participant time for projects but does not provide information on project development costs—a useful item to have. Column C provides for development costs as a separate item, but it still falls short of an ideal situation. There is no way to track evaluation costs, which are becoming a more significant part of the total process. Column D represents an appropriate cost breakdown: assessment, development, participant, implementation, evaluation, and administrative. The administrative costs can be allocated to one of these areas or listed separately as a seventh category.

Needs assessment costs will usually be in the range of 5 to 10 percent of the consulting budget. Development costs may run in the 10 to 15 percent range while implementation is 70 to 80 percent of the budget. Evaluation is usually less than five percent. The actual breakdown will depend on how costs are accumulated in the organization and will vary considerably with each project, particularly in the development and implementation components. In a lengthy project involving a large amount of participant time, the implementation costs may be much higher.

Expense Account Classifications

The most time-consuming step in developing a cost system is defining and classifying the various expenses. Many of the expense accounts, such as office supplies and travel expenses, are already a part of the existing accounting system. However, there may be expenses unique to the consulting practice that must be added to the system. The system design will depend on the organization, the type of projects developed and conducted, and the limits imposed on the current cost-accounting system, if any. Also, to a certain extent, the expense account classifications will depend on how the process/functional categories have been developed, as discussed in the previous section.

Managing Suppliers for Value

Because of the increased use of outsourcing, managing suppliers or vendors becomes a critical issue. When outsourcing a small part of the consulting function, such as the use of specialized facilitators and experts, the issue is not as serious. When outsourcing reaches the point to where much of the function is outsourced to a variety of suppliers (or even one major partner), the accountability of the supplier relationship is critical and the opportunity to add value by managing this relationship properly is vast. Using outsourcing as a way to augment staff and capabilities is an excellent way to leverage the consulting function.

In fact, many internal consulting groups view their associated external consulting resources as "strategic partners" in helping to develop their practice.

Outsourcing Strategy

The extent of outsourcing is usually decided when the strategy of the consulting practice center is defined. Outsourcing is definitely a trend because of the great benefits that can be derived from the process. Outsourcing allows a more flexible and responsive consulting team; in some cases, outsourcing can access capabilities that are not readily available, improving the variety of services and products offered. By outsourcing tasks, key consultants focus their efforts on other value-adding possibilities.

Recently, outsourcing has been explored because of financial consideration—providing services and additional resources either for current service offerings or expertise which has not been developed internally. Cost reduction and/or revenue enhancement can be an important benefit, but only if the process is managed appropriately and the outsourcing partners are selected carefully.

Another key aspect is that by establishing a network of qualified external consultants who can be engaged when additional resources or specialized skills are required, it allows the internal consulting groups to maintain a smaller core staff and still meet their clients' needs.

Outsourcing Decision

The decision to outsource parts—either minor or major—of consulting must be approached carefully and managed properly. It is essential to treat outsourced suppliers as adjunct staff and provide them with knowledge and guidance about the organization. They are dependent on the internal consultants to help them be successful, and if they are successful, the consulting function will be as well. The important element in this process is to ensure that the correct decision is made for the different outsource partners, whether the partner is an expert, a practice that provides the up-front analysis, or a supplier for technology. The selection will rest on several key issues. Table 4.2 presents a checklist of the issues that should be considered in making this selection.

Most of these issues are self-explanatory, but a few deserve some attention. Part A of the table is fairly standard in the supply partner selection. Schedule, fees, and expenses are necessary. Part B contains issues that may not be defined clearly. The most important one is the measurement of success. The supplier should specify what

Table 4.2 Checklist for Selecting Supplier Partner

A	B
• Experience	• Measurement of success
• Credentials	• Reporting and monitoring
• Quality of team	• Deliverables
• Technology capabilities	• Implementation issues
• References	• Schedule
• Work samples	• Reviews
• Demos	• Termination provisions
• Fees and expenses	• Change management expertise

the proposed measure of success will be in the project, in concert with defined requirements. Also, reporting and monitoring will be critical from the supplier's perspective, detailing the specific reports provided and the data monitored to provide a summary of progress made and the success of the project. It is important to define the deliverables. With some suppliers this is easy. For others it may be more difficult (e.g., major consulting projects). In terms of implementation issues, the supplier is indicating what must take place to make the process operate smoothly and efficiently, defining particular problems that may cause a disturbance in the relationship. Private reviews are often inserted to explain the progress and review the relationship. Provisions for termination are necessary in today's legal environment. These issues should not be taken lightly, even when comparing one individual with another to provide consulting or facilitation services.

Managing the Partnership

Managing the on-going relationship is critical. Suppliers are extremely valuable to the consulting practice and they must be managed to obtain maximum value. A checklist for routinely managing these partnerships follows. A few of these issues should be underscored. Appropriate communication channels must be established up front so the supplier always has access to the proper consultants. Expectations for success should be defined up front and on an ongoing basis so that both parties have a clear understanding of the issues.

Managing the Partnership Checklist

- Establishing contacts/communications
- Defining expectations/success
- Clarifying roles and responsibilities
- Minimizing resistance
- Delivering the service
- Aligning methodologies
- Maintaining quality control
- Resolving issues
- Monitoring progress
- Keep communication open
- Provide care to maintain a productive relationship
- Taking action for improvement

Clarifying roles and responsibilities is standard and leads to an important issue: minimizing resistance from the staff. When functions are outsourced, the current staff may be concerned about losing jobs. In some arrangements, the current staff joins the outsource provider. This approach to outsourcing is a major change effort and specific plans and actions should be implemented to ensure that resistance is minimized or removed. Staff members accept outsourcing more readily when they understand the need and advantages, and are involved in some of the issues. Issues must be resolved, progress consistently monitored, and communication left open. Both sides must take care to maintain a productive relationship and be willing to take action when improvements are needed. These partnerships are critical and without the appropriate attention, the value of outsourcing could be missed. In extreme cases, results could be disastrous.

Monitoring Performance

Absent from the previous list is the topic of monitoring performance. Since this is where the value is added, it deserves additional attention. Deliverables are the first issue to consider. Delivery must be on time and include quality commitments. Beyond those items are the routine data that could be captured.

Guaranteeing Results

In the past few years, vendors and suppliers have been a part of fees and expenses, but not all are at risk. Guaranteeing results may be an option. Under this arrangement, results must be clearly defined, in some cases using the actual return on investment. There are a variety of issues, such as what percent to have at risk and the variety of issues that must be detailed to make it successful. The support provided to the supplier must be recommended properly, supported adequately, and all stakeholders understand and respect these roles in success. When applied appropriately, this approach is a tremendous win-win for all parties. It represents the way to achieve maximum value from the supplier. It also keeps the consultants and other stakeholders on the same page, clearly showing what must be done to support the supplier; otherwise, the guarantee is null and void. Other references provide more detail on this concept.[2]

Impact on External Consultants

External consultants who develop a relationship with the internal consulting group will be better positioned to get project work in the organization and work effectively with them to implement the overall initiative. This relationship is also important for externals to meet the increasing expectation that the internal participants (clients and internal consultants), in the projects in which they are involved, be trained in the methodologies being utilized, so they can provide more effective implementation and continuous improvement. The small to medium-sized external firms have a particularly significant opportunity to fit into the growing number of "integrated internal-external consulting staffing models" and complement current internal capabilities and expertise.

Implications for Maximizing Value-Added

The full benefit of developing internal consulting capabilities is realized when it is used not only to provide internal services but also to help maximize the value of the organization's overall consulting investment—and build overall organizational capabilities. We are characterizing this aspirational role as the "maximum value state." Key factors in achieving success in this area are as follows:

- Monitoring external consulting spend
- Ensuring quality consulting contracts
- Managing a combined internal-external staffing model
- Effectively aligning and integrating internal consulting capabilities across the enterprise
- Transferring capabilities and responsibilities to clients
- Enhancing overall organizational change capabilities
- Developing strategic portfolio management approach
- Establishing an economic value tracking system
- Ensuring sustained value from the internal consulting investment

Monitoring External Consulting Spend

Internal consulting groups are increasingly becoming involved in helping to evaluate, organize and monitor the overall investment in consulting services across the enterprise. This is being done both to control cost and to help ensure the maximum benefit for that investment. Recent research has indicated that there is an increasing emphasis on controlling professional services costs in many organizations. This often starts with identifying the aggregate level of such expenditures across the enterprise.

Then procedures are put in place to track the associated activities and institute a process for selecting service providers, including external consultants, and evaluating their performance.

Internal consulting groups, often in concert with the procurement organization, are in a unique position to help the enterprise obtain maximum value by helping to position the right expertise, in the best role and monitoring their performance.

Ensuring Quality Consulting Contracts

Internal consultants also become involved in participating in the contracting for external consulting services. This involvement can assist internal clients in obtaining maximum value for their investment, including these:

- Focusing on deliverables and results
- Specifying the proper knowledge/expertise and experience of resources to be devoted to the project
- Ensuring the needed level of methodology and technology transfer and reuse from the initiative
- Helping to understand the implications of the project for effective implementation planning, execution and continuous improvement

Maximizing a Combined Internal-External Staffing Model

This approach seeks to help effectively integrate and align existing internal consulting resources and expertise with external consulting capabilities both currently engaged and to meet future external needs. This starts with the internal consulting group, in concert with their client organizations, assessing the current and evolving needs for consulting services—and then developing an overall template or framework of expertise and methodologies required to meet them.

Then, relationships are cultivated with external consulting groups and individuals to provide these services on an as needed basis, including project support, business development assistance, external research, and training and coaching. Some of the more well-developed approaches in this area view this as a "capacity free" consulting model. Here, selected externals are integrated into the internal consulting group's consulting services in a variety of roles with overall quality control being the responsibility of internal consulting leadership. Also, in order to create a more consistent approach, externals in this role are often trained in the internal consulting group's methodologies.

Effectively Aligning and Integrating Internal Consulting Capabilities across the Enterprise

These programs, often initiated by the core internal consulting group, endeavor to identify groups providing client advisory services across the enterprise and provide an approach to help create more value from the combined resources and capability. Key steps in this undertaking frequently include the following:

- Identifying functional areas across the organization providing various types of advisory and project management services

- Conducting a survey to obtain more detail on the services provided, methodologies utilized, and skills needed

- Holding a series of meetings with these groups to identify opportunities for alignment and potential integration

- Developing a plan to implement these findings and providing an ongoing coordination and issue resolution capability

This involves helping a variety of internal support groups who are internal consultants "by role but not by title" develop their business partner role with the client organizations they serve.

Included in these groups are human resources and human capital management, quality management, auditing and financial services, and information technology. The alignment and integration process provides a platform for developing client service and planning skills in addition to helping to improve the consistency in tools and techniques utilized. Four specific benefits to be realized from this effort are as follows:

1. Enabling a consistent approach and widespread use of organizational improvement methodologies, such as process redesign or change management— including strategic partnering with externals.

   This is important both for the enterprise to realize the most value from investing in a particular suite of tools/techniques, and also to help ensure a more uniform application across various organizational units. Additional leverage can be gained through the development of a partnering arrangement with externals to complement the internal consulting group's areas of expertise.

2. Driving the effective integration of methodologies in major initiatives.

   The typical internal consulting group has several areas of practice with the need to combine the use of numerous tools and techniques on an individual project. The internal consulting group is also expected to provide insights regarding the proper use of them during the project planning phase.

3. Providing an improved implementation and continuous improvement focus.

   A core value of the internal consulting group is working to ensure effective implementation and transfer of ownership and skills to the project/process owners in order to realize ongoing improvement. This is a unique role that external consultants usually do not fill—either because they don't consider it their role or their clients are not willing to pay for it. In any case, the internal consultants are there for the long haul and must consider this as a key part of their job.

   The internals are also better positioned for this role with their more intimate knowledge of the enterprise and extensive contacts throughout.

4. Stimulating an environment of constant learning and innovation.

   Effective internal consulting groups need to be continually monitoring the evolution of new methodologies and best practice approaches in their application. In addition, a number of internal consulting groups have assumed a leadership position in driving enterprise-wide innovation programs to help the organization revitalize and reframe itself in this challenging environment.

As this strategic role grows, internal consulting groups are increasingly being positioned as a key partner in *enterprise transformation* initiatives with increasing access to and influence on top-level management and cross-organizational leadership roles—and this term has recently been showing up in more titles of the internal consulting groups.

Also, because of this expanding scope and organizational impact, numerous internal consulting groups have been collaborating with corporate training and development groups to include key consulting skills and service offerings into their curriculum.

Transferring Capabilities and Responsibilities to Clients

A key benefit of the overall organization's investment in creating an internal consulting group is their role in transferring skills and capabilities to clients and other stakeholders.

This first occurs as part of the projects in which the internal consulting group is involved. Here, project team members, and those with whom they interact, are trained in key skills needed to effectively execute their associated roles and responsibilities.

Then, during the implementation planning phase, those responsible for executing specific projects are identified and trained in their new responsibilities. In addition, many internal consulting groups have a broader charter to help build related skills across the enterprise. In order to address this need, some of them provide training courses in these areas, which serve not only to build organizational capability, in areas such as process improvement, Lean Six Sigma, or change management, but also to expose the broader organization to improvement opportunities that the internal consulting group can help address.

Another approach for enhancing capabilities for the overall organization is the creation of Centers of Excellence (CoEs) on a widespread basis. These CoEs serve as a network to share experiences, enhance skills, and identify future improvement opportunities.

Enhancing Overall Organizational Change Capabilities

Internal consulting groups are also becoming increasingly involved in leading and coordinating "enterprise-wide change programs." These initiatives have been fostered by the emerging realization that this capability needs to be enhanced across the overall organization and that there needs to be a more consistent approach and an active support network to gain maximum benefit from that endeavor. The return on investment from these programs is largely embedded in the increased level of implementation of projects where the participants have been trained on the change management techniques involved including the following:

- Developing and maintaining sponsorship
- Managing stakeholder involvement
- Training effective project teams
- Overcoming resistance
- Fostering effective communications and feedback

This enterprise-wide approach also reduces problems caused by isolated programs with inconsistent methodologies—and resulting inefficiencies and confusion. Specific measures in this area are aligned with the intangible measures listed in *The Consultant's Scorecard*,[3] including the following categories:

- Level of engagement
- Employee satisfaction
- Leadership effectiveness
- Effective teamwork and cooperation
- Conflict resolution
- Communications quality
- Organizational resilience
- Decision-making quality

Developing a Strategic Portfolio Management Approach

Internal consulting groups can add substantial value to the enterprise by helping to establish and manage a strategic portfolio management system across the organization. Key components of the most successful approaches developed, to date, include the following:

- Strong linkage to the strategic planning process
- Development of streamlined "case for action"
- Cross-organizational prioritization process
- Structured progress monitoring and portfolio updating
- Comprehensive facilitation and coordination role by the internal consulting group including migration from a tactical project management role to a more strategic role

A strong linkage to the strategic planning process at both the enterprise business unit and functional levels is important to help executive-level clients identify key projects and other initiatives that can effectively codify and execute strategic direction. The development of a streamlined case for action provides a consistent high-level description of the project, including expected benefits and resource requirements. This should take the place of lengthy business case development before the project is approved.

Then, a cross-organizational prioritization process provides consistent criteria for evaluation. This is often done by a committee of executive clients from each of the organizations involved with the overall executive responsible acting as the chairperson. After the initial decision is made and projects are initiated, it is important to have a structured process for monitoring their progress, including the achievement of projected benefits within specified timeliness. Then, either coincident with the beginning of the next planning cycle or when a new initiative is required on an urgent basis, the new project should be added to the portfolio and reprioritization conducted.

A key success factor here is the establishment of a comprehensive facilitation and coordination role by the internal consulting group. This helps not only to develop and maintain an effective portfolio management process but also to engage key clients and other stakeholders and maintain objectivity in the evaluation approach.

Establishing an Economic Value Tracking System

One key initiative of several internal consulting groups involves establishing a process for tracking the cost of providing their services on key projects versus the comparable fees charged by leading external consulting firms on similar projects. This often involves the development and maintenance of a competitive fee schedule to represent those external costs, which can also be used as a marketing tool by creating an overview document with a comparison to internal costs.

This comparison can be used both for helping to market internal consulting services on individual projects and to help measure the overall value of the internal consulting group, which is often included in the group's overall performance management scorecard—as described in Chapter 5. One potential future evolution of this approach would be to create a theoretical "profitability tracking" process by using the competitive fee schedule to calculate the revenue that would have been generated by the internal consulting group using external rates on their projects compared to their operating costs.

For those few internal consulting organizations that also receive income from external services and projects, a more formalized profit-center approach could be used at least for that portion of their practice servicing external clients. Dupont, Disney, General Motors, Ford, Microsoft, Cisco, and Xerox are some examples of organizations selling their projects to the public. There are currently a variety of funding approaches utilized for internal consulting groups, including these:

- Being part of corporate overhead or shared services allocation

- Charging back costs to clients—often termed a *cost center approach*

- A hybrid arrangement of charging back certain project costs with other costs of operations considered a corporate expense

A number of factors contribute to the approach utilized, including how top management views the internal consulting function, their areas of practice, and the maturity of their development. However, regardless of the funding mechanism utilized, it is useful for the internal consulting group to be able to demonstrate the financial benefits created. More detail on these various approaches is provided in the extensive benchmarking survey in the book *Internal Consulting Excellence*[4] and the methodologies described in *The Consultant's Guide to Results-Driven Business Proposals.*[5]

Ensuring Sustained Value from the Internal Consulting Investment

A key factor in maximizing the benefit of the internal consulting investment is to help ensure the sustainability of the function and position it for continuing success. Feedback from an extensive survey of more than 1,000 organizations indicated the following key pitfalls that need to be overcome for long-term success:

- Lack of adequate sponsorship during times of organizational change
- Absence of an internal consulting business plan and value proposition
- Insufficient performance measurement
- Inadequate connection with client groups
- Lack of core consulting skills
- Narrow scope of service offerings
- Lack of flexible capacity for handling fluctuations in project demand
- Turf wars with externals
- Not keeping up with important external trends and services

Final Thoughts

This chapter explores four major areas in which the consulting practice can add value by managing costs and enhancing benefits. Setting the budget is the first step to add value. A budget becomes a manager's tool for control. Monitoring and controlling costs on a routine basis is the second step to add value. This is critical to manage processes efficiently. Outsourcing work to suppliers may be another important way to deliver value and is the third step to add value. A key concept is to manage the suppliers to deliver value. Then, key factors for maximizing the value-added of internal consulting provide guidelines to help realize greater benefits for the enterprise.

Utilizing the Consulting Scorecard for the Practice

A key factor in managing a successful consulting practice involves utilizing an effective performance measurement system. The internal consulting scorecard represents a best practice approach to assessing performance utilizing a balanced perspective of both "lead" and "lag" indicators to help achieve long-term value creation.

Feedback received from highly successful internal consulting organizations indicates that they utilize a formalized "scorecard" approach to measuring the performance of their organization as a whole. This is a macro view of the consulting practice. These performance measurement systems have traditionally included four main areas (financial, customer/client, consulting operations, and employee/consultant) with the innovation area gaining additional attention. The scorecard for the consulting project is a micro view and is discussed in the next (and subsequent) chapter.

In recent years, there has been much interest in developing documents that reflect appropriate measures in an organization. Scorecards, such as those originally used in sporting events, provide a variety of measures for top executives. In Kaplan and Norton's landmark book, *The Balanced Scorecard*, the concept was brought to the attention of organizations. Kaplan and Norton suggested that data be organized in four categories: process, operational, financial, and growth.[1]

Scorecards come in a variety of types, whether it is Kaplan and Norton's balanced scorecard or some other kind. Regardless of the type, top executives place great emphasis on the concept of scorecards. In some organizations, the scorecard concept has filtered down to various functional business units and each part of the business has been required to develop scorecards. A growing number of internal consulting practices have developed the scorecard to reflect the contribution of consulting to the business.

The scorecard approach is appealing because it provides a quick comparison of key measures and examines the status of consulting in the organization. As a management tool, scorecards can be very important to shape the direction of the consulting investment and improve or maintain performance of the organization through the implementation of preventive programs.

Several scorecard options exist. Here are a few options that represent different approaches and philosophies for scorecard development. Each has its unique advantages and disadvantages and the list is typically presented in terms of the efforts required to produce them.

Basic IPO Scorecard

One approach is to examine consulting from the perspective of inputs, processes, and outcomes (IPO). As shown in Figure 5.1, the basic IPO scorecard shows inputs such as projects, participants, and money. These inputs are used in a variety of processes to show activity, progress, implementation, and the ultimate outcomes in simple, easy-to-connect-to measures, such as sales, productivity, and job engagement. This approach quickly shows the relationship of input to output, and is a simplistic approach to the process.

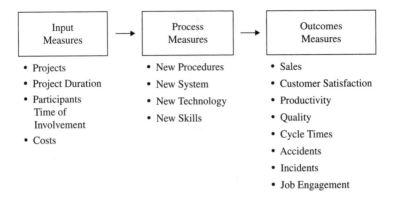

FIGURE 5.1   Tools to Analyze Gaps

The Balanced Scorecard Process

Figure 5.2 shows balanced scorecard categories where human capital measures are shaped into the Kaplan and Norton categories. While this process provides a little more perspective than that contained in the simplistic IPO approach, it is still sometimes awkward to implement. Not all consulting issues fit into these categories and the scorecard fails to offer the kind of balance that may be needed.

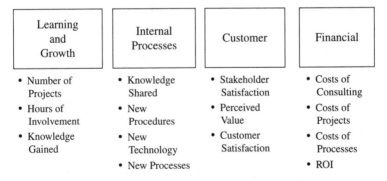

FIGURE 5.2   The Kaplan and Norton Balanced Scorecard

The Causal Chain Scorecard

Figure 5.3 represents a more comprehensive approach, one possessing seven categories of data and reflecting the causal chain of impact that usually takes place in consulting projects. The categories move from inputs to the financial results—ROI. These seven categories represent important measures to the organization, include all types of data (from qualitative to quantitative), and are taken from various perspectives.

The first category—input—shows the scope and the volume of consulting. It divides individuals and projects into a number of categories and tracks their involvement in a variety of activities and the number of hours they spend in different projects.

The second category focuses on costs of consulting projects. The costs are tracked by project, employee, and functional area. The total investment in consulting is included in this category.

The third category tracks participant reactions and their degree of satisfaction with the consulting. This is a critical measure where feedback is obtained about specific projects and information is collected on issues such as relevance, importance, and need.

The fourth category tracks and monitors the learning that takes place in consulting projects and usually involves knowledge and skill gains. This is done in such a way as to show an organization's capabilities. Issues related to readiness are included in this category.

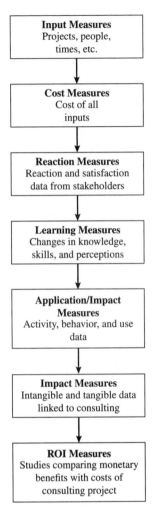

FIGURE 5.3 Scorecard Categories Organized by Causal Chain of Impact

The fifth category, application and implementation, measures processes in place and the degree to which consulting solutions are working effectively. This is similar to the Kaplan and Norton process category but can be much broader.

The sixth category considers impact, particularly impact in the organization as a consequence of the various projects. It may include measures such as sales, productivity, accidents, quality, turnover, and cycle time. The tangible or hard data measures are easily converted to monetary value if the organization so desires. Some measures represent intangible or soft data categories, such as teamwork, image, brand, and reputation. Typically, the mechanisms are not in place to convert these soft data categories into money. Therefore, the measures are purposely not converted to monetary value. However, these intangibles have an important meaning of their own and often drive some consulting solutions.

The seventh and last category is financial results and contains measures to show the payoff of particular projects, including ROI calculations, benefit-cost ratios, and payback period. These measures are usually developed from micro level studies conducted to show the actual cost versus the benefits of a particular solution, as described in later chapters.

These categories are comprehensive and reflect the variety and type of measures linked to consulting in an organization. These measures also reflect the data that are collected to show the impact of a consulting project program. For example, if a retention consulting project creates a solution to improve turnover or termination rate, the success of the solution can be monitored along these seven measures. The following categories would be measured:

- **Inputs** of the number of individuals involved, the duration of the consulting project, and the time to develop the solution

- **Costs** of the project and solution and its parts and components
- **Reaction** from stakeholders to the solution
- **Learning** and changes in knowledge, skills, and perceptions to make the solution successful
- **Application** and **implementation** of the solution
- **Impact** of turnover reduction. The effects of the solution are separated from other influences. Intangibles connected with the process, such as an increase in job satisfaction, stress reduction, and reduced conflicts, are monitored as well.
- **Financial results** showing the cost of the consulting solution compared to the monetary value of the turnover reduction

When a consulting project is implemented to drive a particular measure, a profile of success can be developed to include the seven categories of data shown in Figure 5.3. In essence, a micro-level scorecard analysis can be developed for every consulting project and reported routinely. The data from the micro-level scorecard can be integrated into the macro-level scorecard. For example, the reaction to consulting project can be monitored as reaction and satisfaction data. A single measure such as relevance or importance can be reported in a macro-level scorecard. Thus, it is possible to have both micro-level and macro-level scorecards. Ideally, the same types of data are developed as recommended here. The scorecards must be compatible, at least conceptually, for easy integration.

AIMC Scorecard

A fourth option is a blend of the three previous options. This approach, labeled the AIMC (Association of Internal Management Consultant) scorecard, is used by some highly successful internal consulting practices and by many AIMC members. Figure 5.4 shows the scorecard structure with some typical measures. It is described in more detail here.

FINANCIAL	OPERATIONAL PROCESSES
• Assessment of ROI • Comparison of internal to external fees/costs • Total add-on work to original engagements • Impact on total consulting spend • % utilization of consultants on projects	• % project portfolio considered strategic versus tactical • % large projects with formal contracts • % large projects with standard methodology • % total engagement requests served directly (versus being outsourced and covered by internal consulting group) • % large projects with standard methodology
CUSTOMER/CLIENT	**EMPLOYEE/CONSULTANT**
PROJECT LEVEL • Survey/assessment of quality of consulting contract • Timeliness of completion • Realization of benefits expected OVERALL FEEDBACK (CLIENTS AND OTHER STAKEHOLDERS) • Responsiveness to customer needs • Quality of the consulting process • % repeat business	• % Internal consulting group employee aligned with direction and/or satisfied with their job • % development plans executed as planned • 360-degree assessments of internal consulting group (both group level and individual) • % target competencies realized • Turnover/retention • % projects where client training is included
INNOVATION AND BUSINESS DEVELOPMENT	
• Number of projects with new client groups • % projects using methodologies incorporated in the last 12 months • Number of external presentations or publications generated • % internal consultants considered as thought leaders in their practice areas • Number of target, leading-edge methodologies acquired • Number projects where innovation/creativity skill building training included	

FIGURE 5.4   AIMC Consulting Scorecard

Financial Measures

Financial measures have always been a critical measurement area in evaluating the performance of internal consulting groups and establishing the payback of the investment in providing that capability. The most utilized metric in this area of the AIMC scorecard involves tracking the overall return on investment delivered on projects managed by the internal consulting group. Another metric employed by numerous consulting practices consists of a comparison of internal to external consulting fees/costs. Some groups also track the total amount of add-on work to original engagements.

Customer/Client Feedback

This area endeavors to assess the consultants' performance from the point of view of the clients they serve. These metrics are often packaged in surveys either at the end of an individual project or periodically covering all of the projects managed or supported by the consultants. Specific areas of input include the following:

- Degree to which key objectives were achieved and expected benefits realized
- Timeliness of completion
- Assessment of the performance of the consultants involved
- Assessment of the quality of the consulting process, such as the following:
  - Effectiveness of contracting phase

- Engagement and performance of the project team(s)
- Ability to meet client needs and resolve issues

After-action review sessions are also utilized to gain more in-depth client input and help to gain additional insights. Client/customer loyalty is also often assessed by tracking the percentage of repeat business.

Internal Consulting Operations Measures

This category of measures often involves a variety of measures aimed at assessing the overall quality and rigor of the internal consulting group's operating processes. One area often includes the positioning of the consulting practice and involves tracking the percentage of the consultants overall project portfolio considered to be strategic versus tactical in nature. This helps to indicate the degree to which the consulting practice has been able to gain executive sponsorship and trust in supporting those initiatives most critical to the organization. Other metrics, focusing on the state of the consultants' operational process development include the following:

- Percentage of large projects with formal contracts
- Percentage of engagements where a consistent/ standardized set of methodologies was utilized

Another area of measurement endeavors to track the degree of involvement of the consultants in projects/ initiatives of which they are aware. The specific metrics often utilized assesses the following:

- The percentage of total engagements served directly

- Versus those coordinated with outsourced resources
- Versus those with no involvement by the internal consultants

Consultant Development

In any consulting organization, internal or external, the employees are the most important asset. Therefore, the employee/human capital aspect of their performance measurement is a critical component and also a key lead indicator of future performance. One popular metric here involves consultant satisfaction and alignment. Often administered through a survey tool, this involves questions regarding current job satisfaction and comfort level with development plans and career pathing. A key aspect of this feedback involves an assessment of the consultants' alignment with the positioning and direction of the overall internal consulting group. This involves questions about agreement with the goals, approach, and support provided by the organization.

Another key metric utilized involves tracking the percentage of employee development plans that are executed as planned. It is important for consulting practice to set aside time for consultant development and stick to it even when heavy client demand exists.

A third important metric involves tracking the percentage of target competencies realized. This is preceded by the development of a target competency framework for the overall internal consulting group with desired skills and proficiency in each for every position in the group. The measurement then assesses the gap-closing trend over time.

A fourth area involves monitoring the number of 360-degree assessments conducted for both individual contributors and leadership in the group. This helps promote comprehensive feedback on performance coupled with improvement plans.

Innovation and Business Development

This final major area of performance measurement and management first involves tracking and promoting initiatives to foster a continual stream of innovation in the consulting practice and spread that knowledge throughout the organization.

The first frequently used metric here focuses on the percentage of projects utilizing methodologies recently incorporated by the group (such as in the last 12 months). This helps to focus the consulting practice on continually monitoring emerging tools and techniques, including supporting technologies, to help them do their jobs better and open up new areas of practice.

Another supportive metric is tracking the number of external presentations and publications generated, which helps to stimulate an emphasis on thought leadership. A third related metric utilized by the more well-developed consulting practices involves assessing the percentage of consultants considered thought leaders in their areas of practice (often included in the 360-degree feedback).

The second major area of this measurement category involves tracking the consulting practice's business development efforts. One metric utilized here, often tied to the consulting practice business plan, involves tracking the number of projects with new client groups in the past year.

Another business development-related metric involves tracking the number of projects where consulting skills are transferred to project team members in client organizations. This helps to create an internal network of contacts who often refer additional projects to the consulting practice.

Additional research on leading performance measurement and management programs for internal consultants is contained in Dr. Trotter's book *Internal Consulting Excellence*.[2]

Using the Scorecard

Important reasons for having a scorecard are to manage consulting effectively, optimize the status of consulting, and drive continuous improvement in the use of consulting. Because of this, continuous monitoring and action is required when necessary. The consulting practice will be responsible for monitoring the data and recommending or reporting actions to keep measures where they are or to improve measures that are unacceptable. However, executives should be actively involved in the process. It is too important to delegate this responsibility entirely to the consulting practice. The involvement and commitment of the senior team is essential to ensure appropriate actions are taken and those actions are monitored to check the progress being made. Figure 5.5 shows all the steps needed to drive improvement with the use of scorecards.

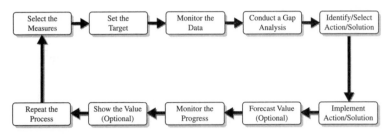

FIGURE 5.5   Using the Scorecard to Drive Improvement

Select the Measures

Earlier in this chapter, specific recommendations for selecting the measures were presented. It is important for all key stakeholders to agree on the measures, so the concerns of the consulting staff and the senior executive team are balanced. After the measures are selected, the format for presentation is determined so that data are routinely, if not instantaneously, available to the management group and the consulting staff.

Set the Target

For each measure on the scorecard, specific target (performance) levels need to be established for almost all measures. The first target level is the minimum acceptable level. This may be developed through operational requirements and guidelines, or perhaps even through benchmarking or industry standards. Anything below this level would be considered unacceptable. Another target could be best practice, which may be above average for the industry or a measure that is found only in best-practice organizations. Finally, targets can be set that represent stretch goals, which only an exceptional performance will deliver. These stretch goals are the measures that truly build excellence in organizations and high-performing consulting groups, exceeding what best practice normally requires.

The typical approach is to set the levels at one of the three targets and take action whenever one of the measures falls below one of the targets, or take action when it is necessary to stay at a desired level. For example, in one organization, action is taken to move a measure to best practice. When best practice is reached, preventive action is needed to keep it at that level. Other kinds of action are needed to move it to a stretch-goal level of performance.

Monitor the Data

Scorecard data can be monitored in a variety of ways depending on the desires of the executive team and the feasibility of presentation. The old way is to send detailed paper-based reports to executives for review and analysis. Brief reports are better; scorecards are much better. In some cases, data are linked to a website where an executive can monitor it at will. The scorecard has drill-down capability to get more detail about a particular measure and its status including trends, forecast, benchmarking comparisons, and so on.

Executives may receive e-mail reports highlighting particular measures, comparing those to target levels, goals, benchmarking data, or other important comparisons. These are sent with routine operational and financial data for the executive.

Still other organizations have color-coded reports where various colors represent different issues. For example, measures that are not doing so well are colored red, while those that are considered to be exceptional and may even be a stretch goal are shown in green. These allow for quick review and often look like scorecards so executives can quickly see that things are okay or that there are signs of trouble.

Conduct a Gap Analysis

Perhaps one of the most difficult, yet critical, issues is to determine what is causing a gap in a specific measure. If a current measure is less than the desired target, this should be cause for concern. The challenge is to determine the cause of the gap so that appropriate, remedial actions can be taken. Collecting the appropriate data to understand the cause is important. Some causes may be obvious; others may be elusive. In some situations, both the problem and solution are equally apparent. A variety of diagnostic tools may be necessary to uncover the exact cause. While several diagnostic processes are available, the following shows an initial list of tools for this type of analysis.

Tools to Analyze Gaps

- Demographic analysis
- Diagnostic instruments
- Focus groups
- Probing interviews
- Employee surveys

- Exit interviews and surveys
- Nominal group technique
- Brainstorming
- Cause-and-effect diagram
- Force-field analysis
- Mind mapping
- Affinity diagrams
- … among others

Identify/Select Action/Solution

The consulting staff is sometimes creative with their approach to the gap analysis, and this results in dozens of solutions that create unintended confusion. While there are specific actions to improve the situation, the challenge is to select the most feasible solution for the organization. This subject is beyond the scope of this book, but a variety of solutions are available. At this stage of analysis, it is helpful to ensure that a range of possibilities is identified and a proper one is selected.

Implement Action/Solution

This step goes hand in hand with the previous one. After the appropriate action or solution is selected, it must be implemented over a predetermined time period to tackle the problem. When attempting to implement the solution, it is important to consider resources, planning, data collection, and reporting.

Forecast the Value

An optional step is to forecast the value of the solution or action, including the impact and ROI. This forecast allows the team to establish priorities, work with a minimum number of solutions and actions, and focus on the solutions for the greatest forecasted return on investment. Forecasting can be difficult, challenging, and even risky. As much data as possible must be accumulated to verify the estimate and build credibility for the process. This step should be reserved for only those solutions that are considered expensive, time consuming, highly visible, or, perhaps, even controversial. Ideally, the forecast should contain an expected return on investment value. This is perhaps one of the most difficult parts of the process and is described in other publications.[3]

Monitor the Progress

Because the gap analysis is conducted only with those areas where the measures are below the target, it may be useful to outline the progress made in these areas. Progress reporting can be conducted either along with the scorecard report or in a report by itself. A progress-in-action report is often generated to complement the human capital scorecard. In web-based scorecards, actions and their progress are detailed when the executive clicks on a particular measure. The detailed information indicates what, if any, actions are in progress, the status of those actions, the estimated completion date, and, if applicable, the forecasted value from the project.

Show the Value

Another optional step is the actual calculation of the impact of the solution to close the gap. This step is often skipped because it can be difficult and time consuming. However, if the solution is very expensive, has a high profile, involves a large number of employees, and perhaps is controversial, it may be beneficial to show the value of the solution. This brings the ROI methodology, described in later chapters, into use to measure the payoff of a particular human capital project. In this context, the project or program is designed to change the measure that is out of alignment.

Repeat the Process

The process should be repeated, making any necessary adjustments in the measures, adjusting targets, monitoring the data, and following the other steps. The improvement process is continuous—the scorecard provides the data and the challenge is to manage it in a proactive way that continues to improve the status, capability, and success of consulting.

Role of External Consultants

It is important for externals who wish to work well with internal consultants to learn about their performance measurement system. This will enable them to align with their key metrics on project work in which they are endeavoring to participate—thereby improving chances of both getting the initial work and developing an ongoing relationship. In addition, they can provide valuable insights into how to effectively manage key project value assessment metrics, such as return on investment and customer satisfaction—particularly for internal consulting groups in their early stages of development.

Final Thoughts

This chapter focuses on utilizing a consulting scorecard as a best practice approach for assessing performance with a balanced perspective. The various types of scorecards are discussed, along with categories of data, metrics, and measures for reporting progress and outcomes. The importance of developing scorecards to meet the needs of the organization is reviewed. The importance of the executive team's collaboration with the consulting practice staff is highlighted. The chapter concludes with a recommended process to utilize the scorecard to set targets, identify gaps, and implement solutions. The next chapter discusses a micro scorecard, the ROI methodology.

6

A Logical Approach to Measure Impact and ROI for Projects

Consultants must address several important accountability issues. For example, a consultant might ask, "What is my role in measuring the impact and ROI? How should I approach evaluation? Is a credible process available? Can it be implemented within my resources? What are the consequences of a negative ROI? What would happen if I do nothing?" These and other critical questions will need attention. This chapter explores each issue and makes the case for consultants to adopt a more comprehensive measurement and evaluation process, including measuring the ROI. A rational, credible approach to measurement and evaluation is presented, showing how the process can be applied within the resources of the consulting team. It shows the various elements and issues needed to build credibility with a proven process. This is an overview of a micro scorecard to show the value of a consulting project, one consulting project at a time. More detail will be presented in the next chapters.

The Case for ROI

Developing a balanced set of measures, including measuring ROI, has already earned a place among the critical issues in the consulting field. The topic appears on conference agendas and comes up at professional meetings. Journals and newsletters embrace the concept with increasing print space. Several consulting experts are recommending ROI calculations. Even top executives have increased their appetite for ROI information, particularly since the global recession.

Although the interest in the topic has heightened and progress has been made, it is still an issue that challenges consulting teams. Some consultants argue that it is not possible to calculate the ROI in consulting, while others quietly and deliberately proceed to develop measures and ROI calculations. Regardless of the position taken on the issue, the reasons for measuring the ROI are still there. Most consultants share a concern that they must eventually show a return on investment for their consulting projects. Otherwise, they won't have the projects and their image may be tarnished.

Although the rationale for focusing on ROI may be obvious, it is helpful to explore the various reasons why now is the time to pursue ROI. The consulting industry has been in existence for many years and has earned an important place in the mainstream activities of medium and large organizations. Why is now the time to begin measuring the success in more detail than ever imagined? Several issues create a logical answer to this question.

Client Demands: "Show Me the Money"

Today, more clients are requesting additional evaluation data, up to and including measuring the ROI. It is common for clients to ask for value at the beginning of most consulting projects, with comments such as "Show me the money," "What is the ROI?," and "Will this be a good return on my investment?" Although this issue has always been there, it has never been present at the level that exists today.

Figure 6.1 illustrates how the "Show me" request has evolved. Two decades ago, clients wanted to see data, resulting in a "Show me data!" request. They wanted to see how well a consulting project was connected to the business. This request evolved into "Show me the money," perhaps even a decade ago. Here, executives recognize that a project is costing money, so they ask "Show me the money I'm getting out of the project." This request evolved into "Show me the real money (only that part that's connected to the project)." This particular request recognizes that many factors can influence a business measure. This issue hasn't been addressed very often, as it is needed to satisfy an executive's request for a

Term	Issue
Show me!	Collect input data
⇩	⇩
Show me the money!	And convert data to money
⇩	⇩
Show me the real money!	And isolate the effects of the project
⇩	⇩
Show me the real money, and make me believe it's a good investment!	And compare the money to the costs of the project

FIGURE 6.1 The "Show-Me" Evolution

credible connection to the business. Finally, particularly since the global recession, executives are asking, "Show me the money and make me believe it's a good investment." Here, the cost of the project must be compared to the monetary benefits derived from it, to present the ultimate evaluation, the financial ROI. Also, it means that it must be a credible process, following conservative standards. This last request is the best way to meet the executive's demands. For consultants, this means that they must focus on the monetary value and return on investment for the project.

When the client suggests, asks for, or requires ROI, it must be explored and implemented, and the process must be credible enough for the client to believe the results. Client questions must be addressed in a simple, rational way. Avoiding the issue will erode the relationship between the client and consultant and ultimately may cause the loss of the project.

Competitive Advantage

Perhaps one of the most important reasons to pursue a more comprehensive measurement and evaluation, including ROI, is to meet or beat the competition. Many progressive consulting teams are beginning to develop the ROI for consulting projects to stay competitive or perhaps stay ahead of others who are developing similar processes. These teams address the issue in a proactive manner with a comprehensive approach to ROI. It just may be the best way to position the consulting team ahead of much of the competition. A database of ROI studies for consulting projects using a credible, undisputed evaluation process can be a crucial advantage and a persuasive selling point.

Increased Revenues and Profits for the Practice

When a consulting team can show the actual contribution of the consulting engagement in monetary terms, an excellent case can be made for additional fees—or at least additional projects. Some teams are taking the process to the level of using it to drive additional bonuses (e.g., discounting regular fees in a consulting project and placing the rest of the compensation at risk with a payoff linked to a target ROI). The payment can be a set amount or savings beyond the target. This approach provides an excellent way to increase revenues and build profits while generating client satisfaction and loyalty. This can work for internal and external consultants.

Satisfaction and Engagement of the Team

Individuals engaged in professional work want to know that their efforts make a difference. Consultants need to see that they are making a contribution in terms that clients and managers respect and appreciate. Showing the ROI on a project may be one of the most satisfying parts of a consulting project. Not only do things go well in terms of schedule, budget, and client feedback, but the value added in monetary terms with an impressive ROI adds the final touch to a major project. This provides additional evidence that what we do does make a difference.

The ROI Challenge

The dilemma surrounding ROI for consulting is a source of frustration with many clients and consultants and even within the consulting field itself. Most clients realize that consulting is a necessity when organizations are experiencing problems, significant growth, or increased competition. In these cases, consultants can prepare employees and the organization to meet competitive challenges. Consultants are also important during business restructuring and rapid change.

While many clients see the need for consulting, they intuitively feel that there is value in a consulting project. They can logically conclude that consulting pays off in important bottom-line measures such as productivity improvements, quality enhancements, cost reductions, and time savings. Also, they believe that a consulting project can enhance customer satisfaction, improve engagement, and build teamwork. Yet the frustration comes from the lack of evidence showing that the process is really working. While the payoffs are assumed to be there, and consulting appears to be needed, more evidence is needed for consulting funds to be allocated in the future. The ROI methodology represents the most promising way to show this accountability through a logical, rational approach.

The Forces Driving ROI

Another important issue to face is examining the rationale for the use of ROI in consulting. Just what is causing so much focus on accountability, including ROI? Several key forces are coming together at this time to create a tremendous pressure to pursue ROI.

Consulting Failures

Let's face it—many consulting projects have not lived up to their promises or expectations. Experienced consultants can identify an uncomfortable number of projects that have not delivered the results that the client and the consulting team expected—at least not in the terms that management understands, primarily bottom-line contributions. As more consulting projects are undertaken, consuming precious resources in an organization, the results have simply not materialized for many projects. And when the results are reported, there is often skepticism and concern about the credibility of the data, objectivity of data, and the thoroughness of the analysis. This has caused many clients to rethink the role of consulting as well as the accountability of consulting and to place more restraints and demands on consultants.

Economic Pressures

As consultants strive to be successful in a global economy, there are tremendous pressures on costs and efficiency. Companies must squeeze all the savings possible out of every process, activity, and resource. They must account for every expenditure and every project. For some, survival is an issue. This competition for resources has caused organizations to examine the payoff of consulting to make sure they are getting the most out of their consulting expenditures.

The pressures to show the value of projects are not just present in an economic slump but instead evolve and grow over time. Prior to the recession, pressures already existed to show the value of all types of projects and programs because of the global, competitive environment and fierce pricing competition in most industries. Organizations have to be efficient and effective in almost everything they do, including consulting projects.

After the recession, there is more pressure to show the value than ever before, up to, and including the forecast of ROI. Some teams are already experiencing this request to show the value before projects are initiated. It's not unusual to see the ROI requirement working its way into the RFP (request for proposal) process.

Budget Growth

With the increased use of consultants comes increased spending for consulting activities. In 2008, when the most recent recession began, external consulting was a big business with $305 billion spent annually, according to Kennedy Consulting Research and Advisory.[1] The recession caused a dip of 5.5 percent. By 2012, consulting had reached $315 billion. Because of this, consulting fees and charges become a target for critics inside the client's organization. It is one thing to spend $50,000 on a consulting project, but it is another to spend $1 million and still have nothing to show for it. Consulting has secured a greater percentage of many teams' operating budgets. They see the percentage of expenditures dedicated to consulting growing significantly, not only in magnitude but also as a percentage of operating costs. This growth makes consulting a likely target for increased accountability—if nothing else—to satisfy critics of the process.

Balanced Measures

For years, there has been debate over what should or should not be measured and how. Some prefer soft data directly from the client or customers. Others prefer hard data focused on key issues of output, quality, cost, and time. Still others have argued for a balance of measures, including financial results. The later camp seems to be winning. Data from a variety of groups at different time frames and for different purposes are collected representing qualitative and quantitative, tangible and intangible, and financial and nonfinancial categories. This mixture of data, often referred to as a balanced approach, is driving the need for the process described in this book and is an important part of consulting accountability.

Executive Interest

ROI for noncapital investments is now enjoying increased interest from the executive suite. Consulting is usually a noncapital expenditure. Top executives who have watched their consulting budgets grow without the appropriate accountability measures have become frustrated and, in an attempt to respond to the situation, have demanded a return on investment for consulting. The payoff of consulting is becoming a conversation topic in executive publications. The *Wall Street Journal*, the *Financial Times*, the *Economist*, *Fortune*, *Businessweek*, and *Forbes* regularly feature articles about consulting and the need for increased accountability. They describe the frustration of senior executives as they search for results from major consulting projects. They describe failures in detail examining complaints, consults, and government regulation.

Fad Surfing in the Boardroom

Finally, ROI applications have increased because of the growing interest in a variety of organizational improvement and change interventions offered by consulting teams, particularly in North America. Organizations have embraced almost any trend that appears on the horizon. Unfortunately, many of these change efforts have not worked and have turned out to be nothing more than passing fads, however well intentioned. Unfortunately, the ROI methodology was not used to measure the accountability of these projects.

The consultants are often caught in the middle of this activity, either by supporting the potential fad with a project or actually coordinating the new fad in these organizations. A process is needed to prevent the implementation of an unnecessary fad. The implementation of the ROI methodology requires a thorough assessment of business needs and significant planning before the ROI is attempted. If these two elements are in place, unnecessary passing fads doomed for failure will be avoided. With the ROI process in place, a new change project that does not connect to business needs will be exposed. Management will be fully aware of it early so that adjustments can quickly be made.

The ROI Methodology

To develop a credible approach for calculating the ROI on consulting, elements must be in place as shown in Figure 6.2. First, there should be an evaluation framework that defines the various levels of evaluation, objectives, and needs assessment and shows the connection between them. Next, an ROI process model is developed that shows a step-by-step procedure for developing the actual ROI calculation. Inherent in this process is the isolation of the effects of consulting from other factors. Next, a set of operating guidelines or operating standards are needed, designed to keep processes on track and build credibility by taking a very conservative approach. There should be ample applications that build experience with a process to show how it actually works in real-world settings. Finally, appropriate resources must be devoted to implementation issues, addressing responsibilities, policies, procedures, guidelines, goals, and internal skill building. Together, these five elements are necessary to develop an evaluation system that contains a balanced set of measures, has

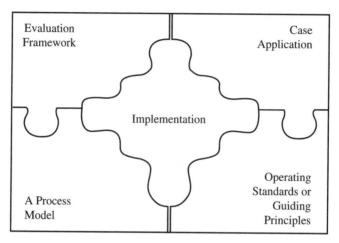

FIGURE 6.2   The Elements of ROI Methodolgy

credibility with the various stakeholders involved, and can be replicated from one group to another. Figure 6.2 offers more details on these five elements.

The Framework: Evaluation Levels

The ROI methodology collects or generates five levels of data. The concept of different levels of evaluation is both helpful and instructive in understanding how the return on investment is calculated. Table 6.1 shows the five-level framework used in this book.

At Level 1, *Reaction* from consulting stakeholders is measured. Almost all consulting projects are evaluated at Level 1, usually with generic questionnaires and surveys. While this level of evaluation is important as a customer satisfaction measure, a favorable reaction does not ensure the project will be successful.

Table 6.1 Measurements in Consulting

Level	Measurement Category	Current Status*	Best Practice†	Comments about Status
1	**Reaction** Measures reaction to the consulting project	100%	100%	94%†
2	**Learning** Measures what consulting participants learned in the project—information, knowledge, skills, and contacts	30–40%	80–90%	Must use simple learning measures 71%†
3	**Application and Implementation** Measures progress with the project—the use of information, knowledge, skills, and contacts	20%	50%	Need more follow-up 44%†
4	**Impact** Measures changes in business impact variables such as output, quality, time, and cost-linked to the consulting project	9%*	30%	This is the connection to business impact 29%
5	**ROI** Compares the monetary benefits of the business impact measures to the costs of the consulting project	2%	15%	The ultimate level of evaluation 18%

*Percentage of projects evaluated at this level
†Best practice benchmarking (user for 5-plus years)

At Level 2, *Learning* measurements focus on what consulting participants and other stakeholders learned to make the project successful. A learning check is helpful to ensure that consulting participants have absorbed new skills and knowledge and know how to use them to make the consulting project successful. However, a positive measure at this level is no guarantee that the project will be successfully implemented.

At Level 3, *Application and Implementation*, a variety of follow-up methods are used to determine if participants applied what is necessary to make the consulting project successful. The frequency and use of knowledge, information, technology, and skills are important measures. In addition, measures at this level include all the steps, actions, tasks, and processes involved in the implementation of the consulting project. While Level 3 evaluation is important to gauge the success of the implementation, it still does not guarantee that there will be a positive impact for the project.

At Level 4, *Business Impact*, the measurement focuses on the business results achieved by the consulting project. Typical Level 4 measures include revenue, productivity, quality, waste, transaction time, cost, cycle time, and customer satisfaction. Although the consulting project may produce a measurable business impact, there is still a concern that the intervention may cost too much and this leads to ROI.

At Level 5, the ultimate level of evaluation, *Return on Investment*, compares the project's monetary benefits with the fully loaded consulting costs. Although the ROI can be expressed in several ways, it is usually presented as a percentage or benefit-cost ratio.

While most consulting teams conduct evaluations to measure reaction, very few conduct evaluations at the ROI level. Perhaps the best explanation for this is that

ROI evaluation is often characterized as a difficult and expensive process. Although business results and ROI are desired, it is very important to evaluate the other levels. A chain of impact should occur through the levels as the skills and knowledge learned (Level 2) in the consulting project are applied as the project is implemented (Level 3) to produce business impact (Level 4). If measurements are not taken at each level, it is difficult to conclude that the results achieved were actually produced by the consulting project. Because of this, it is recommended that evaluation be conducted at all levels when a Level 5 evaluation is planned. Table 6.1 also shows percentages of consulting projects evaluated at each level. The first column is our assessment of how consulting is evaluated now (current status). Best practice is also presented along with the latest benchmarking. The impact level is most desired by top executives, followed by ROI. As this table shows, there are important reasons to focus on Levels 3, 4, and 5.

The ROI Process Model

The ROI process model, presented briefly in this chapter and explored throughout this book, had its beginnings several years ago as the process was applied to a variety of types of projects. Since then, the process has been refined and modified to represent what is presented in Figure 6.3. As the figure illustrates, the process is comprehensive, as data are developed at different times and gathered from different sources to develop the six types of outcome measures (five levels plus intangibles) that are the focal point

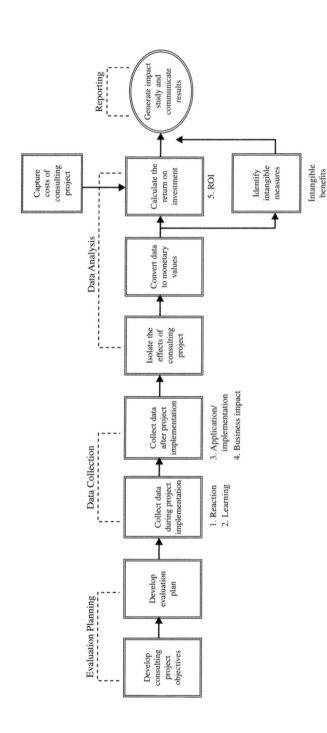

FIGURE 6.3 The ROI Process Model

of this book. To date, more than 400 case studies have been published utilizing the ROI process model, and the number is growing rapidly. It is estimated that 5,000 users conduct 8,000 to 10,000 studies each year. Each part of the process is briefly described here. More detail is provided in later chapters.

Planning the Evaluation

The first two parts of the ROI process model focus on two critical planning issues. The first step is to develop appropriate objectives for the consulting project. These are often referred to as the "objectives of the solution" when a consulting project involves the implementation of a solution. Project objectives range from developing objectives for reaction to developing an objective for the ROI and are defined in more detail in the next chapter.

With the objectives in hand, the next step is to develop a detailed evaluation plan. This involves two important documents. A data collection plan indicates the type of data collected, the method for data collection, data sources, the timing of collection, and the various responsibilities. The next document, the ROI analysis plan, details how the effects of the consulting project are isolated from other influences, how data are converted to monetary values, the appropriate cost categories, the expected intangible measures, and the anticipated target audience for communication. These planning documents are necessary for the process to be implemented appropriately. Additional information on planning is presented in Chapter 9.

Collecting Data

Data collected during the early stages of the project measure reaction (Level 1) and learning (Level 2). Collecting data during the project ensures that adjustments are made and the process is altered as necessary to make sure the project is on track. Reaction and learning data are critical for immediate feedback and are necessary to make the project successful.

Data collection is central to the calculation of the ROI. Post-project data are collected and compared to pre-project situations and expectations. Both hard data (representing output, quality, cost, and time) and soft data (including work habits, work climate, and attitudes) are collected. Data are collected using a variety of methods, such as the following:

- Follow-up surveys to measure reaction and learning from stakeholders.
- Tests and assessments are used to measure the extent of learning (knowledge gained or skills enhanced).
- Follow-up questionnaires uncover specific application issues with consulting projects.
- On-the-job observation captures actual application and use.
- Interviews determine the extent to which the consulting project has been implemented.
- Focus groups determine the degree of application of the consulting project.
- Action plans show progress with implementation on the job and the impact achieved.

- Performance contracts detail specific outcomes expected or obtained from the consulting project.
- Business performance monitoring shows improvement in various performance records and operational data.

The important challenge in data collection is selecting the method or methods appropriate for the setting and the specific intervention, within the time and budget constraints. Data collection methods are covered in more detail in Chapters 10 and 11.

Isolating the Effects of Consulting

An often-overlooked issue in most evaluations is the process of isolating the effects of a consulting project. In this step of the process, specific strategies are explored, which determine the amount of performance improvement directly related to the intervention. This step is essential because there are many factors that will influence performance data after a consulting intervention. The specific strategies in this step will pinpoint the amount of improvement directly related to the intervention. The result is increased accuracy and credibility of the ROI calculation. These strategies have been utilized by organizations to tackle this important issue:

- A pilot group with the consulting initiative is compared to a control group without consulting to isolate the consulting impact.
- Trend lines are used to project business impact measures, and the trend is compared to the actual data after a consulting project is implemented.

- A forecasting model is used to isolate the effects of a consulting project when mathematical relationships between input and output variables are known.

- Participants/stakeholders estimate the amount of improvement related to a consulting project.

- Supervisors and managers estimate the impact of a consulting project on the output measures.

- External studies provide input on the impact of a consulting project.

- Independent experts provide estimates of the impact of a consulting project on the performance variable.

- When feasible, other influencing factors are identified and the impact is estimated or calculated, leaving the remaining unexplained improvement attributable to the consulting project.

- Customers provide input on the extent to which the consulting project has influenced their decision to use a product or service.

Collectively, these strategies provide a comprehensive set of tools to tackle the important and critical issue of isolating the effects of consulting. Chapter 12 provides more information on this important process.

Converting Data to Monetary Values

To calculate the return on investment, business impact data are converted to monetary values and are compared to intervention costs. This requires a value to be placed on each unit of data connected to the consulting project.

Here are the key techniques that are available to convert data to monetary values:

- Output data are converted to profit contribution or cost savings using a standards value.
- The cost of a quality measure, such as a reject, is reported as a standard value.
- Employee time saved is converted to wages and benefits for the time saved.
- Historical costs of a measure are calculated using existing records.
- Internal and/or external experts estimate the value of data item.
- External databases are searched for an approximate value or cost of a data item.
- A hard-to-value measure is linked to other measures where the value is easily developed.
- Participants estimate the cost or value of the data item.
- Supervisors or managers provide estimates of costs or value of the data item.
- The consultant estimates a value of a data item.

The specific strategy selected usually depends on the type of data and the situation.

This step in the ROI model is very important and is absolutely necessary for determining the monetary benefits for the ROI calculation. The process is challenging, particularly with soft data, but can be methodically accomplished using one or more of these strategies. Because of its importance, most of Chapter 13 covers this issue.

Identifying Intangible Benefits

In addition to tangible, monetary benefits, most consulting projects will drive intangible, nonmonetary benefits. During data analysis, every attempt is made to convert all data to monetary values. All hard data such as output, quality, and time are converted to monetary values. The conversion of soft data is attempted for each data item. However, if the process used for conversion is too subjective or inaccurate, and the resulting values lose credibility in the process, then the data are listed as intangible benefits with the appropriate explanation. Intangible benefits include items such as the following:

- Corporate social responsibility
- Brand awareness
- Job satisfaction
- Reputation
- Organizational commitment
- Employee engagement
- Technology leadership
- Stress
- Teamwork
- Culture
- Image

For some consulting projects, intangible, nonmonetary benefits are extremely valuable, often commanding as much influence as the hard data items. Chapter 13 provides more detail on intangible benefits.

Capturing the Cost of the Consulting

The other part of the equation in a benefit-cost analysis is the consulting cost. Capturing the cost involves monitoring or developing all the costs related to the consulting project. A fully loaded approach is recommended where all direct and indirect costs are captured. Here are the cost components that should be included:

- The cost of initial analysis and assessment connected to the consulting project
- The cost to develop consulting solutions, if appropriate
- The cost to acquire technology, equipment, and external services
- The cost of materials and supplies used in the project
- The cost for the use of facilities and support expenses, if appropriate
- The cost for the time of all stakeholders involved in the project
- The cost of application and implementation of the project
- The cost of maintenance and monitoring

- The costs of administration and overhead for the consulting project allocated in some convenient way
- The cost of evaluation and reporting

For internal consulting projects, all these costs are included. For external consulting projects, many of the costs items are included in the consulting fee. Still, the client absorbs other costs. Both groups should be included to develop the ROI from the client perspective. The conservative approach is to include all of these costs so that the total is fully loaded. Chapter 14 provides more detail on this issue.

Calculating the Return on Investment

The return on investment is calculated using benefits and costs of the consulting project. This comparison is made using the benefit/cost ratio (BCR) or the percentage of the return on investment (ROI). The BCR is the monetary benefit of the consulting project divided by the cost of the consulting project. In formula form it is:

$$BCR = \frac{Consulting\ Project\ Monetary\ Benefits}{Consulting\ Project\ Costs}$$

The ROI uses the net monetary benefits divided by consulting costs. The net benefits are the monetary benefits minus the costs, multiplied by 100 to convert the quotient to a percentage. In formula form, the ROI becomes:

$$ROI\% = \frac{Net\ Consulting\ Project\ Monetary\ Benefits}{Consulting\ Project\ Costs} \times 100$$

This is the same basic formula used in evaluating capital investments where the ROI is traditionally reported as earnings divided by investment. The BCR and the ROI present the same general information, but with a slightly different perspective. An example will illustrate the use of these formulas. A wellness and fitness project yielded monetary benefits of $752,000 based on reduced medical expenses, absenteeism, and accidents. The fully loaded costs are $549,000. The BCR is this:

$$BCR = \frac{\$752,000}{\$549,000} = 1.37$$

As this calculation shows, for every $1 invested, $1.37 in benefits is returned. In this example, net benefits are $752,000 − $549,000 = $203,000. Thus, the ROI is this:

$$ROI\% = \frac{\$203,000}{\$549,000} \times 100 = 37\%$$

This means that for each $1 invested in the consulting project, there is a return of $0.37 in *net* benefits, after costs are covered. The benefits are usually expressed as annual benefits for short-term consulting projects, representing the amount saved or gained for a complete year after the consulting project has been implemented and the business impact has occurred. While the benefits may continue after the first year, the impact usually diminishes and is omitted from calculations in short-term situations. For long-term projects, the benefits are spread over several years. The number of years is determined at the beginning of the project, with a view of being conservative. This conservative approach is used throughout the application of the ROI process described in this book.

Chapter 14 provides more detail on the BCR and ROI calculations.

Reporting Results

A final operational step of the ROI process model is to generate an impact study to document the results achieved by the consulting project and communicate results to various target audiences. The impact study presents the process used to generate the six measures of outcome data. The methodology, assumptions, key concepts, and guiding principles are all outlined before the results are presented. Next, the six categories of data, beginning with reaction and moving through to ROI and intangible measures, are presented in a rational, logical process, showing the building blocks to measure the success of the study. This becomes the official document of the complete assessment of success of the consulting project. Its length ranges from 20 to 30 pages for a small project to 200 to 300 pages for a substantial, long-term consulting impact study. A variety of methods are used to communicate results to several target audiences. Chapter 15 is devoted to communicating results.

The Operating Standard: Guiding Principles

To ensure that each study takes the same conservative philosophy and to increase the likelihood of replication, a set of guiding principles has been developed for the consulting ROI process. The following list presents the guiding principles used throughout this book: While the principles may be obvious, each will be explored and revisited throughout the book. Collectively, these principles will ensure that the proper conservative approach is taken and that the impact ROI study can be replicated and compared to others.

1. When a higher-level evaluation is conducted, data must be collected at lower levels.

2. When an evaluation is planned for a higher level, the previous level of evaluation does not have to be comprehensive.

3. When collecting and analyzing data, use only the most credible sources.

4. When analyzing data, select the most conservative alternative for calculations.

5. At least one method must be used to isolate the effects of the project.

6. If no improvement data are available for a population or from a specific source, it is assumed that little or no improvement has occurred.

7. Estimates of improvements should be adjusted for the potential error of the estimate.

8. Extreme data items and unsupported claims should not be used in ROI calculations.

9. Only the first year of benefits (annual) should be used in the ROI analysis of short-term solutions.

10. Costs of a solution, project, or program should be fully loaded for ROI analysis.

11. Intangible measures are defined as measures that are purposely not converted to monetary values.

12. The results from the ROI methodology must be communicated to all key stakeholders.

Implementation of the Process

The best tool, technique, or model will be unsuccessful unless it is properly utilized and becomes a routine part of the consulting process. As a new process, both the consultants and clients may resist it, just as with any other significant change. Consultants may fear it; clients may not trust it. Some of the resistance is based on realistic barriers, while some will be based on misunderstandings and perceived problems that may be mythical. In either case, specific steps must be taken to overcome the resistance by carefully and methodically implementing the ROI process. Implementation involves many issues, including assigning responsibilities, building the necessary skills, and developing the plans and goals around the process. It will also involve preparing the environment, individuals, and support teams for this type of comprehensive analysis. The consulting teams with the most success with this process are those that have devoted adequate resources to implementation and deliberately planned for the transition from the current state to where they desire the organization to be in terms of accountability.

Applications

It is recommended that the material and content in this book be put into practice quickly. This ensures that there is successful application of learning from the book to actual consulting projects. This quick application comes to life in the ROI Institute's certification process. The business model of the ROI Institute is to transfer the capability to conduct ROI studies to organizations through the ROI certification process, which began in 1995. Since then, more than 10,000 people have participated in the process, resulting in 4,000 achieving the status of Certified ROI Professional. To achieve that designation, the individual must complete a study meeting the standards of the ROI Institute. Based on our experience at the ROI Institute, when people have conducted one study, they are more apt to do more. The value of the ROI methodology is in its use, in systematically and routinely changing practices and approaches, and in showing the value of projects along the way.

Application of the ROI Process: A Case Study

To illustrate how the data collected in the consulting ROI is reported, an example is presented. The problem addressed by the consulting team focuses directly on alternative work solutions with a work-at-home project for employees. A health and insurance company is seeking ways to increase efficiency, productivity, and retention of claims processors and examiners. In addition, executives are interested in doing its share to help with the environment. For top executives, this may be the most important issue.

At Family Mutual Insurance Company (FMI), work-at-home opportunities appeared to be a very effective solution from several perspectives. First, productivity was not at the level executives thought it should be in two job categories, claims processors and claims examiners. Claims processors process the claims as they are filed, ensuring that all paperwork is proper, procedures are followed, and the process is consistent with specifications. Claims examiners review claims only when there is a challenge or complaint. They essentially examine what has been done and then work directly with the customer to ensure that they are satisfied. Both of these groups have high turnover, and a work-at-home option seemed to be a great way to minimize this, as many individuals see this option as an attractive offer.

At the same time, the company is growing and it has reached maximum working capacity with the current office space. Consequently, more real estate space is needed. This project would free up office space that may be used by others to accommodate the growth without additional construction or leasing other buildings. Finally and foremost, the team wanted to take an important stand in helping the environment. They realize that one of the best ways to help the environment is to reduce carbon emissions by decreasing or eliminating the amount of travel of employees who come to work, thus reducing pollution and congestion.

The consultants were asked to analyze the causes of the problem, develop the best solution, and implement the solution to improve costs, productivity, and retention. A summary of the project is presented in the below case study.

A Case Study: Family Mutual Health and Life Insurance Co.

Project Profile

Title: Alternative Work Solutions: Work at Home

Target Audience: Claims processors and claims examiners (950)

Duration: Six months—from initial analysis and assessment, solution development, and implementation

Overall Objective: Explore the feasibility of working at home for this group and recommend a specific solution, and implement the solution.

Origination: Management directive with needs analysis and assessment

Coordination: HR Managers

Detailed Objectives

After implementing this project:

(Continued)

(Continued)

Project Profile

Reaction

Employees should react favorably to the work-at-home project in terms of satisfaction and motivation.

Managers must see this project as important and necessary.

Learning

Employees must understand the roles and responsibilities for success.

Managers must be able to discuss performance issues related to working at home.

Managers must be able to explain company's policy for working at home.

Application

Managers should conduct a meeting with direct reports to discuss policy, expected behavior, and actions.

At least 30 percent of eligible employees should volunteer for work-at-home assignments.

Work-at-home employees should work effectively at home.

The workplace at home should be free from distractions and conflicting demands.

Managers will administer the company's policy properly.

Managers should manage the remote employees effectively.

Project Profile

Impact

The office expense per person should reduce by 20 percent in six months.

The productivity of participants should increase by 5 percent in six months.

Employee turnover for this target group should reduce to 12 percent in six months.

The company's image as a green company should improve.

Employee engagement should improve.

ROI

Achieve a 25 percent Return on Investment

Data Collection during Project

Interview

Questionnaires

Business performance monitoring

Data Collection after Implementation

Questionnaires

Interviews

Business performance monitoring

Isolating the Effects of the Consulting Project

Productivity—control group comparisons,
participant estimates as a backup

Turnover—control group comparisons,
participant estimates as a backup

Office expenses—control group comparisons;
expert estimates,
participant estimates as a backup

(Continued)

(Continued)

Project Profile

Converting Data to Monetary Values: Techniques

Office expenses — standard values based on historical costs and expert input

Turnover— external studies, same industry

Productivity—standard values from finance and accounting

Level 1 Results: From Participating Employees

Rating of 4.6 out of 5 on satisfaction with new work arrangement

Rating of 4.1 out of 5 on motivational effect of new work arrangement

Level 1 Results: From Managers

Rating of 4.2 out of a 5 on importance of the work alternative

Rating of 4.3 out of 5 on the need for the work alternative

Level 2 Results: From Employees

Rating of 4.3 of 5 on roles and responsibilities

Level 2 Results: From Managers

Rating of 4.2 of 5 on knowing the policy for working at home

Rating of 3.9 of 5 on ability to explain policy

Successful skill practice demonstration on remote performance discussions

---

Project Profile

Level 3 Results: Key Issues

93 percent of managers conducted meetings with
employees to discuss working at home.

36 percent of eligible employees volunteered for
at-home-work assignments (342 participants).

Work-at-home employees rate 4.3 out of 5 on
working effectively at home.

95 percent of employees report that workplace is
free of distractions and conflict.

Managers rate 4.1 out of 5 on administering policy
properly.

Managers rate 3.8 out of 5 on managing remote
employees effectively.

Level 4 Results

Business Performance	Work-at-Home Group	Comparison Group	Change	Number of Participants
Daily claims processed	35.4	33.2	2.2	234
Daily claims examined	22.6	20.7	1.9	77
Office expense per person	$12,500	$17,000	$4,500	311
Turnover* (*Processors and Examiners)	9.1%	22.3%	13.2%	311

(Continued)

(Continued)

Monetary Benefits from Productivity Improvement

Value of one claim = $10.00

Value of one disputed claim = $12.00

Daily improvement = 2.2 claims per day

Daily improvement =1.9 disputed claims per day

Annual value = 234 × 220 work days × 2.2 × 10.00
= $1,132,560

Monetary Benefits from Office Expense Reduction

Office expenses in company office: per person $17,000 annually

Office expenses at home office: per person $12,500 first year; $3,600 second year

Net improvement: $4,500

Total annual value = 311 × $4,500 = $1,399,500

Monetary Benefits from Turnover Reduction

Value of one turnover statistic = $25,400

Annual improvement related to program = 45 turnovers (prevented), first year

Annual value = $25,400 × $45 = $1,143,400

Level 5 Results

Monetary Benefits

Productivity = $1,132,560 + 386,232 = $1,518,792

Office Expense = $4,500 × 311 = $1,399,500

Turnover = $1,143,000

Total   = $4,061,292

Consulting Project Costs

Initial Analysis and Assessment	$ 21,000
Solution Development	35,800
IT Support and Maintenance	238,000
Administration and Coordination	213,000
Materials (400 @ $50)	20,000
Facilities and Refreshments:	
21 meetings	12,600
Salaries plus benefits for employee	
and manager meetings	418,280
Evaluation and reporting	33,000
Total First Year Costs	**$991,680**

ROI Calculation

$$BCR = \frac{\text{Consulting project monetary benefits}}{\text{Consulting project costs}}$$

$$= \frac{\$4,061,292}{\$991,680} = 4.10$$

$$ROI = \frac{\text{Net consulting project benefits}}{\text{Consulting project costs}}$$

$$= \frac{\$4,061,292 - \$991,680}{\$991,680} = 310\%$$

(*Continued*)

(Continued)

Intangible Benefits
Reduced commuting time
Reduced carbon emissions
Reduced fuel consumption
Reduced sick leave
Absenteeism reduction
Stronger job engagement
Improved image as environmentally friendly
   company
Increased corporate social responsibility
Improved job satisfaction
Reduced stress
Improved recruiting image

As the case summary illustrates, the project involved the employees in claims processing and claims examiner job categories. The approach was comprehensive and was based on an analysis to develop a solution and implement those solutions. Detailed objectives were developed at Levels 1 through 5. The above case study also presents the methods selected for data collection during the project as well as after the implementation of the solution. In addition, the methods used to isolate the effects of consulting and the methods to convert data to monetary values are shown.

The results are then presented, beginning with Level 1, and working through Level 5, and the intangibles. The monetary benefits are based on a one-year time frame achieved from improving office expenses, turnover, and productivity. The cost of the project is presented in the case study and shows a fully loaded cost profile. A very high ROI was achieved.

This brief example shows the richness of this approach in terms of presenting a comprehensive profile of success, ranging from reaction to ROI and intangible benefits. Additional detail on this case study is found in other parts of the book.

Final Thoughts

This chapter provides a brief overview of the ROI process presented in other chapters of the book. The chapter underscores the urgency of the challenge from the consultant's perspective, and now is the time to use a comprehensive measurement and evaluation process, including the ROI for consulting. Several forces are creating this important need for more accountability. The ROI methodology presented in the book is defined with five important elements: framework, ROI process model, application, implementation, and guiding principles. When combined with determination, a reliable, credible process is developed that can be replicated from one project to another. Some detail on the ROI process is provided along with the benefits of using it. A sample case study highlights all of the issues in the chapter. This produces a micro-level scorecard for a particular project. The next chapter focuses on setting objectives.

Developing Powerful Objectives at Multiple Levels

Consulting projects need objectives. Most consultants know this. However, objectives at certain levels are often missing. Objectives at the different levels define success throughout the project, from initial reaction of individuals involved in the project, all the way through to the financial ROI. Specifically, objectives need to be written with the kind of precision to provide direction, guidance, and clarity. They need to be SMART (Specific, Measureable, Achievable, Realistic, and Time-Bound). Without SMART objectives, consulting projects tend to go astray and not deliver the desired results. With SMART objectives, the project becomes clearly focused, communicating to all stakeholders why the project is needed, where the project is going, and what will be the measures of success along the way. This chapter explains how to develop objectives at five levels, corresponding to the levels of evaluation introduced in the previous chapter.

Overall Project Goal

The goal for the consulting project, indicates specifically what will be accomplished and delivered in the consulting project. This is sometimes referred to as the purpose, overall objective, or aim of the project. Every consulting project should have a goal, and in some cases, multiple goals. These goals should be as specific as possible and focused directly on the overall assignment. Examples of project goals are presented in the following list. As this list illustrates, the goal is very broad in scope, outlining from an overall perspective what is to be accomplished within basic parameters. The details of timing, specifications, and specific deliverables come later. Project goals are critical because they bring focus to the project quickly, often serving as the beginning point in the discussion of the consulting project.

Examples of Project Goals

- Evaluate the feasibility of three alternative approaches to new product development and rollout. For each approach, provide data on projected success, resources required, and timing.
- Implement a new accounts payable system that will maximize cash flow and discounts and minimize late-payment penalties.
- Identify the causes of excessive, unplanned absenteeism, and recommend solutions with costs and timetable.
- Design, develop, and implement an automated sales-tracking system that will provide real-time information on deliveries, customer satisfaction, and sales forecasts.
- Enhance the productivity of the call center staff as measured in calls completed, without sacrificing service quality.
- Build a customer feedback and corrective action system that will meet customer needs and build customer relationships.

- Explore the feasibility of a work-at-home program to improve productivity, efficiency, and retention, while helping to protect the environment.

- Reorganize the sales and marketing division from a product-based unit to a regional-based, fully integrated structure.

- Provide review, advice, and oversight input during the relocation of the headquarters staff. Input is provided by memo each week. The project will address concerns, issues, problems, and delays.

- Recommend and implement a social media marketing approach, given our current marketing strategy and customer base.

Levels of Project Objectives

Most consulting projects lead to solutions. In some situations, the consulting project is aimed at solving a particular problem, preventing a problem, or taking advantage of an opportunity. In other situations, the initial consulting project is designed to develop a range of feasible solutions, or one desired solution prior to implementation. Whatever the case, these solutions or opportunities should have multiple levels of objectives, as described in Table 7.1. These levels of objectives, ranging from qualitative to quantitative, define precisely what will occur as a particular project is implemented in the organization. These objectives reflect the levels of evaluation and types of data described in Chapter 6. They are so critical that they need special attention in their development and use.

Table 7.1   Multiple Levels of Objectives

Levels of Objectives	Focus of Objectives
Level 1 Reaction	Defines a specific level of reaction to the consulting project as it is launched and communicated to the stakeholders.
Level 2 Learning	Defines specific levels of knowledge, information, and skills for the stakeholders to learn how to make the consulting project successful.
Level 3 Application and Implementation	Defines specific measures and levels of success with application, uses, and implementation of project.
Level 4 Impact	Defines the specific levels business measures will change or improve as a result of the project's implementation.
Level 5 ROI	Defines the specific return on investment from the project, comparing costs with monetary benefits from the project.

Reaction Objectives

For any project to be successful, various stakeholders must react to the project favorably, or at least not negatively. Ideally, the stakeholders should be satisfied with the project since the best project solutions offer win-win outcomes for the client and consultant. The stakeholders are those who are directly involved in implementing the project, usually referred to as participants in the project. This diverse group can be the employees who are involved in implementing the new system, team leaders who are responsible for the change process, customers who must use a redesigned product, suppliers who must follow a new system, citizens who must use a new procedure, or volunteers who must adjust to a new protocol. Stakeholders could also be managers who must support or assist the project in some way.

Table 7.2 shows a few of the typical areas for specific reaction objectives with examples. This type of information should be collected routinely through a consulting

Table 7.2   Reaction Objectives

Typical Areas

- Usefulness of project
- Relevance to our needs
- Feasibility of project
- Difficulty of project
- Necessity of project
- Importance of project
- Perceived value of project
- Appropriateness of project
- Overall satisfaction with the project

- The project is challenging.
- The project is rewarding.
- The project is motivational.
- The project is fair.
- The project is a good investment for my organization.
- The project is a good use of my time.
- Intent to make this project successful

Examples

1. Citizens should perceive the new recycling process as useful to them with a rating of a 4 on a 5-point scale.
2. Sales team should rate the new tracking as relevant to their needs, scoring 4.5 on a 5-point scale.
3. Suppliers should view the new sustainability requirement as necessary with a 5 rating on a 7-point scale.
4. Construction workers should see the new safety harness system as important to keep them safe with a rating of 4.2 out of 5.

project so that feedback can be used to make adjustments, keep the project on track, and perhaps even redesign certain parts of it. These are necessary to maintain proper focus. Unfortunately, many consulting projects do not have specific objectives at this level and data collection mechanisms are not put in place to ensure appropriate feedback for making needed adjustments.

Learning Objectives

Almost every consulting project will involve a learning objective. In some cases, involving major change projects or new technology implementations, the learning component is quite significant. To ensure that the various stakeholders have learned what they need to learn to make the project successful, learning objectives are developed. Learning objectives are critical because they communicate expected outcomes from the learning component of the project, the information needed, the desired competence, or the required performance to make the consulting project successful. These objectives provide a basis for evaluating the learning since they often reflect the type of measurement process. Learning objectives clearly indicate what participants must learn—sometimes with precision. Table 7.3 show typical action verbs and examples of typical learning objectives.

The three types of learning objectives are often defined. These include the following:

1. Awareness: Familiarity with terms, concepts, and processes

2. Knowledge: General understanding of concepts, processes, or procedures

3. Performance: Ability to demonstrate skills at least on a basic level

Table 7.3   Learning Objectives and Typical Action Verbs

Action Verbs

• Name	• Explain	• Complete
• Write	• Search	• State
• Prepare	• Sort	• Build
• Describe	• Locate	• Start up
• Recite	• Stop	• List
• Reboot	• Solve	• Compare
• Differentiate	• Calculate	• Recall
• Identify	• Eliminate	• Contrast
• Load	• Construct	• Use
• Score	• Determine	• Document

Typical Learning Objectives

After completing the project, participants will be able to

- Identify the six features of the new ethics policy in two minutes.
- Complete each software routine in the standard time for the routine.
- Use problem-solving skills, given a specific problem statement.
- Determine whether they are eligible for the early retirement program.
- Score 80 percent or better in 10 minutes on the new-product test.
- List all five customer-interaction skills.
- Explain the five types of value of diversity in a work group.
- Document suggestions for award consideration without assistance.
- Score at least 9 out of 10 on a sexual harassment policy quiz.
- Identify five new features of the redesigned system.
- Name the six pillars of the division's new strategy.
- Complete the leadership simulation in 15 minutes.

The best learning objectives describe observable, measurable behavior or performance that is necessary for the success of the consulting project. They are often outcome-based, clearly worded, and specific. They specify what the particular stakeholder must know and do to implement the project successfully. Learning objectives can have three components:

1. Performance: What the participant or stakeholder will be able to do to as a result of the consulting project

2. Conditions under which the participant or stakeholder will perform the various tasks and processes

3. Criteria: The degree or level of proficiency necessary to perform a new task, process, or procedure that is part of the solution

Application Objectives

As a consulting project is implemented, it should be guided by application objectives that define clearly what is expected of participants and often to what level of performance. Application objectives reflect the action desired from the project. They also involve particular milestones, indicating specifically when steps or phases of the process are completed. Application objectives are critical because they describe the expected outcomes in the intermediate area, that is, between learning what is necessary to make the project successful and the actual impact that will be improved because of it. Application objectives describe how people should perform, processes should evolve, or technology should be used as the project is implemented. The emphasis is on actions, activities, and tasks.

The best application objectives identify behaviors that are observable and measurable or action steps in a process that can easily be observed, measured, or checked. They specify what the various stakeholders will change or have changed as a result of the consulting project. As with learning objectives, application or implementation objectives may have three components: performance, condition, and criteria.

Table 7.4 shows typical key questions asked at this level and typical application objectives. Application objectives have almost always been included to some degree in consulting projects, but have not been as specific as they could be or need to be. To be effective, they must clearly define the environment where the project is successfully implemented.

Impact Objectives

Almost every consulting project should have an impact, even in the public sector and among nonprofits and non-government organizations. Business impact is expressed in the key business measures that should be improved as the application objectives are achieved. The impact objectives are critical to measuring business performance because they define business-unit performance that should be connected to the consulting project. Above

Table 7.4 Application Objectives

Typical Questions for Application Objectives

1. What new or improved knowledge will be applied on the job?
2. What is the frequency of skill application?
3. What specific new tasks will be performed?
4. What new steps will be implemented?
5. What action items will be implemented?
6. What new procedures will be implemented or changed?
7. What new guidelines will be implemented?
8. What new processes will be implemented?
9. Which meetings need to be held?
10. Which tasks, steps, or procedures will be discontinued?

Typical Application Objectives
When this project is implemented

- At least 99.1 percent of software users will be following the correct sequences after three weeks of use.

- Within one year, 10 percent of employees will submit documented suggestions for saving costs.

- The average 360-degree leadership assessment score will improve from 3.4 to 4.1 on a 5-point scale in 90 days.

- 95 percent of high-potential employees will complete individual development plans within two years.

- Employees will routinely use problem-solving skills when faced with a quality problem.

- Sexual harassment activity will cease within three months after the zero-tolerance policy is implemented.

- 80 percent of employees will use one or more of the three cost-containment features of the health-care plan in the next six months.

- In three months, 50 percent of sales team will use insight selling with every customer.

- By November, pharmaceutical sales reps will communicate adverse effects of a specific prescription drug to all physicians in their territories.

- Managers will initiate three workout projects within 15 days.

- Within three weeks, customer service representatives will use all five interaction skills with at least 70 percent of the customers each day.

---

all, they place emphasis on achieving bottom-line results that key client groups expect and demand.

The best impact objectives contain data that are easily collected and are well known to the client group. They are results-based, clearly worded, and specify what the stakeholders have ultimately accomplished in the business unit as a result of the consulting project.

The four major categories of hard data impact objectives are output, quality, cost, and time. Major categories of soft data impact objectives are customer service, work climate, and image. Typical measures that frame the objectives are presented in the next chapter. The following list offers examples of impact objectives.

Typical Business Impact Objectives
After project completion, the following conditions should be met:

- After nine months, grievances should be reduced from three per month to no more than two per month.

- The average number of new accounts should increase from 300 to 350 per month in six months.

- Medical treatment cases should decrease by 20 percent within the next five months.

- A 25 percent reduction in overtime should be realized for front-of-house managers in the third quarter of this year.

- Employee complaints should be reduced from an average of three per month to an average of one per month.

- By the end of the year, the average number of product defects should decrease from 214 per month to 150 per month at all plants in the Midwest region.
- The employee engagement index should rise by one point during the next calendar year.
- Sales expenses for the sales team should decrease by 10 percent in the fourth quarter.
- There should be a 10 percent increase in Pharmaceuticals, Inc. brand awareness among physicians during the next two years.
- Customer returns per month should reduce by 15 percent in six months.

Return on Investment Objectives

A fifth level of objectives for consulting projects is the expected return on investment. These objectives define the expected payoff from the consulting project and compare cost of the consulting project with the monetary benefits from the consulting project. This is typically expressed as an acceptable ROI percentage that compares the annual monetary benefits minus the cost, divided by the actual cost, and multiplied by 100. A 0 percent ROI indicates a breakeven of a consulting project. A 50 percent ROI indicates that the cost of the consulting is recaptured and an additional 50 percent "earnings" is achieved.

For many consulting projects, the ROI objective is larger than might be expected from the ROI of other expenditures, such as the purchase of a new company, a new building, or major equipment, but the two are related. In many organizations the ROI objective for a consulting project is set slightly higher than the ROI expected from capital investments because of the relative newness of applying the ROI concept to consulting. For example, if the expected ROI from the purchase of a new company is 20 percent, the ROI from a consulting project might be set at the 25 percent range. Ideally, the ROI objective should be established up front and in discussions with the client.

Importance of Specific Objectives

Developing specific objectives at all levels, including application and impact, for consulting projects provides important benefits. First, they provide direction to the consultants directly involved in the process to help keep them on track. Objectives define exactly what is expected at different time frames from different individuals. These objectives provide guidance to the support staff as they offer assistance to the consultants. Impact objectives help the client to fully understand the ultimate goal and impact of consulting. These objectives provide the focus and motivation for the consultants who must achieve success with the project. In most consulting projects, the participants are actively involved and will influence the results of the project. They will clearly see the gains that should be achieved. Objectives provide important information for all stakeholder groups to clearly understand what the landscape will look like when the consulting is complete. Finally, from an evaluation perspective, the objectives provide a basis for measuring success.

Final Thoughts

This brief chapter shows how the objectives are developed to provide guidance and direction to consulting projects. SMART (Specific, Measurable, Achievable, Realistic, and Time-bound) objectives need to be established for at least four levels (reaction, learning, application, and impact). When an ROI calculation is to be delivered, a fifth-level ROI objective should be added. These objectives provide the direction from the consultant to the participants (or users) involved in the consulting project, to the other important stakeholders supporting the consulting project, and to the major sponsor or funder for the project.

Aligning Projects to the Business

The previous chapter defines the objectives needed for a project to give it direction and focus. This chapter describes how to develop those objectives and align the project to business issues. Alignment occurs at three points. The first is at the beginning of the project where the project is aligned directly to the business and the consulting solution is connected directly to the business measure. The alignment is continued during the project with the business impact objectives described in the previous chapter. The alignment is validated in the follow-up to determine the extent to which the consulting project has influenced the business measure. When the project is isolated from other influences, alignment is then validated. This chapter shows how alignment is achieved through five levels of needs assessment, beginning with payoff needs and moving through to preference needs.

Introduction to the V Model

Where do objectives come from? A distinct link between objectives and needs should exist for each consulting project. Chapter 6 focuses on the five levels of evaluation and explains how they are critical to providing an overall assessment of the impact of a consulting project—particularly when a solution is implemented as part of the consulting project. Chapter 7 shows the importance of setting objectives for the consulting project at different levels. This chapter makes a further connection to the original needs assessment. Figure 8.1 shows the connection between evaluation and needs assessment

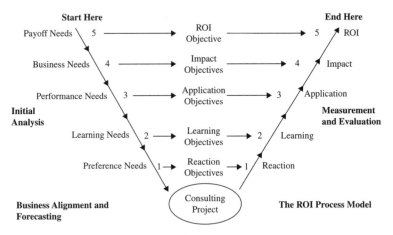

FIGURE 8.1   Consulting Alignment with the V Model

for consulting projects. This figure shows the important links from the initial problem or opportunity that created the need for consulting to the evaluation of the project. Level 5 defines the potential payoff and examines the possibility for a return on investment before the project is even pursued. Level 4 analysis focuses directly on the business needs that precipitated the need for consulting. At Level 3, the specific performance or action is defined that must change to meet the business needs. At Level 2, the specific information, knowledge, or skills that are needed to address the performance needs are identified. Finally, the preferences for the project implementation define the Level 1 needs. This connection is very important to understand how alignment is achieved with consulting projects.

An example will help illustrate this linkage. Figure 8.2 shows an example of linking needs assessment with the evaluation for a consulting project. This

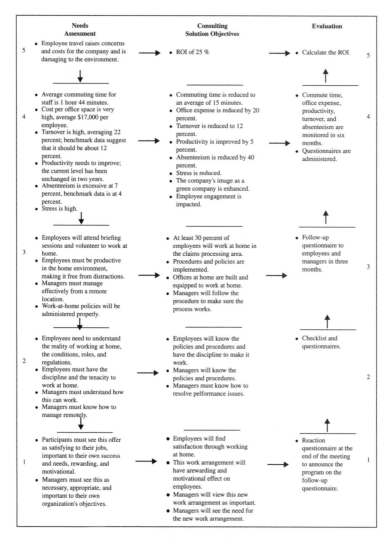

FIGURE 8.2 Alignment for Consulting

particular project is designed to create a work-at-home solution for an organization. In this project, several business input measures, such as productivity, office expenses, and employee turnover are identified. Also there are many intangibles that should be connected to this solution. These include reduction of carbon emissions as employees drive less, job satisfaction and stress reduction, as well as increased physical well-being and other benefits. As the figure shows, the first step is to see if this is a problem worth solving or an opportunity worth pursuing. This usually validates the problem using Level 4 data. In this example, the payoff need is based on the problem of employees having to travel long distances that generate costs to them and damage to the environment. The average commuting time for the team is almost two hours. At Level 4, the problem unfolds with more detail, and it is obvious that this is worth solving. Office expenses are very high and increasing as staff additions are made. Turnover, which is expensive, is extremely high, averaging 22 percent, while benchmark data suggests that it should be about 12 percent or lower. Productivity needs to improve; it has not increased in the past two years. Absenteeism is excessive, and stress is high. When all these measures are considered, this presents a serious problem, and to a certain extent it is also a great opportunity for improvement.

With the confirmation in Level 4 that there is a problem, a potential payoff can be estimated. This involves estimating the cost of the measures of office expenses, turnover, and lost productivity, and estimating the reduction that can come from the consulting project. This develops a profile of potential payoff to see if the problem is worth solving.

At Level 3, the causes of the problem are explored using a variety of techniques.

Ideally, each measure should be analyzed to see what is causing it to be where it is (i.e., why is productivity not improving, what is the cause of the excessive turnover, etc.?). For this project, the consultants conducted interviews and focus groups, examined exit interview data, and administered surveys to understand why business measures are at the current level. Some causes of the problem were obvious, for example, office expenses are incurred due to growth and the increasing costs of real estate and leasing.

The key issue is to identify the solution to the problem. The commuting time will not get better unless the office space is either moved to the people, the people are moved closer to the office, or they're allowed to work from home. The turnover issue has many components, but having an alternative work schedule, such as working at home, would reduce turnover significantly according to an analysis of exit interviews. Some employees have left to work either closer to home or at home. The productivity issue is a little more confusing. It could be better, but it is not clear as to how this should be addressed. Interviews and focus groups hint that working at home might raise the productivity. Absenteeism is traced to problems that could be solved if there were some flexibility in work arrangements. Flexibility in their work arrangements may help avoid this stress, and it appears that it could be resolved with a work-at-home situation as well.

At the next level, Level 2, the learning issue is explored. Do employees understand what's necessary to make this work? Are employees confident that they can work at home? Are they fully aware of all the issues and the ramifications of working at home? Do the managers understand what's involved in this arrangement, and can they adapt to a work-at-home arrangement? These issues involve the content of the project, detailing what people must know to work successfully at home.

At Level 1, the desired reaction must be detailed. At first, a realistic picture of the work-at-home environment must be presented so that individuals may understand this choice may not be for everyone. Also, when the ground rules are fully understood, employees must see this as helpful, necessary, and, for some, even motivational. Managers must see this as a tool to help them and the organization, not as a process that's going to cause them to lose control. These perceptions are very important and must be approached very deliberately.

These five levels provide an overall profile for determining if the problem is worth solving, align the project solution with key measures, and identify the issues necessary to develop the objectives. The consulting project objectives for each level are shown in the figure as well, along with the evaluation method to verify that the objectives were met. This process is important to the development and implementation of a consulting project. Many consulting projects are involved in developing a solution and implementing the solution, as in this particular example. When this occurs, the above linkage connects the needs to objectives and then to evaluation.

The solution to the problem or opportunity to pursue is an important part of this linkage. Some consulting projects may be involved in uncovering needs with the initial analysis to determine the causes of the problem and then recommend solutions. In those situations, it is up to the client to then implement the solution, or implementation becomes part of another consulting project. In either case, the solutions are ultimately developed for a complete consulting project. If this has not been accomplished, multiple levels of analysis may be necessary for the project. While there are other references that focus more specifically on the performance analysis to uncover different levels of needs, a brief summary is presented here.

Payoff Needs

The first part of the process is to determine if the problem is worth solving or the opportunity warrants serious consideration. In some cases, this is obvious when there are serious problems that are affecting the organization's operations and strategy. Still others may not be so obvious.

The following list shows some requests for consulting that represent obvious payoff opportunities, and thus, have business value written all over them. These payoff opportunities make it clear that this is a problem that needs to be solved or an opportunity that should be pursued with a clearly identified business need.

Obvious Payoff Opportunities

- System downtime is at its highest level, up to 36 percent from last year.

- Carbon footprint is excessive for this type of organization, and increasing rapidly.

- Excessive turnover of critical talent: 35 percent above benchmark data

- Very low market share in a market with few players

- Inadequate customer service: 3.89 on a 10-point customer satisfaction scale

- Safety record is among the worst in the industry.

- This year's out-of-compliance fines total $1.2 million, up 82 percent from last year.

- Excessive product returns: 30 percent higher than previous year.

- Excessive absenteeism in call centers is 12.3 percent, compared to the 5.4 percent industry average

- Revenue is declining for top two projects, although the overall market is growing.

- Sexual harassment complaints per 1,000 employees are the highest in the industry.

- Grievances are up 38 percent from last year.

- The health care, legal, administrative, and incarceration costs for each homeless person are averaging $78,000 per year.

Some requests represent not-so-obvious payoff opportunities, such as those presented in the following list. In each of the situations, it is not clear what business measures will actually change as a result of this project.

The focus moves to the next level in order to clearly define the business measure or variety of measures. In the previous project of converting employees from a work to work-at-home arrangement, the initial request was not so obvious: to reduce employee travel time, to lower costs, and to have a positive impact on the environment. A work-at-home solution was anticipated. Additional detail was needed, and this need led to the connection of several measures. These requests may be difficult to address because the not-so-obvious opportunities may raise concerns. The project may not be connected to business needs, and if so, the client should be made aware of this.

Not-So-Obvious Payoff Opportunities

- Become a technology leader.
- Create an efficient supply chain.
- Organize a business development conference.
- Establish a project management office.
- Launch a new product.
- Provide job training for unemployed workers.
- Create a green company.
- Create a conservative risk management system.
- Develop highly effective employees.
- Provide shelter for the homeless.
- Implement a sexual harassment project for all associates.
- Develop an "open-book" company.

- Implement the same workout process that GE has used.

- Improve leadership competencies for all managers.

- Create a great place to work.

- Implement a transformation program involving all employees.

- Implement a career advancement program.

- Create a wellness and fitness center.

- Build capability for future growth.

At this level, it is important not only to identify business measures that need to improve, but to also convert them into monetary values, so the anticipated improvement can be converted to money. The company requirement to "show me the money" is occurring more often. The second part of the process is to develop an approximate cost for the entire consulting project. This could come from a detailed proposal or may be a rough estimate. At this stage only an estimate is needed. The projected cost of the project is then compared to the potential monetary benefits to show the ROI forecast. A forecast of ROI is important in very expensive, strategic, or critical projects. This step may be omitted in situations when the problem must be solved regardless of the cost, or if it becomes obvious that it is a high-payoff activity. Still, other projects may be initiated, and the potential payoff is not desired. For example, as an organization strives to be a technology leader, it may be difficult to place a value on that goal for executives.

Business Needs

At Level 4, business data are examined to determine which measures need to improve. This involves a review of organizational records and reports, examining all types of hard and soft data. It is usually the performance of one of the data items that triggers the consulting project. For example, when market share is not as much as it should be, operating costs are excessive, product quality is deteriorating, or productivity is low, the business measure is easily pinpointed. These are the key issues that come directly from the data in the organization and are often found in the operating reports or records.

Table 8.1 shows examples of business needs ranged in categories of hard data to include output, quality, cost, and time. These measures exist in any type of organization, even in the public sector and in nonprofits and nongovernmental organizations (NGOs). These measures often attract the attention of executives, as they represent the effects on business. An important goal is to connect the consulting project to one or more of these issues.

Table 8.2 shows measures with softer effects, including some of the more common measures, such as those involving customer service, image, and work climate. Although these may be perceived as not as important as hard data, they are important, and in some cases, a consulting project will be connected to one of these soft data items. This book defines a soft measure that can be converted to money as a tangible. If it cannot be converted to money credibility with a minimum amount

Table 8.1 Examples of Hard Data

Output	Quality	Costs	Time
• Completion Rate	• Failure Rates	• Shelter Costs	• Cycle Time
• Units Produced	• Dropout Rates	• Treatment Costs	• Equipment Downtime
• Tons Manufactured	• Scrap	• Budget Variances	• Overtime
• Items Assembled	• Waste	• Unit Costs	• On-time shipping
• Money Collected	• Rejects	• Cost by Account	• Time to Project Completion
• Items Sold	• Error Rates	• Variable Costs	• Processing Time
• New Accounts Generated	• Rework	• Fixed Costs	• Supervisory Time
• Forms Processed	• Shortages	• Overhead Costs	• Time to Proficiency
• Loans Approved	• Deviation from Standard	• Operating Costs	• Learning Time
• Inventory Turnover	• Product Defects	• Project Cost Savings	• Meeting Schedules
• Patients Visited	• Product Failures	• Accident Costs	• Repair Time
• Applications Processed	• Inventory Adjustments	• Program Costs	• Efficiency
• Students Graduated	• Time Card Corrections	• Sales Expense	• Work Stoppages
• Tasks Completed	• Incidents	• Participant Costs	• Order Response
• Output Per Hour	• Compliance Discrepancies		• Late Reporting
• Productivity	• Agency Fines		• Lost Time Days
• Work Backlog			
• Incentive Bonus			
• Shipment			

Table 8.2   Examples of Soft Data

Work Habits	Employee Development/Advancement
Tardiness	Promotions
Visits to dispensary	Capability
Violations of safety rules	Intellectual capital
Communication breakdowns	Programs completed
Excessive breaks	Requests for transfer
Conflicts	Performance appraisal ratings
	Readiness
Work Climate/Satisfaction	Networking
Grievances	
Discrimination charges	**Creativity/Innovation**
Employee complaints	Creativity
Job satisfaction	Innovation
Organization commitment	New ideas
Employee engagement	Suggestions
Employee loyalty	
Intent to leave	**Image**
Stress	Brand awareness
	Reputation
Customer Service	Leadership
Customer complaints	Social responsibility
Customer satisfaction	Environmental friendliness
Customer dissatisfaction	Social consciousness
Customer impressions	Diversity
Customer loyalty	External awards
Customer retention	
Customer value	
Lost customers	
New products and suggestions	
Trademarks	
Copyrights and patents	
Process improvements	
Partnerships	
Alliances	

of resources, it is left as an intangible. This definition means that most of the hard data categories are usually converted to money and are thus tangible.

The supporting data may come not only from the operating reports, but from annual reports, marketing data, industry data, major planning documents, or other important information sources that clearly indicate operating performance.

Performance Needs

The Level 3 analysis involves determining performance needs. The task is to determine what is causing the problem (or creating the opportunity) identified at Level 4 (i.e., what is causing the business measure to not be at the desired level). Something in the system is not performing as it should, and this may be caused by one or more of the following:

- Inappropriate behavior
- Dysfunctional behavior
- Ineffective systems
- Improper process flow
- Ineffective procedures
- Unsupported processes
- Inappropriate technology
- Inaction of stakeholders

The analysis usually reveals that a group of people are not performing as they should. The reason for this inadequate performance is the basis for the solution, the consulting project. For example, if employee health-care costs are increasing more than they should, and sick leave usage is increasing, this may be caused by the unhealthy habits of employees. A wellness and fitness project may be needed.

Performance needs will have to be uncovered using a variety of problem-solving or analysis techniques, such as those listed in the following list. This may involve the use of data collection techniques discussed in this book, such as surveys, questionnaires, focus groups, or interviews. It may involve a variety of problem-solving or analysis techniques such as root-cause analysis, fishbone diagrams, and other analysis techniques. Whatever is used, the key is to determine all of the causes of the problem so that solutions can be developed. Often, multiple solutions are appropriate.

Diagnostic Tools

- Statistical process control
- Brainstorming
- Problem analysis
- Cause-and-effect diagram
- Force-field analysis
- Mind mapping
- Affinity diagrams
- Simulations
- Diagnostic instruments
- Focus groups
- Probing interviews

- Job satisfaction surveys
- Engagement surveys
- Exit interviews
- Exit surveys
- Nominal group technique

Learning Needs

The analysis at Level 3 usually uncovers specific learning needs with the people who would be involved in the project. It may be that learning deficiencies, in terms of knowledge and skills, may contribute to the problem if they are not the major cause of it. In other situations, the solution will need a learning component as participants learn how to implement a new process, procedure, or technology. The learning would typically involve acquisition of knowledge or the development of skills necessary to improve performance. In some cases, perceptions or attitudes may need to be altered to make the process successful in the future. The extent of learning required will determine whether formalized training is needed or if more informal, on-the-job methods can be utilized to build the necessary skills and knowledge to make the project successful.

Preference Needs

The final level is to consider the preference for the project solution. This involves determining the preferred way in which those involved in the process will need or want it to be implemented. A fundamental issue at this level is the perceived value of the project. Typical questions that surface are, "Is this important?" "Is this necessary?" and "Is it relevant to me?" Preference needs may involve implementation and/or learning issues. Learning issues may involve decisions such as when learning is expected and in what amounts, how it is presented, and the overall time frame. Implementation issues may involve issues such as timing, support, expectation, and other key factors. The important issue is to try to determine the specific preferences to the extent possible so that the complete profile of the solution can be developed based on all of the needs.

Final Thoughts

This chapter describes the initial analysis needed for proper alignment. The initial analysis includes five levels of needs, beginning with payoff needs and progressing to preference needs. When these needs are complete, a project is aligned to the business need at the beginning, which is a critical element in the initial success of the project. The alignment continues when the project is implemented with impact objectives described in previous chapter. Alignment is validated with follow-up evaluation as described in later chapters. The next chapter describes the tools needed for planning an ROI study.

Planning the Evaluation

Few things are more important in a consulting process than the initial planning and, in particular, the planning for evaluation processes. When attempting to measure the success of consulting after the project is complete—as an add-on, follow-up assignment—the need for more planning is often obvious. The initial planning involves several key issues explored in this chapter.

Initial Planning for Success

An important ingredient in the success of the use of the ROI methodology is to properly plan for the ROI study early in the consulting cycle. Appropriate up-front attention will save much time later when data are collected and analyzed, thus improving accuracy and reducing the cost of the ROI study. Planning also avoids any confusion surrounding what will be accomplished, by whom, and at what time. Four planning documents are necessary and should be completed before the consulting project is initiated.

Data Collection Plan

Figure 9.1 shows a completed data collection plan for the work-at-home consulting project described previously. The project was initiated to reduce turnover, reduce office expenses, and improve productivity. An ROI calculation was planned to show the value of this project.

This document provides a place for the major elements and issues regarding collecting data for the five

Evaluation Purpose: Measure Success of Program

Program: FMI Work-at-Home Project			Responsibility: HR/Consultants		Date: March 30
Level	**Broad Program Objective(s)**	**Measures**	**Data Collection Method/Instruments**	**Data Sources**	**Timing**
1	*Reaction and Planned Action* • Employees should react favorably to the work-at-home project in terms of satisfaction and motivation. • Managers must see this project as important and necessary.	• Rating scale (4 out of 5)	• Questionnaires • Interviews	• Participants • Managers	• 30 days • 30 days
2	*Learning and Confidence* • Employees must understand the roles and responsibilities for success. • Mangers must be able to discuss performance issues related to working at home. • Managers must be able to explain company's policy for working at home.	• Rating scale (4 out of 5)	• Questionnaires • Interviews	• Participants • Managers	• 30 days • 30 days
3	*Application and Implementation* • Managers should conduct a meeting with all employees to discuss policy and expected behavior and actions. • At least 30 percent of eligible employees volunteer for work-at-home assignments. • Work-at-home employees should work effectively at home. • The workplace at home should be free from distractions and conflicting demands. • Managers will administer the company's policy properly. • Managers should manage the remote employees effectively.	• Checklist • Sign Up • Rating scale (4 out of 5)	• Data Monitoring • Questionnaires	• Company Records • Participants • Managers	• 30 days • 90 days
4	*Business Impact* • The office expense per person should decrease by 70 percent. • The productivity of participants should increase by 10 percent. • Employee turnover for this target group should decrease 15 percent. • The company's image as a green company should improve. • Employee engagement should improve.	• Direct costs • Claims per day • Voluntary turnover • Rating scale (4 out of 5) • Rating scale (4 out of 5)	• Business Performance Monitoring • Survey	• Company Records • Participants • Managers	• 6 months • 6 months • 6 months • 90 days • 90 days
5	ROI 25 %	Baseline Data:			

FIGURE 9.1   Data Collection Plan

evaluation levels. In the first column, specific project objectives are stated. In the second column, the specific measures or data descriptors are indicated when they are needed to explain the links from objectives to the data collection. In the next column, the specific data collection method is briefly described using standard terminology. Next, the source of the data is entered. Data sources will vary considerably but usually include participants, team leaders, company records, and/or the client. In the next column, the timeframe for data collection is listed, usually referenced from the beginning of the project. Finally, the responsibility for data collection is noticed.

The objectives for reaction usually include the desired reactions to the consulting project and suggested improvements. Planned actions may be included here. Reaction data may be collected at different intervals. In this example, feedback is taken only at one time, when the work-at-home project is implemented.

Because Level 2 evaluation focuses on the measures of learning, specific objectives include those areas where participants are expected to learn new tasks, procedures, technology knowledge, skills, or processes. The data collection method is the specific way in which learning is assessed, in this case using a self-assessment questionnaire. The timing for Level 2 evaluation is during the implementation of the project.

For application evaluation, the objectives represent key areas of application, including significant on-the-job activities and implementation steps. In this example, the methods include questionnaires, surveys, and monitoring company records. This information is usually collected a matter of months after the implementation. Because responsibilities are often shared among several groups, including the consulting staff, it is important to clarify this issue early in the process. The timing depends on the scope and nature of the project, and is usually in the range of three weeks to three months after the launch of the project.

For impact evaluation, objectives focus on business impact measures influenced by the consulting project. The measures/data column includes the specifics and may provide a hint about the location of the measure. For example, if one of the objectives is to improve productivity, a specific measure would indicate how productivity is actually measured. In the example, productivity is measured for each group, processors and examiners. The preferred evaluation method is performance monitoring, though other methods may be appropriate. The sources of data utilized at this level are the company records. The timing depends on how quickly the intervention can generate a sustained impact on the three measures—usually a matter of months after the consulting project is completed. In this example, data are collected at six-month intervals. A project evaluator is responsible for data collection at this level. If appropriate, an ROI objective (Level 5) is included.

The data collection plan is an important part of the evaluation strategy, and it should be completed prior to moving forward with the consulting project; the plan is completed before pursuing an ROI evaluation. The plan provides a clear direction of what types of data will be collected, how they will be collected, where they will be collected, when they will be collected, and who will collect them.

ROI Analysis Plan

Figure 9.2 shows a completed ROI analysis plan for the same project. This planning document is the continuation of the data collection plan presented in Figure 9.1 and captures information on several key items that are necessary to develop the actual ROI calculation. In the first column, significant business impact data items are listed. These items will be used in the ROI analysis. The method for isolating the effects of consulting is listed next to each data item in the second column. For most projects, the method will be the same for each data item, but there could be variations. For example, if no historical data are available for one data item, then trend line analysis is not possible for that item, although it may be appropriate for other items. In this example, a control group arrangement was feasible, and a trend line analysis was also considered. Participant estimates were used as a backup.

The method for converting data to monetary values is included in the third column. In this example, office expenses are converted to monetary values with two approaches: using costs in the company records and collecting expert input from the staff directly involved in the process. The cost categories planned for capture are outlined in the fourth column. Instructions about how certain costs should be prorated are noted here. Normally the cost categories will be consistent from one consulting project to another. However, a specific cost that is unique to this consulting project is also noted. The anticipated intangible benefits expected from this project are outlined in the fifth column. This list is generated from discussions about the project with sponsors, subject matter experts, and other stakeholders.

Program: FMI Work-at-Home Project			Responsibility: HR/Consultants			Date: _____
Data Items (Usually Level 4)	**Methods for Isolating the Effects of the Program/Process**	**Methods of Converting Data to Monetary Values**	**Cost Categories**	**Intangible Benefits**	**Communication Targets for Final Report**	**Other Influential issues During Application**
Office expenses	• Control group • Expert estimates	• Standard value based on costs	• Initial analysis and assessment • Solution development • IT support and maintenance • Administration and coordination • Materials • Facilities and refreshments • Meetings • Salaries plus benefits for employee and manager meetings • Evaluation and reporting	• Reduced carbon emissions • Reduced fuel consumption • Reduced sick leave • Absenteeism reduction • Job engagement • Community image • Environmental friendly company • Corporate social responsibility • Job satisfaction improvement • Stress reduction • Recruiting image	• Participants • Managers • HR team • Executive group • Consultants • External groups	• Must observe marketing and economic forces • Search for barriers/obstacles for progress
Productivity	• Control group • Participant estimates	• Standard values				
Turnover	• Control group • Participant estimates	• External studies				

FIGURE 9.2 ROI Analysis Plan

Communication targets are outlined in the sixth column. Although there could be many groups that should receive the information, four target groups are always recommended: senior management, consulting participants, managers of participants, and the consulting staff. Each of these four groups needs to know about the results of the ROI analysis. Finally, other issues or events that might influence the success of the consulting project are highlighted in the last column. Typical items include the capability of participants, external issues, the degree of access to data sources, political influence, and unique data analysis issues.

The ROI analysis plan, when combined with the data collection plan, provides detailed information on calculating the ROI, illustrating how the process will develop from beginning to end. When completed, these two plans should provide the direction necessary for the ROI evaluation and should integrate with the overall project plan.

Communication Plan

Although communicating the results of a consulting project is often the most neglected step, it is the most important. A golden rule of evaluation: If you ask for the data, do something with them. In order to do something constructive, the right people must know the results. The plan goes from describing target audiences to purpose, communication time line, distribution channel, and responsibility. The plan also includes a place for communication status. Figure 9.3 shows the communication plan for the work-at-home project. In this example, the results were communicated to the board of directors.

Target Audience	Purpose of Communication	Communication Time line	Distribution Channel	Responsibility	Status
Senior Executives	1. Present results. 2. Gain support for project.	End of project	Live briefing Complete report	Consultant	
Managers Involved in the Project	1. Highlight their success. 2. Reinforce the process used in the project.	One week after completing final report	Brief summary	HR Team	
Employees Working Remotely	1. Highlight their success. 2. Reinforce decision to work at home.	One week after completing final report	Brief summary	HR Team	
Analytics Team	1. Underscore the importance of measuring results. 2. Explain the techniques used to measure results.	Three weeks from end of project	Meeting with complete report	Analytics Project Team	
HR Team	1. Demonstrate accountability for expenditures. 2. Show the complete results of the project.	Within three weeks of the project	Meeting with complete study	HR Executive	
Board of Directors	1. Gain support for project. 2. Corporate social responsibility.	Next board meeting After end of project	Meeting with brief summary	HR Executive	

FIGURE 9.3 Communication Plan

Project Plan

The final planning document is the project plan, which maps each step of the evaluation process. Figure 9.4 shows an example. This plan is a culmination of the previously described plans, plus the detailed steps. The project plan begins with project approval and ends with communication and follow-up activities. As you complete each chapter in the book, the steps in the project plan will become clear. The first step is the project go-ahead, followed by problem definition, business alignment, and setting objectives. The project plan includes these steps, as well as steps to design the data collection instruments and to administer the data collection process. The final section of the project plan includes any follow-up activity after you have communicated results.

	F	M	A	M	J	J	A	S
Decide to Conduct Project	▓							
Define/Align the Problem/Opportunity	▓							
Set Objectives	▓							
Form an On-Board Project Team		▓						
Design Data Collection		▓						
Collect Data (L1–L2)		▓	▓					
Collect Data (L3–L4)					▓			
Complete Preliminary Data Analysis					▓			
Complete Data Analysis						▓		
Write Report						▓		
Print Report						▓		
Communicate Results							▓	
Initiate Improvements							▓	
Complete Implementation								▓

FIGURE 9.4 Project Plan

The project plan helps track resources. Accounting for resources expended while implementing the project is a plus. It will save you time as you go. There are a variety of useful tools available to help plan a comprehensive consulting project. It allows you automatically to account for the costs of people involved in the evaluation, as well as the cost of other resources. However, spreadsheet tools such as Microsoft Excel work just fine, or your organization may have an internal project planning tool. Microsoft Word is even a sufficient tool to develop a project plan, although it does lack some of the calculation capabilities. Nevertheless, the plan should represent an operational tool. Develop it by using the best tool for you and your team. It will save you time, money, and frustration!

ROI Planning Meeting

The plans are developed, completed, and finalized in a project planning meeting (although some of the input will be known and developed before this meeting). This crucial meeting brings together the various stakeholders. Four important issues must be addressed:

1. Who should be involved in the planning meeting?
2. What are the success factors? (credible sources, access to data, etc.)
3. What is the agenda?
4. Who will approve the project plan?

Planning Participants

Participants of the planning meeting vary according to project. It is essential for the consultant to participate. This person will drive the consulting project. Next is the evaluator who will actually collect and analyze the data. The evaluator(s) could be the consultant or a member of the consulting team. In the work-at-home example, it is the person who manages the HR analytics process inside the organization. The client, who would represent the interests of the particular business unit, would also be involved in the meeting. In the case of the work-at-home project, it is the HR executives and others on the HR team who are familiar with the various issues with working at home. A subject matter expert who understands the work-at-home process should participate, as well as another who understands the dynamics of working at home. Finally, someone from finance and accounting should be involved, ideally.

Success Factors

To make the planning meeting successful, several issues have to be addressed or be in place. This meeting must involve people with credible sources of information. Sometimes for a planning session like this, representatives are sent who are not necessarily the best and most credible people for the task. Access to the data is another issue. When business impact is needed, it should be readily available to the team, or at least the capture process should be known to the group. Also, the group must cover all the issues, so no key participants can be missing. In terms of duration, this meeting can last anywhere from an hour for small projects to four hours for more involved projects. The key is to move swiftly and have the data prepared ahead of time, if possible. It is important to consider the output to be a draft at this point, which could be adjusted when additional information is known.

Agenda

The meeting agenda is straightforward. The purpose of the meeting must first be explained. Next on the agenda are the objectives of the project. The project description itself can be detailed, as are the objectives for the particular elements of the project. For a solution-focused project, such as the work-at-home example, the objectives need to be detailed. Objectives should be developed ahead of time. Then a step-by-step description of the data collection plan, the analysis plan, the communication plan, and the project plan are presented. In each case, it is helpful to have documents that are almost fully completed before the meeting so that the team is merely filling in the gaps. After the planning documents are complete, a quick review of the next steps would be in order.

Approval

Now that the plans are complete, the adjustments are made based on any other feedback. The key is to seek commitment from key stakeholders so that they understand what their role will be and the roles of those whom they represent. Their commitment is critical. Then, perhaps one of the most important points is to get the client to sign off on the project. Signing off can be a simple process in which you obtain agreement for the plan of action. It is helpful in this discussion to point out those things that might be considered weaknesses in the project, controversies around the project, or the difficult parts of the project. Finally, if budgets need to be secured (many times they do), they need to be secured at this time. The project planning meeting often yields an estimate of project cost. In all, this is one of the most important meetings related to a particular consulting project.

Final Thoughts

This chapter presents planning for the evaluation of a consulting project. Four evaluation planning tools are introduced: the data collection plan, ROI analysis plan, communication plan, and project plan. It is also important to integrate an effective change management process into the overall project plan, including stakeholder management, issue resolution approach, and implementation planning and transfer of ownership activities. When the ROI process is thoroughly planned, taking into consideration all potential strategies and techniques, it becomes manageable and achievable. The next few chapters focus on the major elements of this process.

10

Methods of Data Collection

With the planning accomplished, the project is ready for execution. From the evaluation perspective, data collection becomes the first task after execution. Essentially, data are collected at four different levels (reaction, learning, application, and impact), matching the levels described in previous chapters. This chapter presents the methods of data collection that span all levels. The list is comprehensive, beginning with questionnaires and ending with monitoring business performance data from the system and records. The chapter concludes with tips on selecting the data collection methods to use on specific projects.

Using Questionnaires and Surveys

The questionnaire is probably the most common data collection method. Questionnaires come in all sizes, ranging from short surveys to detailed instruments. They can be used to obtain subjective data about participants' perceptions as well as to document data for use in a projected ROI analysis. With this versatility and popularity, it is important for questionnaires and surveys to be designed properly to satisfy both purposes.

Types of Questions and Statements

Five basic types of questions or statements are available. Depending on the purpose of the evaluation, the questionnaire may contain any or all of the following types of questions:

1. **Open-ended question.** Has an unlimited answer. The question is followed by ample blank space for the response.
2. **Checklist.** A list of items. A participant is asked to check those that apply to the situation.
3. **Range of responses.** Has alternate responses, a yes/no, or other possibilities. This type of question can also include a range of responses from disagree to agree.
4. **Multiple-choice question.** Has several choices, and the participant is asked to select the most appropriate.
5. **Ranking scales.** Requires the participant to rank a list of items.

Figure 10.1 shows examples of each of these types of questions.

Design Issues

Questionnaire design is a simple and logical process. An improperly designed or worded questionnaire will not collect the desired data and is confusing, frustrating, and potentially embarrassing. The following steps will help ensure that a valid, reliable, and effective instrument is developed.

- **Determine the information needed.** The first step of any instrument design is to itemize the topics, issues, and success factors for the project. Questions are developed later. It might be helpful to develop

1. Open-Ended Question:

   What problems will you encounter when attempting to use the system implemented in this project?

2. Checklist:

   For the following list, check all of the business measures that may be influenced by the application of the system in this project:

   ☐ Responsibility   ☐ Cost Control
   ☐ Productivity   ☐ Response Time
   ☐ Quality   ☐ Customer Satisfaction
   ☐ Efficiency   ☐ Job Satisfaction

3. Range of Responses:

   As a result of this project, I have a better understanding of my job as a customer service representative.

   ☐ Yes   ☐ Maybe   ☐ No

4. Multiple Choice Question:

   Since the project has been initiated, the customer response time has

   a. Increased
   b. Decreased
   c. Remained the same
   d. Don't know

5. Ranking Scales:

   The following list contains five important factors that will influence the success of this project. Place a one (1) by the item that is most influential, a two (2) by the item that is second most influential, and so on. The item ranked five (5) will be the least influential item on the list.

   Rewards Systems   _____   Training   _____
   Job Responsibility _____   Management Support   _____
   Communications   _____   Resources   _____

FIGURE 10.1 Types of Questions

this information in outline form so that related questions can be grouped together.

- **Select the type(s) of questions.** Determine whether open-ended questions, checklists, ranges, multiple-choice questions, or a ranking scale is most appropriate for the purpose of the questions. Take into consideration the planned data analysis and variety of data to be collected.

- **Develop the questions—keep it simple.** The next step is to develop the questions based on the types of questions planned and the information needed.

The questions should be simple and straightforward enough to avoid confusion or leading the participant to a desired response. Unfamiliar terms or expressions should be avoided.

- **Test the questions.** After the questions are developed, they should be tested for understanding. Ideally, the questions should be tested on a small sample of participants in the project. If this is not feasible, the questions should be tested on employees at approximately the same job level as the participants. Collect as much input and criticism as possible, and revise the questions as necessary.

- **Prepare a data summary.** A data summary sheet should be developed so data can be tabulated quickly for summary and interpretation. This step will help ensure that the data can be analyzed quickly and presented in a meaningful way.

A Detailed Example

One of the most difficult tasks is to determine specific issues that need to be addressed on a follow-up questionnaire. Although the content items on a follow-up questionnaire can be the same as questionnaires used in measuring reaction and learning, the following content items are more desirable for capturing application and impact information (Level 3 and 4 data). Figure 10.2 presents a questionnaire used in a follow-up evaluation of a consulting project on building a sales culture. The evaluation was designed to capture the ROI, with the primary method of data collection being the follow-up

Are you currently in a sales capacity at a branch?   Yes   ☐   No   ☐

1.   Listed below are the objectives of the sales culture project. After reflecting on this project,
      please indicate the degree of success in meeting the objectives. Use the following scale:

      1 = No success
      2 = Limited success
      3 = Moderate success
      4 = Generally successful
      5 = Very successful

As a result of this project, branch employees will	1	2	3	4	5
a. Use the tools and techniques to determine customer needs and concerns.	☐	☐	☐	☐	☐
b. Match needs with specific projects and services.	☐	☐	☐	☐	☐
c. Use the tools and techniques to convince customers to buy/use Progress Bank products and services.	☐	☐	☐	☐	☐
d. Build a productive, long-term relationship with customers.	☐	☐	☐	☐	☐
e. Increase sales of each product line offered in the branch.	☐	☐	☐	☐	☐

2.   Did you implement an on-the-job action plan for this project?

      Yes   ☐   No   ☐

      If yes, please describe the nature and outcome of the plan. If not, explain why. _____
      _____
      _____
      _____

3.   Please rate the relevance to your job of each of the following components of the project using
      the following scale:

      1 = No relevance
      2 = Limited relevance
      3 = Moderate relevance
      4 = General relevance
      5 = Very relevant

	1	2	3	4	5
Job Aids	☐	☐	☐	☐	☐
Group Learning Activities	☐	☐	☐	☐	☐
Incentive Opportunities	☐	☐	☐	☐	☐
Networking Opportunities w/Other Branches	☐	☐	☐	☐	☐
Reading Material/Videos	☐	☐	☐	☐	☐
Coaching Sessions	☐	☐	☐	☐	☐
Software/System Changes	☐	☐	☐	☐	☐
Database Enhancements	☐	☐	☐	☐	☐

4.   Have you used the job aids provided during the project?

      Yes   ☐   No   ☐

      Please explain. _____
      _____
      _____
      _____

FIGURE 10.2   Example of Questionnaire

(Continued)

5.   Please indicate the change in the application of knowledge and skills as a result of your participation in the sales culture project. Use the following scale:

    1 = No change
    2 = Limited change
    3 = Moderate change
    4 = Much change
    5 = Very much change

	1	2	3	4	5	No Opportunity to Use Skill
a. Probing for customer needs	□	□	□	□	□	□
b. Helping the customer solve problems	□	□	□	□	□	□
c. Understanding the features and benefits of all products and services	□	□	□	□	□	□
d. Comparing products and services to those of competitors	□	□	□	□	□	□
e. Selecting appropriate products and services	□	□	□	□	□	□
f. Using persuasive selling techniques	□	□	□	□	□	□
g. Using follow-up techniques to stay in touch with the customer	□	□	□	□	□	□
h. Using new software routines for data access and transactions	□	□	□	□	□	□

6.   What has changed about your work (actions, tasks, activities) as a result of this project?

_____
_____
_____
_____

7.   Indicate the extent to which you think this program has influenced each of these measures in your branch. Use the following scale:

    1 = No influence
    2 = Limited influence
    3 = Moderate influence
    4 = Much influence
    5 = Very much influence

	1	2	3	4	5
a. New Accounts	□	□	□	□	□
b. Sales	□	□	□	□	□
c. Customer Response Time	□	□	□	□	□
d. Cross-Sales Ratio	□	□	□	□	□
e. Cost Control	□	□	□	□	□
f. Employee Satisfaction	□	□	□	□	□
g. Customer Satisfaction	□	□	□	□	□
h. Customer Complaints	□	□	□	□	□
i. Customer Loyalty	□	□	□	□	□

FIGURE 10.2   (*Continued*)

8. Please define the most improved measure above. Use a unit of value such as one sale, one new account, one customer complaint.

_____
_____
_____
_____

9. Provide the actual change in the unit measure since the project began. This would take the pre-program baseline data and subtract it from the current level to indicate a change.

_____
_____
_____
_____

10. Indicate the actual unit value for the specific measure in question. If it is a measure that is desired to improve, indicate the value-add, such as one additional sale. If it is a value that needs to be minimized, such as one customer complaint, indicate the money saved when the customer complaint is avoided. Although this can be very difficult, please follow the instructions of how this value may be obtained.

_____
_____
_____
_____

11. Provide the basis for the above unit value. If it is a standard value, please indicate that it is a standard value; if it is an expert input, indicate that it is an expert input; if it is based on an estimate, indicate how the estimate was derived.

_____
_____
_____
_____

12. Provide the total impact of the change. This involves taking the unit value times the change in the value for one year. This takes into account the frequency. If it is a monthly data item, then it would be times 12. If it is a weekly value, it would be times 52.

_____
_____
_____
_____

13. List other factors that could have influenced this improvement. Be very thoughtful and specific in listing the other influences.

_____
_____
_____
_____

14. Indicate the percent of improvement directly related to this project using a scale of 0% to 100%. Zero percent is no improvement connected to the project. One hundred percent is all the improvement is connected to the project.

_____
_____
_____
_____

FIGURE 10.2 (*Continued*)

15. What level of confidence do you place in the above estimations? (0% = No confidence, 100% = Certainty) _____%

Please explain. _____
_____

Note: Participants may cycle through questions 8-15 with other measures.

16. Do you think the sales culture project represented a good investment for Progress Bank?

Yes ☐   No   ☐

Please explain. _____
_____
_____
_____

17. Please rate the success of the immediate project team and the quality of the team's leadership. Use the following scale:

1 = No success
2 = Limited success
3 = Moderately successful
4 = Generally successful
5 = Very successful

Team Characteristic	1	2	3	4	5
Capability	☐	☐	☐	☐	☐
Motivation	☐	☐	☐	☐	☐
Cooperation	☐	☐	☐	☐	☐
Communication	☐	☐	☐	☐	☐

Leadership Quality	1	2	3	4	5
Leadership Style	☐	☐	☐	☐	☐
Organization	☐	☐	☐	☐	☐
Communication	☐	☐	☐	☐	☐
Team Support	☐	☐	☐	☐	☐
Team Training	☐	☐	☐	☐	☐

18. What barriers, if any, have you encountered that prevented this project from being successful. Please explain, if possible.

_____
_____
_____
_____

19. What has helped this project be successful? Please explain.

_____
_____
_____
_____

20. Which of the following statements best describes the level of management support?

☐ There was no management support.
☐ There was limited management support.
☐ There was a moderate amount of management support.
☐ There was much management support.
☐ There was very much management support.

FIGURE 10.2   (*Continued*)

21. Could other program solutions have been effective in meeting the business need(s)?

    Yes ☐   No ☐

Please explain. _____
_____
_____
_____

22. What specific suggestions do you have for improving this project?

_____
_____
_____

23. Other comments about this project:

_____
_____
_____

FIGURE 10.2   (*Continued*)

questionnaire. This example will be used to illustrate many of the issues involving potential content items for a follow-up questionnaire.

Progress Bank, following a carefully planned growth pattern through acquiring smaller banks, initiated a consulting project to develop a strong sales culture. The project involved four solutions. Through a competency-based learning intervention, all branch personnel were taught how to aggressively pursue new customers and cross-sell to existing customers in a variety of product lines. The software and customer database were upgraded to provide faster access and enhanced routines to assist selling. The incentive compensation system was also redesigned to enhance payments for new customers and increase sales of all branch products. Finally, a management coaching and goal-setting system was implemented to ensure that ambitious sales goals were met. All branch employees were involved in the project.

Six months after the project was implemented, an evaluation was planned. Each branch in the network had a scorecard that tracked performance through several measures such as new accounts, total deposits, and growth by specific products. All product lines were monitored. All branch employees provided input on the questionnaire shown in Figure 10.2. Most of the data from the questionnaire covered application and impact. This type of feedback helps consultants know which parts of the intervention are most effective and useful.

Improving the Response Rate for Questionnaires and Surveys

Given the wide range of potential issues to explore in a follow-up questionnaire or survey, asking all of the questions can cause the response rate to be reduced considerably. The challenge, therefore, is to approach questionnaire and survey design and administration for maximum response rate. This is a critical issue when the questionnaire is a key data collection activity and much of the evaluation hinges on the questionnaire results. The following actions can be taken to increase response rate. Although the term *questionnaire* is used, the same rules apply to surveys.

- **Provide advance communication.** If appropriate and feasible, consulting participants and other stakeholders should receive advance communications about the plans for the questionnaire or survey. This minimizes some of the resistance to the process, provides an opportunity to explain in more detail the circumstances surrounding the evaluation, and positions the evaluation as an integral part of the consulting project rather than an add-on activity that someone initiated three months after the project is completed.

- **Communicate the purpose.** Stakeholders should understand the reason for the questionnaire, including who or what initiated this specific evaluation. They should know if the evaluation is part of a systematic process or a special request for this consulting project only.

- **Explain who will see the data.** It is important for respondents to know who will see the data and the results of the questionnaire. If the questionnaire is anonymous, it should clearly be communicated to participants what steps will be taken to ensure anonymity. If senior executives will see the combined results of the study, the respondent should know it.

- **Describe the data integration process.** The respondents should understand how the questionnaire results will be combined with other data, if available. Often the questionnaire is only one of the data collection methods utilized. Participants should know how the data are weighted and integrated into the entire impact study, as well as interim results.

- **Keep the questionnaire/survey as simple as possible.** A simple questionnaire does not always provide the full scope of data necessary for a comprehensive analysis. However, the simplified approach should always be kept in mind when questions are developed and the total scope of the questionnaire is finalized. Every effort should be made to keep it as simple and brief as possible.

- **Simplify the response process.** To the extent possible, it should be easy to respond to the questionnaire. If appropriate, a self-addressed stamped envelope should be included. Perhaps e-mail could be used for responses, if it is easier. In still other situations, a response box is provided near the project work area.

- **Utilize local management support.** Management involvement at the local level is critical to response-rate success. Managers can distribute the questionnaires themselves, make reference to the questionnaire in staff meetings, follow up to see if questionnaires have been completed, and generally show support for completing the questionnaire. This direct managerial support will prompt many participants to respond with usable data.

- **Let the participants know they are part of the sample.** For large consulting projects, a sampling process may be utilized. When that is the case, participants should know they are part of a carefully selected sample and that their input will be used to make decisions regarding a much larger target audience. This action often appeals to a sense of responsibility for participants to provide usable, accurate data for the questionnaire.

- **Consider incentives.** A variety of incentives can be offered, and they usually are found in three categories.

First, an incentive is provided in exchange for the completed questionnaire. For example, if participants return the questionnaire personally or through the mail, they will receive a small gift, such as a T-shirt or mug. If identity is an issue, a neutral third party can provide the incentive. In the second category, the incentive is provided to make participants feel guilty about not responding. Examples are money clipped to the questionnaire or a pen enclosed in the envelope. Participants are asked to "take the money, buy a cup of coffee, and fill out the questionnaire." A third group of incentives is designed to obtain a quick response. This approach is based on the assumption that a quick response will ensure a greater response rate. If an individual delays completing the questionnaire, the odds of completing it diminish considerably. The initial group of participants may receive a more expensive gift, or they may be part of a drawing for an incentive. For example, in one project, the first 25 returned questionnaires were placed in a drawing for a $400 gift certificate. The next 25 were added to the first 25 in the next drawing. The longer a participant waits, the lower the odds of winning.

- **Have an executive sign the introductory letter.** Participants are always interested in who sent the letter with the questionnaire. For maximum effectiveness, a senior executive who is responsible for a major area where the participants work should sign the letter. Employees may be more willing to respond to a senior executive than to a member of the consulting team.

- **Use follow-up reminders.** A follow-up reminder should be sent a week after the questionnaire is received and another sent two weeks later. Depending on the questionnaire and the situation, these times can be adjusted. In some situations, a third follow-up is recommended. Sometimes the follow-up is sent in a different media. For example, a questionnaire may be sent through regular mail, whereas the first follow-up reminder is from the immediate supervisor, and a second follow-up is sent via e-mail.

- **Send a copy of the results to the participants.** Even if it is an abbreviated report, participants should see the results of the questionnaire. More important, participants should understand that they will receive a copy of the impact study when they are asked to provide the data. This promise will often increase the response rate, as some individuals want to see the results of the entire group along with their particular input.

- **Estimate the length of time to complete the questionnaire.** Respondents often have a concern about the time it may take to complete the questionnaire. A very lengthy questionnaire may quickly discourage the participants and cause it to be discarded. Sometimes lengthy questionnaires can be completed quickly because they contain forced-choice questions or statements that make it easy to respond. However, the number of pages may put off the respondent. Therefore, it is helpful to indicate the estimated length of time needed to complete the questionnaire, perhaps in the letter itself or at least noted in the communications. This provides extra information so that respondents can decide if they are willing to invest the required amount of time in the process. A word of caution: the amount of time must be realistic. Purposely underestimating it can do more harm than good.

- **Explain the timing of the planned steps.** Sometimes the respondents want to learn more about the process, such as when they can see the results. It is recommended that a time line of the different phases be presented, showing when the data will be analyzed, when the data will be presented to different groups, and when the results will be returned to the participants in a summary report. This provides some assurance that the process is well organized and professional and that the length of time to receive a data summary will not be too long. Another word of caution: The timetable must be followed to maintain the confidence and trust of the individuals.

- **Make it appear professional.** While it should not be an issue in most organizations, unfortunately, there are too many cases in which a questionnaire is not developed properly, does not appear professional, or is not easy to follow and understand. The participants must gain respect for the process and for the organization. To do this, a sense of professionalism must be integrated throughout data collection, particularly in the appearance and accuracy of the materials. Sloppy questionnaires will usually elicit sloppy responses, or no response at all.

- **Explain the questionnaire during the project meetings.** Sometimes it is helpful to explain to the participants and other key stakeholders that they will be required or asked to provide certain types of data. When this is feasible, questionnaires should be reviewed question by question so that the participants understand the purpose, the issues, and how to respond. This will take only 10–15 minutes but can increase the response rate, enhance the quality and quantity of data, and clarify any confusion that may exist on key issues.

- **Collect data anonymously, if necessary.** Participants are more likely to provide frank and candid feedback if their names are not on the questionnaire, particularly when the project is going astray or is off target. When this is the case, every effort should be made to protect the anonymous input, and explanations should be provided as to how the data are analyzed while minimizing the demographic makeup of respondents so that the individuals cannot be identified in the analysis.

Collectively, these items help boost response rates of follow-up questionnaires. Using all of these strategies can result in a 70–90 percent response rate, even with lengthy questionnaires that might take 30 minutes to complete.

Using Interviews

Another helpful collection method is the interview, although it is not used as frequently as the questionnaire. The consultants, the client's staff, or a third party can conduct interviews. Interviews can secure data not available in performance records, or data difficult to obtain through written responses or observations. Also, interviews can uncover success stories that can be useful in communicating evaluation results. Consulting participants may be reluctant to describe their results in a questionnaire but will volunteer the information to a skillful interviewer using probing techniques. The interview is versatile and appropriate for reaction, learning, and application data. A major disadvantage of the interview is that it is time consuming. It also requires time and training of interviewers to ensure that the process is consistent.

Types of Interviews

Interviews usually fall into two basic types: structured and unstructured. A structured interview is much like a questionnaire. Specific questions are asked with little room to deviate from the desired responses. The primary advantages of the structured interview over the questionnaire are that the interview process can ensure the questionnaire is completed and that the interviewer understands the responses supplied by the participant.

The unstructured interview permits probing for additional information. This type of interview uses a few general questions, which can lead to more detailed information, as important data are uncovered. The interviewer must be skilled in the probing process. Typical probing questions are as follows:

- Can you explain that in more detail?
- Can you give me an example of what you are saying?
- Can you explain the difficulty that you say you encountered?

Interview Guidelines

The design steps for interviews are similar to those of the questionnaire. A brief summary of key issues with interviews is outlined here.

- **Develop questions to be asked.** After the decision has been made about the type of interview, specific questions need to be developed. Questions should be brief, precise, and designed for easy response.
- **Test out the interview.** The interview should be tested on a small number of participants. If possible, the interviews should be conducted as part of the early stages of the project. The responses should be analyzed and the interview revised, if necessary.
- **Prepare the interviewers.** The interviewer should have appropriate skills, including active listening, the ability to form probing questions, and the ability to collect and summarize information into a meaningful form.
- **Provide clear instructions.** The consulting participant should understand the purpose of the interview

and know what will be done with the information. Expectations, conditions, and rules of the interview should be thoroughly discussed. For example, the participant should know if statements will be kept confidential. If the participant is nervous during an interview and develops signs of anxiety, he or she should be encouraged to relax and feel at ease.

- **Administer interviews with a plan in mind.** As with other evaluation instruments, interviews need to be conducted according to a predetermined plan. The timing of the interview, the person who conducts the interview, and the location of the interview are all issues that become relevant when developing an interview plan. For a large number of stakeholders, a sampling plan may be necessary to save time and reduce the evaluation cost.

Using Focus Groups

As an extension of the interview, focus groups are particularly helpful when in-depth feedback is needed. The focus group involves a small group discussion conducted by an experienced facilitator. It is designed to solicit qualitative judgments on a planned topic or issue. Group members are all required to provide their input, as individual input builds on group input.

When compared to questionnaires, surveys, or interviews, the focus group strategy has several advantages. The basic premise of using focus groups is that when quality judgments are subjective, several individual judgments are better than only one. The group process, where participants often motivate one another, is an effective method for generating new ideas and hypotheses. It is less expensive than the interview and can be quickly planned and conducted. Its flexibility makes it possible to explore a consulting project's unexpected outcomes or applications.

Applications for Evaluation

The focus group is particularly helpful when qualitative information is needed about the success of a consulting project. For example, the focus group can be used in the following situations:

- Assessing the potential impact of the project
- Evaluating the reaction to the consulting project and the various components of it
- Assessing learning of specific procedures, tasks, schedules, or other components of the project
- Assessing the implementation of the consulting project as perceived by the participants immediately following the project's completion
- Sorting out the causes of success

Essentially, focus groups are helpful when evaluation information is needed but cannot be collected adequately with a simple questionnaire or survey.

Guidelines

While there are no set rules on how to use focus groups for evaluation, the following guidelines should be helpful:

- **Plan topics, questions, and strategy carefully.** As with any evaluation instrument, planning is the key. The specific topics, questions, and issues to be discussed must be carefully planned and sequenced. This enhances the comparison of results from one group to another and ensures that the group process is effective and stays on track.

- **Keep the group size small.** While there is no magical group size, a range of 8 to 12 seems appropriate for most focus group applications. A group has to be large enough to ensure different points of view but small enough to give every participant a chance to talk freely and exchange comments.

- **Ensure a representative sample of the target population.** It is important for groups to be stratified appropriately so that participants represent the target population. The group should be homogeneous in experience, rank, and influence in the organization.

- **Insist on facilitators with appropriate expertise.** The success of a focus group rests with the facilitator, who must be skilled in the focus group process. Facilitators must know how to control aggressive members of the group and diffuse the input from those who want to dominate the group. Also, facilitators must be able to create an environment in which participants feel comfortable to offer comments freely and openly. Consequently, some organizations use external facilitators.

In summary, the focus group is an inexpensive and quick way to determine the strengths and weaknesses of projects. However, for a complete evaluation, focus group information should be combined with data from other instruments.

Measuring with Tests

Testing is important for measuring learning in project evaluations. Pre- and postproject comparisons using tests are very common. An improvement in test scores shows the change in skill, knowledge, or capability of the participant attributed to the consulting project. The questionnaires and surveys, described earlier, can be used in testing for learning.

Performance testing allows the participant to exhibit a skill (and occasionally knowledge or attitude) that has been learned in a consulting project. The skill can be manual, verbal, or analytical, or a combination of the three. For example, computer systems engineers are participating in a system-reengineering project. As part of the project, participants are given the assignment to design and test a basic system. The consultant observes participants as they check out the system, then carefully builds the same design, and compares his results with those of the participants. These comparisons and the performance of the design provide an evaluation of the project and represent an adequate reflection of the skills learned in the project.

Measuring with Simulation

Another technique for measuring learning is job simulation. This method involves the construction and application of a procedure or task that simulates or models the work involved in the consulting project. The simulation is designed to represent, as closely as possible, the actual job situation. Participants try out their performance in the simulated activity and have it evaluated based on how well the task is accomplished. Simulations may be used during the project, or as part of a follow-up evaluation.

Task Simulation

One approach involves a participant's performance in a simulated task as part of an evaluation. For example, in a new system implementation, users are provided a series of situations and they must perform the proper sequence of tasks in a minimum amount of time. To become certified to use this system, users are observed in a simulation, where they perform all the necessary steps on a checklist. After they have demonstrated that they possess the skills necessary for the safe performance of this assignment, they are certified by the consultant. This task simulation serves as the evaluation.

Business Games

Business games have grown in popularity in recent years. They represent simulations of a part or all of a business organization. Participants change the variables of the business and observe the effects of those changes. The game not only reflects the real-world situation, but may also represent a consulting project. The participants are provided certain objectives, play the game, and have their output monitored. Their performance can usually be documented and measured. Typical objectives are to maximize profit, sales, market share, or operating efficiency. Participants who maximize the objectives are those who usually have the highest performance.

Role-Playing/Skill Practice

When skill building is part of the consulting project, role-playing may be helpful. This is sometimes referred to as *skill practice*: Participants practice a newly learned skill and are observed by other individuals. Participants are given their assigned role with specific instructions, which sometimes include an ultimate course of action. The participants then practice the skill with other individuals to accomplish the desired objectives. This is intended to simulate the real-world setting to the greatest extent possible. Difficulty sometimes arises when other participants involved in the skill practice make the practice unrealistic by not reacting in the same way that individuals would in an actual situation. To help overcome this obstacle, trained role players (nonparticipants trained for the role) may be used in all roles except that of the participant. This can possibly provide a more objective evaluation.

Using Observation

Observing participants and recording changes in behavior and specific actions taken may be appropriate to measure application. This technique is useful when it is important to know precisely how the consulting participants are using new skills, knowledge, tasks, procedures, or systems. For example, participant observation is often used in sales and sales support projects. The observer may be a member of the consulting staff, the participant's supervisor, a member of a peer group, or an external resource, such as a mystery customer.

Guidelines for Effective Observation

Observation is often misused or misapplied to evaluation situations, forcing some to abandon the process. The effectiveness of observation can be improved with the following guidelines:

- **Observers must be fully prepared.** Observers must fully understand what information is needed and what skills are covered in the intervention. They must be prepared for the assignment and provided a chance to practice observation skills.
- **The observations should be systematic.** The observation process must be planned so that it is executed effectively without any surprises. The individuals observed should know in advance about the observation and why they are being observed, unless the observation is planned to be invisible. In this case, the individuals are monitored unknowingly. Observations are planned when work situations are normal. Eight steps are necessary to accomplish a successful observation:
    1. Determine what behavior will be observed.
    2. Prepare the forms for the observer's use.

    3. Select the observers.

    4. Prepare a schedule of observations.

    5. Prepare observers to observe properly.

    6. Inform participants of the planned observation, providing explanations.

    7. Conduct the observations.

    8. Summarize the observation data.

- **The observers should know how to interpret and report what they see.** Observations involve judgment decisions. The observer must analyze which behaviors are being displayed and what actions the participants are taking. Observers should know how to summarize behavior and report results in a meaningful manner.

- **The observer's influence should be minimized.** Except for "mystery" or "planted" observers and electronic observations, it is impossible to completely isolate the overall effect of an observer. Participants will display the behavior they think is appropriate, performing at their best. The presence of the observer must be minimized. To the extent possible, the observer should blend into the work environment and be unnoticeable.

- **Select observers carefully.** Observers are usually independent of the participants. They are typically members of the consulting staff. The independent observer is usually more skilled at recording behavior and making interpretations of behavior and is usually unbiased in these interpretations. Using an independent observer reduces the need to prepare observers. However, the independent observer has the appearance of an outsider, and participants may resent the observer. Sometimes it is more feasible to recruit observers from inside the organization.

Observation Methods

Five methods of observation are suggested and are appropriate depending on the circumstances surrounding the type of information needed. Each method is briefly described below.

- **Behavior checklist and codes**. A behavior checklist is useful for recording the presence, absence, frequency, or duration of a participant's behavior or action as it occurs. A checklist does not provide information on the quality, intensity, or possible circumstances surrounding the behavior observed. The checklist is useful, though, since an observer can identify exactly which behaviors should or should not occur. The behaviors listed in the checklist should be minimized and listed in a logical sequence if they normally occur in a sequence. A variation of this approach involves coding behaviors or actions on a form. While this method is useful when there are many behaviors, it is more time consuming because a code is entered that identifies a specific behavior or actions instead of checking an item. A variation of this approach is the 360-degree feedback process in which surveys are completed on other individuals based on observations within a specific time frame.

- **Delayed report method.** With a delayed report method, the observer does not use any forms or written materials during the observation. The information is either recorded after the observation is completed or at particular time intervals during an observation. The observer tries to reconstruct what has been witnessed during the observation period. The advantage of this approach is that the observer is not as noticeable, and there are no forms being completed or notes being taken during the observation. The observer becomes more a part of the situation and less of a distraction. This approach is typical of the mystery shopper for retail stores. An obvious disadvantage is that the information written may not be as accurate and reliable as the information collected at the time it occurred.

- **Video recording.** A video camera records behavior or actions in every detail. However, this intrusion may be awkward and cumbersome, and the participants may be unnecessarily nervous or self-conscious while they are being videotaped. If the camera is concealed, the privacy of the participant may be invaded. Because of this, video recording of on-the-job behavior is not frequently used.

- **Audio monitoring.** Monitoring conversations of participants is an effective observation technique. For example, in a large communication company's telemarketing department, sales representatives were prepared to sell equipment by telephone. To determine if employees were using the skills and procedures properly, telephone conversations were monitored on a randomly selected basis. While this approach may stir some controversy, it is an effective way to determine if skills and procedures are being applied consistently and effectively. For it to work smoothly, it must be fully explained and the rules clearly communicated.

- **System monitoring.** For employees who work regularly with checklists, tasks, and technology, system monitoring is becoming an effective way to "observe" participants as they perform job tasks. The system monitors times, sequence of steps, use of routines, and other activities to determine if the participant is performing the work according to specific steps and guidelines of the consulting intervention. As technology continues to be a significant part of the workplace, system monitoring holds much promise.

Using Action Plans

In some cases, follow-up assignments can develop application and impact data. In a typical follow-up assignment, the consulting participant is asked to meet a goal or complete a particular task or project by a set date. A summary of the results of the completed assignments provides further evidence of the success of the consulting project.

With this approach, participants are required to develop action plans as part of the consulting project.

Action plans contain detailed steps to accomplish specific objectives related to the project. The process is one of the most effective ways to enhance support for a consulting project and build the ownership needed for the successful application and impact of the project.

The plan is typically prepared on a printed form, such as the one shown in Figure 10.3. The action plan shows what is to be done, by whom, and the date by which the objectives should be accomplished. The action-plan approach is a straightforward, easy-to-use method for determining how participants will implement the project and achieve success with consulting.

Using Action Plans Successfully

The development of the action plan requires two major tasks: determining what measure to improve and writing the action items to improve it. As shown in Figure 10.3, an action plan can be developed for a safety consulting project. The plan presented in this figure requires participants to develop an objective, which is related to the consulting project. In this example, the objective is to reduce the slips and falls on a hospital floor from 11 to 2 in six months. In some cases, there may be more than one objective, which requires additional action plans. Related to the objective are the improvement measure, the current levels, and target of performance. This information requires the participant to anticipate the application of the consulting project and set goals for specific performances that can be realized. In another example, an objective may be to reduce equipment

Safe Workplace Action Plan

Name: _Ellie Hightower_   Facilitator Signature: _____   Follow-Up Date   _2 June_

Objective: _Improve workplace safety_

Improvement Measure: _Monthly slips and falls_   Evaluation Period: _December_ to _May_

	Current Performance	Target Performance	
	11/six months	_2/six months_	

Action Steps

1. _Meet with team to discuss reasons for slips and falls._   2 Dec

2. _Review slip and fall records for each incident with safety—look for trends and patterns._   18 Dec

3. _Make adjustments based on reasons for slips and falls._   22 Dec

4. _Counsel with housekeeping and explore opportunities for improvement._   5 Jan

5. _Have safety conduct a brief meeting with team members._   11 Jan

6. _Provide recognition to team members who have made extra efforts for reducing slips and falls._   As needed

7. _Follow up with each incident and discuss improvement or lack of improvement and plan other action._   As needed

8. _Monitor improvement and provide adjustment when appropriate._   As needed

Intangible Benefits: _Image, risk reduction_

Analysis

A. What is the unit of measure? _1 slip and fall_

B. What is the value (cost) of one unit? _$1,750_

C. How did you arrive at this value? _Safety and Health—Frank M._

D. How much did the measure change during the evaluation period? (monthly value) _8_

E. What other factors could have caused this improvement? _A new campaign from safety and health_

F. What percent of this change was actually caused by this program? _70%_

G. What level of confidence do you place on the above information? (100% = Certainty and 0% = No confidence) _80%_

FIGURE 10.3   Action Plan Example

downtime for the printing press. The measure is the average hours of downtime with the current performance at six hours per week and a target of two hours per week.

The action plan is completed during the early stages of the consulting project, often with the input, assistance, and facilitation of the consultant. The consultant actually approves the plan, indicating that it meets the particular requirements of being very Specific, Measurable, Achievable, Realistic, and Time-bound (SMART). The plan can actually be developed in a one- to two-hour time frame and often begins with action steps related to the implementation of the project. These action steps are actually Level 3 activities that detail the application of the consulting project. All of these steps build support for, and are linked to, business impact measures:

- **Define the unit of measure.** The next important issue is to define the actual unit of measure. In some cases, more than one measure may be used and will subsequently be contained in additional action plans. The unit of measure is necessary to break the process down into the simplest steps so that the ultimate value of the project can be determined. The unit can be output data, such as an additional unit manufactured or additional hotel room rented. In terms of quality, the unit can be one reject, error, or defect. Time-based units are usually measured in minutes, hours, days, or weeks, such as one minute of downtime. Units are specific to their particular type of situations, such as one turnover of key talent, one customer, complaint, or one escalated call in the call center. The important point is to break them down into the simplest terms possible.

- **Require participants to provide monetary values for each improvement.** During the consulting project, participants are asked to determine, calculate, or estimate the monetary value for each improvement outlined in the plan. The unit value is determined using standard values, expert input, external databases, or estimates (the consultant will help with this). The process used to arrive at the value is described in the action plan. When the actual improvement occurs, participants will use these values to capture the annual monetary benefits of the plan. For this step to be effective, it is helpful to provide examples of common ways in which values can be assigned to the actual data.

- **Participants implement the action plan.** Participants implement the action plan during the consulting project, which often lasts for weeks or months following the intervention. Upon completion, a major portion, if not all, of the consulting project is slated for implementation. The consulting participants implement action-plan steps and the subsequent results are achieved.

- **Participants estimate improvements.** At the end of the specified follow-up period—usually three months, six months, nine months, or one year—the participants indicate the specific improvements made, sometimes expressed as a monthly amount. This determines the actual amount of change that has been observed, measured, or recorded. It is important for the participants to understand the necessity for accuracy as data are recorded. In most cases only the changes are recorded, as those amounts are needed to calculate the value of the project. In other cases, before and after data may be recorded, allowing the evaluator to calculate the actual differences.

- **Ask participants to isolate the effects of the project.** Although the action plan is initiated because of the project, the improvements reported on the action plan may be influenced by other factors. Thus, the action planning process, initiated in the consulting project, should not take full credit for the improvement. For example, an action plan to reduce employee turnover in a division could take only partial credit for an improvement because of the other variables that affect the turnover rate. While there are several ways to isolate the effects of a consulting project, participant estimation is usually most appropriate in the action-planning process. Consequently, participants are asked to estimate the percentage of the improvement actually related to this particular intervention. This question can be asked on the action plan form or in a follow-up questionnaire.

- **Ask participants to provide a confidence level for estimates.** Because the process to convert data to monetary values may not be exact and the amount of the improvement actually related to the project may not be precise, participants are asked to indicate their level of confidence in those two values, collectively. On a scale of 0 to 100 percent, where 0 percent means no confidence and 100 percent means the estimates represent certainty, this value provides participants a mechanism for expressing their uneasiness with their ability to be exact with the process.

- **Collect action plans at specified time intervals.** An excellent response rate is essential, so several steps may be necessary to ensure that the action plans are completed and returned. Usually participants will see the importance of the process and will develop their plans in detail early in the consulting project. Some organizations use follow-up reminders by mail or e-mail. Others call participants to check progress. Still others offer assistance in developing the final plan as part of the consulting project. These steps may require additional resources, which must be weighed against the importance of having more data.

- **Summarize the data and calculate the ROI.** If developed properly, each action plan should have annualized monetary values associated with improvements. Also, each individual should have indicated the percentage of the improvement directly related to the project. Finally, participants should have provided a confidence percentage to reflect their uncertainty with the process and the subjective nature of some of the data that may be provided.

Advantages/Disadvantages of Action Plans

Although there are many advantages to using action plans, there are at least two concerns:

1. The process relies on direct input from the participant. As such, the information can sometimes be inaccurate and unreliable. Participants must have assistance along the way.

2. Action plans can be time consuming for the participant and, if the participant's manager is not involved in the process, there may be a tendency for the participant not to complete the assignment.

As this section has illustrated, the action-plan approach has many inherent advantages. Action plans are simple and easy to administer, are easily understood by participants, are suitable in a wide variety of consulting, and are appropriate for all types of data.

Because of the tremendous flexibility and versatility of the process and the conservative adjustments that can be made in analysis, action plans have become important data collection tools for consulting project evaluation.

Using Performance Contracts

The performance contract is essentially a slight variation of the action-planning process. Based on the principle of mutual goal setting, a performance contract is a written agreement between a participant, the participant's manager, and the consultant. The participant agrees to improve performance on measures related to the consulting project. The agreement is in the form of a goal to be accomplished during or after the consulting project. The agreement spells out what is to be accomplished, at what time, and with what results.

The process of selecting the area for improvement is similar to the process used in the action-planning process. The topic selected should be stated in terms of one or more objectives. The objectives should state what is to be accomplished when the contract is complete. The objectives should be as follows:

- Written
- Understandable by all involved
- Challenging (requiring an unusual effort to achieve)
- Achievable (something that can be accomplished)
- Largely under the control of the participant
- Measurable and dated

The details required to accomplish the contract objectives are developed following the guidelines for action plans presented earlier.

Monitoring Business Performance Data

Data are available in every organization to measure business performance. Monitoring performance data enables management to measure performance in terms of output, quality, costs, time, job engagement, and customer satisfaction. When determining the source of data in the evaluation, the first consideration should be existing databases and reports. In most organizations, performance data suitable for measuring improvement from a consulting project are available. If not, additional record-keeping systems will have to be developed for measurement and analysis. At this point, the question of economics surfaces. Is it economical to develop the record-keeping systems necessary to evaluate a consulting project? If the costs are greater than the expected return for the entire project, then it is pointless to develop those systems.

Existing Measures

Existing performance measures should be researched to identify those related to the proposed objectives of the project. In many situations, it is the performance of these measures that has created the need for the project. Frequently, an organization will have several performance measures related to the same item. For example, the efficiency of a production unit can be measured in several ways, some of which are outlined below:

- Number of units produced per hour
- Number of on-schedule production units
- Percentage of utilization of the equipment
- Percentage of equipment downtime
- Labor cost per unit of production
- Overtime required per unit of production
- Total unit cost

Each of these, in its own way, measures the efficiency of the production unit. All related measures should be reviewed to determine those most relevant to the consulting intervention.

Occasionally, existing performance measures are integrated with other data, and it may be difficult to keep them isolated from unrelated data. In this situation, all existing related measures should be extracted and tabulated again to be more appropriate for comparison in the evaluation. At times, conversion factors may be necessary. For example, the average number of new sales orders per month may be presented regularly in the performance measures for the sales department. In addition, the sales costs per sales representative are also presented. However, in the evaluation of a consulting project, the average cost per new sale is needed. The average number of new sales orders and the sales cost per sales representative are required to develop the data necessary for comparison.

Developing New Measures

In some cases, data are not available for the information needed to measure the effectiveness of a consulting project. The consulting staff must work with the client organization to develop record-keeping systems, if economically feasible. In one organization, a turnover problem with new professional staff prompted a consulting project to fix the problem. To help ensure success of the project, several measures were planned, including early turnover defined as the percentage of employees who left the company in the first three months of employment. Initially this measure was not available. When the intervention was implemented, the organization began collecting early turnover figures for comparison.

Several questions regarding this issue should be addressed:

- Which department will develop the measurement system?
- Who will record and monitor the data?
- Where will it be recorded?
- Will new forms or documentation be needed?

These questions will usually involve other departments or a management decision that extends beyond the scope of the consultants. Often the administration department, operations, or the information technology unit may be instrumental in helping determine whether new measures are needed and, if so, how they will be developed.

Selecting the Appropriate Method for Each Level

This chapter and the previous chapter presented several methods to capture data. Collectively, they offer a wide range of opportunities for collecting data in a variety of situations. Eight specific issues should be considered when deciding which method is appropriate for a situation. These should be considered when selecting data collection methods for other evaluation levels as well.

Type of Data

Perhaps one of the most important issues to consider when selecting the method is the type of data to be collected. Some methods are more appropriate for Level 4, while others are best for Level 3, 2, or 1. Table 10.1 shows the most appropriate types of data for specific methods of data collection at all levels. Follow-up surveys, observations, interviews, and focus groups are best suited for Level 3 data, sometimes exclusively. Performance monitoring, action planning, and questionnaires can easily capture Level 4 data.

Participants' Time for Data Input

Another important factor in selecting the data collection method is the amount of time participants must spend with data collection and evaluation systems. Time requirements should always be minimized, and the method should be positioned so that it is a value-added

Table 10.1   Collecting Application and Impact Data

Method	Level 1	Level 2	Level 3	Level 4
Surveys	✓	✓	✓	
Questionnaires	✓	✓	✓	✓
Observation		✓	✓	
Interviews	✓	✓	✓	
Focus Groups		✓	✓	
Tests		✓		
Simulations		✓		
Action Planning			✓	✓
Performance Contracting			✓	✓
Performance Monitoring			✓	✓

activity (i.e., the participants understand that this activity is something valuable so they will not resist). This requirement often means that sampling is used to keep the total participant time to a minimum. Some methods, such as performance monitoring, require no participant time, while others, such as interviews and focus groups, require a significant investment in time.

Manager Time for Data Input

The time that a participant's direct manager must allocate to data collection is another important issue in the method selection. This time requirement should always be minimized. Some methods, such as performance contracting, may require much involvement from the supervisor before and after the intervention. Other methods, such as questionnaires administered directly to participants, may not require any supervisor time.

Cost of Method

Cost is always a consideration when selecting the method. Some data collection methods are more expensive than others. For example, interviews and observations are very expensive. Surveys, questionnaires, and performance monitoring are usually inexpensive.

Disruption of Normal Work Activities

Another key issue in selecting the appropriate method—and perhaps the one that generates the most concern with managers—is the amount of disruption the data collection will create. Routine work processes should be disrupted as little as possible. Some data collection techniques, such as performance monitoring, require very little time and distraction from normal activities. Questionnaires generally do not disrupt the work environment and can often be completed in only a few minutes, or even after normal work hours. On the other extreme, some items such as observations and interviews may be too disruptive to the work unit.

Accuracy of Method

The accuracy of the technique is another factor to consider when selecting the method. Some data collection methods are more accurate than others. For example, performance monitoring is usually very accurate, whereas questionnaires can be distorted and unreliable. If actual on-the-job behavior must be captured, observation is clearly one of the most accurate methods.

Utility of an Additional Method

Because there are many different methods to collect data, it is tempting to use too many data collection methods. Multiple data collection methods add to the time and costs of the evaluation and may result in very little additional value. Utility refers to the added value of the use of an additional data collection method. As more than one method is used, this question should always be addressed. Does the value obtained from the additional data warrant the extra time and expense of the method?

If the answer is no, the additional method should not be implemented.

Cultural Bias for Data Collection Method

The culture or philosophy of the organization can dictate which data collection methods are used. For example, some organizations are accustomed to using questionnaires and find the process fits in well with their culture. Some organizations will not use observation because their culture does not support the potential invasion of privacy often associated with it.

Final Thoughts

This chapter outlines techniques for data collection—a critical issue in determining the success of the project. These essential measures determine not only the success achieved but areas where improvement is needed and areas where the success can be replicated in the future. Several techniques are available, ranging from questionnaires to action planning and business performance monitoring. The method chosen must match the scope of the project resources available and the accuracy needed. Complicated projects require a comprehensive approach that measures all of the issues involved in application and impact. Simple projects can take a less formal approach and collect data from only a questionnaire. The next chapter explores the issues of collecting data at the different levels.

Data Collection at All Four Levels

This chapter describes the issues surrounding data collection at each of the levels. The previous chapter focused on the specific methods of data collection. This chapter explores issues about the measurement at each level, describing why it is important, the methods that are most useful, some of the data that must be collected, and the sources of the data. When combined with the previous chapter, these two chapters provide the essentials for collecting all of the data needed through Level 4.

Sources of Data

When considering the possible data sources for collecting data in a consulting project, the categories are easily defined. Here are the major categories of stakeholders.

Client/Senior Managers

One of the most useful data sources for ROI analysis is the client group, usually a senior management team. Whether an individual or a group, the client's perception and understanding is critical to project success. Clients can provide input on all types of issues and are usually available and willing to offer feedback. Collecting data from this source is preferred, because the data usually reflect what is necessary to make adjustments and measure success.

Consulting Participants

The most widely used data source for an ROI analysis is the consulting participants, who are directly involved in the consulting project. They usually work for the client. They must use the skills and knowledge acquired via the project and apply them on the job. Sometimes they are asked to explain the potential impact of those actions. Participants are a rich source of data for almost every issue or part of the project. They are credible, since they are the individuals who make the project work. Also, they are often the most knowledgeable of the processes and other influencing factors. The challenge is to find an effective and efficient way to capture data in a consistent manner.

Consulting Team

In situations where teams of consultants are involved in the consulting project, all team members can provide information about reaction and learning by the consulting project. Input is appropriate for issues directly involved in their work on the project. In many situations, they observe the participants as they attempt to use the knowledge and skills acquired in the project. Consequently, they can report on the successes linked to the project as well as the difficulties and problems associated with it.

Internal Customers

The individuals who serve as internal customers of the consulting participants are another source of data for a few types of projects. In these situations, internal customers provide input on perceived changes linked to the consulting project. This source of data is more appropriate when consulting projects directly affect the internal customers.

They report on how the project has (or will) influence their work or the service they receive. For example, consider a project involving the implementation of a new Enterprise Resource Planning (ERP) system. The participants are the users of the system. The internal customers are the individuals who receive the information and reports from the system.

The Importance of Measuring Inputs, Level 0

As described in the previous chapters, the inputs to a consulting project begin at Level 0; measurements at this level does not reflect contribution or outcomes, but only the inputs. These are very important because they define who is involved, when they are involved, where they are involved, for how long, and at what costs.

Define the Project

This level is the basic definition of the project. The critical measure is the budget of the consulting project or the cost of the project throughout all of the phases and stages. The budget is usually based on the direct costs, but in today's environment, sometimes indirect costs are tracked. For ROI evaluation, they are needed—to show the financial ROI, the total cost of the project is necessary. Another measure defines who is involved, an important ingredient to the project's success. An important part of any project is defining all of the resources needed, including the people who must be involved, when they are involved, and where they are involved. Not having the right people in the right place at the right time can quickly destroy the project. These three issues stand at the top of the lists of reasons for project failures. Finally, measurement at this level reflects different efficiencies that may be employed to move the project along in a very timely manner. This is captured in typical project planning tools.

Reflects Commitment

The inputs reflect commitments in terms of resources allocated to the project and specific budgets for the project. Resources, including budgets and staffing levels, are probably the most impressive way to describe an executive's commitment to the project. The more resources allocated, the more commitment is there, at least in the beginning of the project.

Facilitates Benchmarking

Measurements at this level often provide data that can compare one project to another so that projects internally can be benchmarked for processes, efficiencies, times, involvement, and cost. This measurement sets the stage to benchmark with projects externally.

Issues in Measuring Input

A variety of issues should be addressed to properly measure the inputs. Some are essential; others are optional.

Some measures would be appropriate to try as inputs in the consulting project. The nine measures are as follows:

1. The type of project
2. The functions in the organization where the project is located
3. The users of the project, the people directly involved (the participants)
4. The support staff and others who may be involved
5. The timing of involvement of all parties
6. The duration of the involvement
7. The place of involvement
8. The cost of the project, including direct and indirect costs
9. The inefficiencies surrounding the project

Some of the input data are measured before the project, in terms of the proposed project. The remainder is captured during the project as resources are used and individuals become involved. The source of data would usually be the records of the organization to reflect who is involved and the cost.

Importance of Measuring Reaction, Level 1

Collecting reaction and data during the first operational phase of the ROI process is critical. Client feedback data are powerful for making adjustments and measuring success. It would be difficult to imagine a consulting project being conducted without collecting feedback from those involved in the project, or at least from the client. Client feedback is critical to understanding how well the process is working or to gauge its success after it has been completed. It is always included in every consulting project because of its crucial importance. Here are a few reasons why measuring reaction is important.

Customer Satisfaction Is Essential

Without sustained, favorable reactions to projects, it would be difficult for a consulting team to continue in business. Three important categories of customers exist for almost every consulting project. First, there are those directly involved in the project. These individuals have a direct role in the project and are often referred to as the consulting participants. They are key stakeholders who are directly affected by the consulting project and often have to change processes and procedures and make other job adjustments related to the project. In addition, they often have to learn new skills, tasks, and behaviors to make the project successful. Their feedback is critical to make adjustments and changes in the project as it unfolds and is implemented.

The second category of customers is the supporters, who are on the sidelines, not directly involved, but have some interest in the project. Their perception of the success of the project or potential success is important feedback, as this group will be in a position to influence the project in the future. The third set of stakeholders is the client, the individual, or group of individuals who request consulting projects, approve project budgets, allocate resources, and ultimately live with the success or failure of the project. This important group must be completely satisfied, or it will not have to pay for the project.

Making Adjustments Early

Projects can go astray quickly, and sometimes a specific project is the wrong solution for the specified problem. A project may be mismatched from the beginning, so it is essential to get feedback early in the process so that adjustments can be made. This helps avoid misunderstandings, miscommunications, and, more important, misappropriations, as an improperly designed project is altered or changed quickly before more serious problems are created. Obtaining feedback, making changes, and reporting changes back to the groups who provide the information should be routine.

Benchmarking Data from Other Projects

Some consultants collect reaction data from several sources using standard questions, and the data are then compared with data from other projects so that norms and standards can be developed. This is particularly helpful at the completion of a project as client satisfaction is gauged and correlation between reaction data is compared to the success of other projects. Sometimes an overall project success is developed. Some teams even base part of their consulting fee on the level of client satisfaction, making reaction data very critical to the success of every project. Data collection must be deliberately pursued in a systematic, logical, rational way.

The Importance of Measuring Learning, Level 2

It may seem unnecessary to measure learning in a consulting project. However, projects can fail because those involved did not know what to do to make the project successful. This is particularly important in projects where there is a significant amount of job changes, procedure changes, new tools, new processes, and new technology. The extent to which the participants involved in a project actually learn their new jobs and new processes is an important success factor for the project.

Knowledge Management Is Important

Many organizations are increasing their attention to the areas of knowledge, expertise, and competencies. Consulting projects may involve developing expertise with employees using tools and techniques not previously used. Some projects focus directly on core competencies and building important skills, knowledge, and behaviors into the organization. With a continuous focus on knowledge management, participants understand and acquire a vast array of information, assimilate it, and use it in a productive way.

Learning Is Critical for Complex Projects

Although some consulting projects may involve new equipment, processes, procedures, and new technology, the human factor is still critical to the process. The participants must learn new systems, complex procedures, comprehensive processes, and innovative technology. Whether there is significant restructuring or the addition of new systems, employees must learn how to work in the new environment and develop new knowledge and skills. Learning is becoming a larger part of consultation. Automation has its limitation. Instead, there are complex environments with confusing processes and complicated tools that must be used in an intelligent way to reap the benefits of consulting.

Employees must learn in a variety of ways, not just in a formal classroom environment, but also through technology-based learning and on-the-job assistance. Also, the project team leaders and managers of participants often serve as reinforcers, coaches, or mentors in some projects. In a few cases, learning coaches or on-the-job trainers are used as a part of the consulting project to ensure that learning is acquired so that it can be transferred to the job and the project is implemented as planned.

Topics for Reaction and Learning

Many topics are critical targets for reaction and learning because there are so many issues and processes involved in a typical consulting project. Feedback is needed in almost every major issue, step, or process to make sure things are moving forward properly. The following list shows the typical major areas of feedback for most projects. The key success factors in a consulting project are shown, beginning with the objectives of the project and concluding with the likelihood of success. Different stakeholders react to the project and the progress made. The relevance and importance of the project are critical. Knowledge, skills, capability, and capacity are important learning measures. For a particular project, there can be other issues, and each can have specific parts. Each step, element, task, or part of the project represents an opportunity for feedback. The challenge is to sort out those things that are most important, so the participants and others can provide valuable input.

Areas for Reaction
- Intent to implement the project successfully
- Feasibility of schedule
- Progress made
- Relevance of project
- Importance of project
- Support for project
- Resources for project
- Integration of project
- Project leadership
- Project staffing
- Project coordination

- Project communication
- Motivation of project participants
- Cooperation of project participants
- Knowledge about the project
- Capability of project participants
- New skills acquired
- Capacity achieved
- Likelihood of project success

Using Reaction and Learning Data

Sometimes consulting reaction and learning data are solicited, tabulated, summarized, and then disregarded. The information must be collected and used for one or more of the purposes of evaluation. Otherwise, the exercise is a waste of the time. Too often, project evaluators use the material to feed their egos and let it quietly disappear into their files, forgetting the original purposes behind its collection. Here are a few of the more common uses of reaction and learning data.

Monitor Customer Satisfaction

Because this input is the principal measure taken from the stakeholders, it provides a good indication of the reaction to, and satisfaction with, the project. Thus, project leaders and owners will know how satisfied the customers actually are with the project. Data should be reported to clients and other key stakeholders.

Identify Strengths and Weaknesses of the Project

Feedback is extremely helpful in identifying weaknesses as well as strengths in the project. Feedback on weaknesses can often lead to adjustments and changes. Identifying strengths can be helpful in future designs, so processes can be replicated.

Develop Norms and Standards

Because reaction and learning evaluation data can be automated and are collected in nearly 100 percent of projects, it becomes relatively easy to develop norms and standards throughout the organization. Target ratings can be set for expectations; particular course results are then compared to those norms and standards.

Evaluate Consultants

Perhaps one of the most common uses of reaction and learning data is consultant evaluation. If properly constructed and collected, helpful feedback data can be provided to consultants so that adjustments can be made to increase effectiveness. Some caution needs to be taken, though, since consultant evaluations can sometimes be biased, so other evidence may be necessary to provide an overall assessment of consultant performance.

Identify Planned Improvements for a Forecast

Reaction and learning can provide a profile of planned actions and improvements to use in a forecast or impact and ROI. Also this data can be compared with on-the-job actions as a result of the project. This provides a rich source of data in terms of what participants may be changing or implementing because of what they have learned.

Marketing Future Projects

For some organizations, reaction and learning data provide helpful marketing information. Participants' quotes and reactions provide information that may be convincing to potential participants. Learning measures help to validate the effectiveness of the project. Consulting marketing brochures often contain quotes and summaries of feedback data.

Providing Individual Feedback to Build Confidence

Learning data, when provided directly to participants, provides reinforcement for learning and enhances learning for the solutions. This reinforces the learning process and provides much-needed feedback to participants in consulting projects.

The Importance of Measuring Application and Implementation, Level 3

The two previous measures, reaction and learning, occur during the early stages of the consulting project where there is more attention and focus directly on what must be accomplished in the consulting project. Measuring

Level 3, application and implementation data, occurs at later stages and even after the project has been implemented. The focus is on the measures of the success of the implementation. Sometimes, this level of evaluation measures the degree to which the project is handed off to those who are charged with its success. This is a key transition process with measures that follow the project until it has been fully implemented. Here are a few reasons to measure at this level.

The Value of the Data

The value of the information increases as progress is made through the chain of impact from Level 1 to Level 5. Thus, data concerning application and implementation (Level 3) are more valuable to the client than reaction (Level 1) and learning (Level 2). While these two levels are important, measuring the extent to which the consulting project is implemented properly provides critical data for executives at this level; the success of the project includes the factors that contributed to the success, as the consulting process is fully implemented.

It's the Key Focus of Many Projects

Many consulting projects focus directly on implementation. The project sponsor often speaks in these terms and is concerned about these measures of success (e.g., the system was fully implemented, the new product was successfully launched). Even a comprehensive consulting project, designed to transform an organization, will have key issues for application and implementation.

The sponsor will be interested in knowing the extent to which all of the key stakeholders are adjusting to, and properly implementing, the desired new behaviors, processes, systems, and procedures. This interest in application and implementation often drives the project.

Barriers and Enablers

When a consulting project goes astray, the first question is usually, "What happened?" More important, when a project appears not to be adding value, the first question should be, "What can we do to change the direction of the project?" In either scenario, it is critical to have information that identifies barriers to success, problems encountered in implementation, and obstacles to the application of the process. It is at Level 3, measuring application, that these barriers are identified and examined for reduction or elimination. Sometimes, it's a matter of going around the barrier. In many cases, the key stakeholders directly involved in consulting provide important input into the recommendations for making changes or for using a different approach in the future.

When there is success, the obvious question is, "How can we repeat this success or even improve on this in the future?" The answer to this question is usually found at Level 3. Identifying the factors that contribute directly to the success of the project is critical since those same items can be used to replicate the process to produce specific results in the future and to enhance results. When key stakeholders identify those issues, it not only makes the project successful but provides an important case history of what is necessary for success.

Rewards for Success

Measuring application and implementation allows the client and consulting team to reward those who are doing the best job of applying the processes and implementing the consulting project. Measures taken at this level provide clear evidence of various efforts and roles, providing an excellent basis for performance review or special recognition. Sometimes the consultants are rewarded for implementation (e.g., the project was completed on time, system is operational, or the procedure is working properly). This often has reinforcing value for keeping the project on track and communicating a strong message for future improvements.

Types of Data

The types of data needed are directly related to the objectives of the project. At Level 3, application and implementation, data reflect what participants have accomplished in the project. The outcomes of applications are easy to observe and evaluate. Table 11.1 shows the variety of data for this level of analysis. It's all about action and activity.

The Importance of Measuring Business Impact, Level 4

A logical extension of application is the corresponding business impact. Although there are several obvious reasons for measuring impact, several issues support the

Table 11.1 Examples of Coverage Areas for Application

Action	Explanation	Example
Increase	Increase a particular activity or action.	Increase the frequency of the use of a particular skill.
Decrease	Decrease a particular activity or action.	Decrease the number of times a particular process has to be checked.
Eliminate	Stop or remove a particular task or activity.	Eliminate the formal follow-up meeting, and replace it with a virtual meeting.
Maintain	Keep the same level of activity for a particular process.	Continue to monitor the process with the same schedule as previously used.
Create	Design, build, or implement a new procedure, process, or activity.	Create a procedure for resolving the differences between two divisions.
Use	Use a particular process, procedure, or activity.	Use the new procedure in situations when it is appropriate.
Perform	Conduct or do a particular task, process, or procedure.	Perform a postaudit review at the end of each activity.
Participate	Become involved in various activities, projects, or programs.	Each associate should submit a suggestion for reducing costs.
Enroll	Sign up for a particular process, program, or project.	Each associate should enroll in the career advancement program.
Respond	React to groups, individuals, or systems.	Each participant in the project should respond to customer inquiries within 15 minutes.
Network	Facilitate relationships with others who are involved or have been affected by the project.	Each project participant should continue networking with contacts on, at least, a quarterly basis.

rationale for collecting business impact data related to a consulting project.

Higher-Level Data

Following the assumption that higher-level data create more value for the client, the business impact measures in a five-level framework offer more valuable data. They are the data considered to be the consequence of the successful application and implementation of a consulting project. This level responds to "So what?" and "What if?" questions. The product was successfully launched, so what are the results (i.e., sales, profits, etc.)? What if the system is implemented on time (i.e., productivity and quality improve)? These consequences often represent the bottom-line measures that are positively influenced when a project is successful. For most executives, this is the most important data set, but only if the amount of improvement can be pinpointed to the project.

The Business Driver for Projects

For most consulting projects, the business impact data represent the initial drivers for the project. The problem of deteriorating or less-than-desired performance may have perpetuated the need for the project (e.g., a quality problem or a retention problem). The opportunity for improvement of a business measure may lead to a consulting project (e.g., improving customer satisfaction or market share). If the business needs defined by business measures are the drivers for a project, then the key measures for evaluating the project are the same business measures. The extent to which measures actually have changed is the key determinant of the success of the project.

It's the Payoff for Clients

Business impact data often reflect key payoff measures from the perspective of the client. These are the measures often desired by the client and what he or she wants to see changed or improved. They often represent hard, indisputable facts that reflect performance critical to the business and operating unit level of the organization. And these measures are the ones converted to money to calculate the ROI. Without impact data, a credible ROI calculation cannot be delivered.

Easy to Measure

One unique feature about business impact data is that they are often very easy to measure. Hard and soft data measures at this level often reflect key measures that are found in plentiful numbers throughout an organization. A typical large organization will have hundreds or even thousands of business measures reflecting output, quality, cost, time, job satisfaction, and customer satisfaction. The challenge is to connect the consulting project to the appropriate business measures. This is easily accomplished at the beginning of the consulting project because of the availability and ease with which many of the data items can be located.

Types of Data

To help focus on the measures for impact, a distinction is made in two general categories of data: hard data and soft data. Hard data are the primary measurements of improvement, presented through rational, undisputed facts that are easily gathered. They are the most desirable type of data to collect. The ultimate criteria for measuring the effectiveness of management rest on hard data items, such as productivity, profitability, cost control, and quality control.

Hard data are

- Easy to measure and quantify
- Relatively easy to convert to monetary values
- Objectively based
- Common measures of organizational performance
- Credible with management

Hard data can be grouped into four categories—output, quality, costs, and time—and are typical performance measures in almost every organization. Table 11.2 shows examples of these four categories.

There are times when hard, rational numbers just do not exist. When this is the case, soft data may be meaningful in evaluating consulting projects. Table 11.3 shows common types of soft data, categorized or subdivided into five areas: work climate/satisfaction, employee development/advancement, customer service, initiative/innovation, and image. There may be other ways to divide soft data into categories. Due to the many types of soft data, the possibilities are almost limitless.

Table 11.2 Examples of Hard Data

Output	Time
Sales	Cycle Time
Completion Rate	Equipment Downtime
Units Produced	Overtime
Tons Manufactured	Delivery Time
Items Assembled	Time to Project Completion
Money Collected	Processing Time
Items Sold	Employee Time
New Accounts Generated	Time to Proficiency
Forms Processed	Response Time
Loans Approved	Meeting Time
Inventory Turnover	Repair Time
Patients Discharged	Efficiency
Applications Processed	Recruiting Time
Students Graduated	Average Delay Time
Projects Completed	Late Reporting
Output per Hour	Lost Time Days
Productivity	
Work Backlog	**Quality**
Incentive Bonus	Failure Rates
Shipments	Dropout Rates
	Scrap
Costs	Waste
Shelter Costs	Rejects
Treatment Costs	Reject Rates
Budget Variances	Error Rates
Unit Costs	Rework
Cost by Account	Shortages
Variable Costs	Product Defects
Fixed Costs	Deviation from Standard
Overhead Costs	Product Failures
Operating Costs	Inventory Adjustments
Project Cost Savings	Accidents
Accident Costs	Incidents
Program Costs	Compliance Discrepancies
Sales Expense	Agency Fines
Participant Costs	Penalties

Table 11.3 Examples of Soft Data

Work Climate/Satisfaction	Customer Service
Job Satisfaction	Customer Complaints
Organization Commitment	Customer Satisfaction
Employee Engagement	Customer Dissatisfaction
Employee Loyalty	Customer Impressions
Tardiness	Customer Loyalty
Grievances	Customer Retention
Discrimination Charges	Customer Value
Employee Complaints	Lost Customers
Intent to Leave	
Stress	**Employee Development/Advancement**
Teamwork	
Communication	Promotions
Cooperation	Capability
Conflicts	Intellectual Capital
	Requests for Transfer
Initiative/Innovation	Performance Appraisal Ratings
Creativity	Readiness
Innovation	Networking
New Ideas	
Suggestions	**Image**
New Products	Brand Awareness
New Services	Reputation
Trademarks	Leadership
Copyrights	Social Responsibility
Patents Process	Environmental Friendliness
Patents Improvements	Social Consciousness
Partnerships	Diversity
Alliances	External Awards

Data Collection Key Issues

When collecting application and impact data, several key issues should be addressed. While these are very similar to measuring reaction and learning, a few are different due to the later collection time for this type of data and the importance of the results at this level.

Timing of Data Collection

The timing of data collection revolves around particular events connected with the consulting project. Any particular activity, implementation issue, or milestone is an appropriate time to collect reaction and learning data. Figure 11.1 shows the timing of feedback on a six-month project. This particular project has preproject data collection. This is important to make sure that the environment is proper and supportive of the project. A preproject assessment can be an eye-opening exercise, as particular inhibitors and barriers can be identified that will need adjusting or altering in the project to achieve success. In this particular example, assessment is taken at the beginning of the project as the announcement is made and the project is fully described. Next, a one-month follow-up is taken, followed by a four-month follow-up (which occurs three months later). Finally, at the end of the project, the sixth month, an assessment is taken.

Sources

For application, the sources of data mirror those identified earlier for reaction and satisfaction. Essentially,

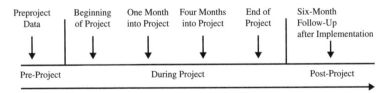

FIGURE 11.1 Project Timetable

all key stakeholders are candidates for sources of data. Perhaps the most important source is those who are actually involved in the application and implementation. It may involve the entire team, or team leaders charged with the responsibility of implementation. For impact data, sources include reports, records, and data in operating reports.

Final Thoughts

This chapter presents the issues involved in collecting data at all levels of outcomes of projects, including reaction, learning, application, and impact. It also explores and addresses the issue of collecting data for the inputs of the process, which is Level 0. The chapter presents some of the reasons for collecting data and some of the issues involved in collecting the data. The next chapter begins the analysis phase of the ROI methodology, sorting out the effects of consulting.

CHAPTER

12

Isolating the Effects of Consulting

When a significant increase in a business measure is noted after a consulting project has been conducted, the two events appear to be linked. The client asks, "How much of this improvement was caused by the consulting project?" When this potentially challenging question is posed, it is not always answered with the accuracy and credibility needed. While the change in the business measure may be linked to the consulting project, other nonconsulting factors usually contribute to the improvement as well. This chapter explores useful techniques for isolating the effects of consulting. This step must always be taken to have a credible analysis at Levels 4 and 5.

The Importance of Isolating the Effects of Consulting Projects

In almost every consulting project multiple influences will drive the business measures targeted by the consulting project. With multiple influences present, it is critical to measure the actual effect of each of the different factors, or at least the improvements that can be attributed to the consulting project. Without this isolation step, the consulting project's success will be in question. The results will be overstated if it is suggested that all of the change in the business impact measure is attributed to the actual consulting project. When this issue is ignored, the impact study is considered invalid and inconclusive. This harsh reality places tremendous pressure on consultants to show the business value of consulting when compared to other factors.

Preliminary Issues

The cause-and-effect relationship between consulting and business performance can be very confusing and difficult to prove but can be developed with an acceptable degree of accuracy. The challenge is to develop one or more specific techniques to isolate the effects of consulting early in the process, usually as part of an evaluation plan. Up-front attention ensures that appropriate techniques will be used with minimum costs and time commitments. Here are the most important issues when isolating the effects of a consulting project.

Early Evidence: Chain of Impact

Before presenting the isolation techniques, it is helpful to examine the chain of impact implied in the different levels of evaluation. Measurable results achieved from a consulting project should be derived from the application of the consulting recommendations over a specified period of time after the project has been completed. Application is Level 3 in the five evaluation levels. Continuing with this logic, successful application of the project should stem from participants learning new skills or acquiring new knowledge from the consulting project, which is a Level 2 evaluation. For participants to learn new information and skills, they must see the project as important and relevant, which is Level 1 evaluation.

Therefore, for a business impact improvement from the project (Level 4 evaluation), this chain of impact implies that measurable application and implementation are realized (Level 3 evaluation), new knowledge and skills are acquired (Level 2 evaluation), and the participant must see value in the project. Without this preliminary evidence, it is difficult to isolate the effects of a consulting project. In other words, if there is an adverse reaction and there is no learning and application, it is virtually impossible to conclude that any performance improvements were caused by the consulting project. From a practical standpoint, this issue requires data collection at four levels for an ROI calculation.

If data are collected on business impact, they should also be collected for other levels of evaluation to ensure that the consulting project helped produce the business results. While this requirement is a prerequisite to isolating the effects of a consulting intervention, it does not prove that there was a direct connection, nor does it pinpoint how much of the improvement was caused by the consulting project. It merely shows that without improvements at previous levels, it is difficult to make a connection between the ultimate outcome and the consulting project.

Identifying Other Factors: A First Step

A first step in isolating a consulting project's impact on performance is to identify the factors that may have contributed to the performance improvement. This step underscores that consulting is not the sole source of improvement and that the credit for improvement is shared with several possible sources—an approach that is likely to gain the respect of the client.

Several potential sources are available to identify major influencing variables. In many situations, the client may be able to identify factors that will or already have influenced the business measure. The client usually is aware of other projects, events, initiatives, or promotions that may be present and have an influence on the output.

Participants in the consulting project are usually aware of other influences that may have caused performance improvement. After all, it is the impact of their collective efforts that is being monitored and measured. In many situations, they have witnessed previous changes in the business measures and can pinpoint reasons for the changes.

Project consultants are another source for identifying variables that impact results. Although the needs analysis will usually uncover these influencing variables, consultants usually analyze these variables while addressing the issues in the consulting project implementation.

In some situations, immediate managers of participants (e.g., work unit managers) may be able to identify variables that influence the performance improvement. This is particularly useful when participants are nonexempt employees (operatives) who may not be fully aware of the variables that can influence performance.

Finally, subject matter experts may be able to identify other influences based on their experience and knowledge of the situation. In the role of expert, they have monitored, examined, and analyzed the variables previously.

The authority of these individuals often increases the data's credibility.

Taking time to focus attention on variables that may influence performance brings additional accuracy and credibility to the process. It moves beyond presenting results with no mention of other influences—a situation that often destroys the credibility of a consulting impact study. It also provides a foundation for some of the techniques described in this book by identifying the variables that must be isolated to show the effects of a consulting project.

Use of Control Groups

The most accurate approach for isolating the impact of a consulting project is the use of control groups in an experimental design process. This approach involves the use of an experimental group that experiences the consulting project and a control group that does not. The composition of both groups should be as identical as possible and, if feasible, each group should be selected randomly from a list of potential candidates. When this is achieved, and both groups are subjected to the same environmental influences, the difference in the performance of the two groups can be attributed to the consulting project.

Sometimes the use of control groups may create an image that consultants are producing a laboratory setting, which can cause a problem for some executives. To avoid this stigma, consultants use the term *pilot project* instead of *experimental group*. A similarly matched, nonparticipating group is referred to as the *comparison group*. For example, in a consulting project for a major U.S.-based computer company, a pilot group was used. The consulting project involved regional and local sales managers, account managers, account executives, account representatives, and sales representatives. The business measures involved profit-margin quota attainment, total revenue attainment, profit margin, and various sales volumes. A comparison group (the control group) was carefully matched with the initial pilot group. The same number of participants for the comparison group was selected at random using the company database. This effort ensured that the comparison group and the pilot group had equivalent job roles. A distinct difference in the two groups emerged after the project was implemented.

The control arrangement does have some inherent issues that may make it difficult to apply in practice. The first major issue is the selection of the groups. From a theoretical perspective, it is virtually impossible to have identical control and experimental groups. Dozens of factors can affect business performance, some of them individual, others contextual. To address this issue on a practical basis, it is best to select four to six variables that will have the greatest influence on performance. For example, in a consulting project designed to boost direct sales in a large retail store chain, three stores were selected, and their performances were compared to three similar stores that constituted the control group. The selection of these particular groups of stores was based on four variables store executives thought would have the greatest influence on sales performance from one store to another: the household income in market area, store size, customer traffic, and previous store performance. Although there are other factors that could have influenced performance, these four variables were used to make the selection.

Another issue is contamination, which can develop when participants in the consulting group (experimental group) communicate with others who are in the control group. Sometimes the members of the control group model the actions of the consulting project. In either case, the experiment becomes contaminated as the influence of the consulting intervention is passed on to the control group. This can be minimized by ensuring that control groups and consulting groups are at different locations, (i.e., stores, branches, plants, cities, etc.) have different shifts, or are on different floors in the same building. When this is not possible, it may be helpful to explain to both groups that one group will be involved in the consulting project now, and the other will be involved at a later date if it works. It is not unusual to try a new system, process, or procedure in one area first, and then implement the change in other areas if it is successful. Also, it may be helpful to appeal to the sense of responsibility of those involved in the consulting project and ask them not to share the information with others.

Another issue surfaces when the different groups function under different environmental influences. This is usually the case when groups are at different locations. Sometimes the selection of the groups can help prevent this problem from occurring. Another tactic is to use more groups than necessary and discard those with some environmental differences.

Consider this example of a control group arrangement. In a manufacturing unit, work teams are averaging 31 hours of overtime a week, which is much too high for the executives. In the experimental group, a consultant was involved with one team to see if the overtime could be corrected with a new scheduling process. The team was carefully matched with another group with the same overtime performance and the same types of processes. Figure 12.1 shows the two teams. The control group is a group that did not get the project, and the experimental group did. The control consulting project was implemented and the results were captured in seven weeks. After seven weeks, the difference in the control group and experimental group was eight hours of overtime. The interesting thing that occurred was that other influences were also lowering the overtime so that the control group actually went down from 31 to 25, while the experimental group (the one involved in the consulting) went from 31 to 17. Thus an improvement of

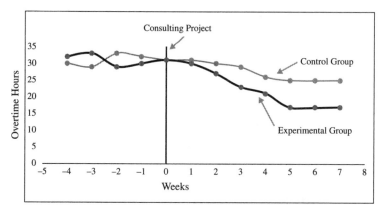

FIGURE 12.1   Control Group Example

eight hours per week is the difference attributed to this consulting project.

Because the use of control groups is an effective approach for isolating the impact of consulting, it should be considered as a technique when a major ROI impact study is planned. In these situations, it is important that the consulting impact is isolated with a high level of accuracy, and the primary advantage of the control group process is accuracy. Best practice data, among the users of the ROI methodology, shows that about 30 percent of the ROI studies are using this isolation technique.

Analytical Approaches

The control group is the most credible process if it works. If it does not work, the next set of approaches is categorized as analytical approaches, because they involve various mathematical relationships and calculations. Three approaches are in this category: trend-line analysis; forecasting, which can involve regression analysis; and calculating the effects of other factors.

Trend-Line Analysis

A useful technique for approximating the impact of consulting is trend-line analysis. With this approach, a trend line is drawn to project the future, using previous performance as a base. When the consulting project is conducted, actual performance of the business measure is compared to the trend-line projection. Any improvement of performance over what the trend line predicted can then be reasonably attributed to the consulting project. While this is not an exact process, it provides a reasonable estimation of consulting impact.

Figure 12.2 shows an example of a trend-line analysis taken from a processing unit of a financial services company. Error rates are increasing and excessive, averaging about 25 per month for the six-month period prior to consulting. Data are presented before and after the consulting project was implemented in June. As shown in the figure, there was an upward trend on the data prior to the consulting. Although the consulting apparently had an effect on errors, the trend line shows a more dramatic improvement. Based on the trend that had previously been established, the error rate would be at 40 per month at month 5 (the average of month 5 and 6.) It is tempting to measure the improvement by comparing

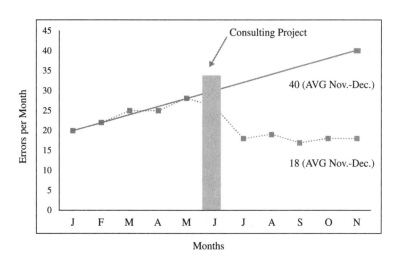

FIGURE 12.2　Example of a Trend Line

the average six months' errors prior to the project (25) to the value six months after the project (18), yielding a 7 error difference. However, a more accurate comparison is the value after the project (18) compared to the trend line (40). In this example, the difference is 22. Using this measure increases the accuracy and credibility of the process to isolate the impact of consulting.

A primary disadvantage of the trend-line approach is that it is not always accurate. This approach assumes that the events that influenced the business measure prior to the consulting project are still in place after the project is implemented (i.e., the trends that were established prior to consulting will continue in the same relative direction). Also, it assumes that no new influences entered the situation at the time consulting was conducted. This may not always be the case. These two conditions must be met to use this isolation technique.

The primary advantage of this approach is that it is simple and inexpensive. If historical data are available, a trend line can quickly be drawn and differences estimated. While not exact, it does provide a quick assessment of the consulting impact.

Relationship Modeling

A more analytical approach to trend-line analysis is the use of a mathematical relationship that predicts a change in performance variables. This approach represents a mathematical interpretation of the trend-line analysis when other factors (variables) enter a situation at the time the consulting project is implemented. With this approach, the business measure targeted by consulting is forecasted based on the influence of other variables (from a mathematical relationship) that have changed during the implementation or evaluation period of the consulting project. The actual value of the measure is compared to the forecasted value. The difference reflects the contribution of consulting.

An example will help illustrate the effect of the forecasting. One healthcare organization was focusing on decreasing length of stay. In June, a new consulting project involved changing several procedures that made the diagnosis, treatment, and healing process faster, with various ways to recognize improvement quickly and make decisions and adjustments accordingly. All of these procedures were aimed at reducing the average length of stay. Figure 12.3 shows that the length of stay prior to the change in medical procedures and the actual data shows a significant downward improvement in the nine

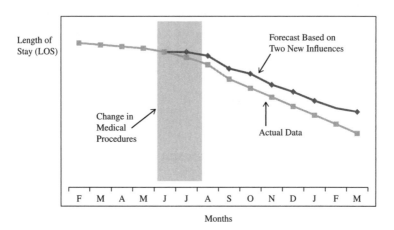

FIGURE 12.3 Forecasting Example

months since the project was implemented. However, two important changes occurred about the same time that the new project was implemented. A major provider reissued a maximum length of stay that they would reimburse for specific illnesses. This influence has a tendency to cause organizations to focus more intensely on getting patients discharged as quickly as possible. At the same time, the severity of the influx of patients had slightly decreased. The types of illnesses dramatically affect the length of stay. The analysts in the business process improvement department developed a forecast showing the effects of the provider reimbursement process and the change in the illnesses of the patients upon admission. They were able to develop a multiple variable analysis to forecast the LOS, as shown in the figure. The data from February show the difference in the forecasted value and the actual value. That difference after nine months represents the impact of the new medical procedures, because they were not included in the forecasted value.

With the relationship model approach, a major disadvantage occurs when several variables enter the process. The complexity multiplies, and the use of sophisticated statistical packages for multiple variable analysis is necessary. Even then, a good fit of the data to the model may not be possible. Unfortunately, some organizations have not developed mathematical relationships for business measures as a function of one or more inputs, and without them, the forecasting method is difficult to use.

The primary advantage of this process is that it can accurately predict business performance measures without the consulting, if appropriate data and models are available. Many organizations are investing in analytics teams to develop these types of models. The presentation of specific methods is beyond the scope of this book. More detailed information on this important subject can be found in the book *Making Human Capital Analytics Work* by Patricia and Jack Phillips.[1]

Calculating the Impact of Other Factors

Although not appropriate in all cases, sometimes it is possible to calculate the impact of factors (other than consulting) that influence a portion of the improvement and credit the consulting project with the remaining portion. In this approach, the consulting project takes credit for improvement that cannot be attributed to other factors.

An example will help explain the approach. In a consulting project to improve consumer loans for a large bank, a significant increase in consumer loan volume was generated after the consulting project was completed. Part of the increase in volume was attributed to consulting, and the remaining was due to the influence of other factors in place during the same time period. Two other factors were identified: an increase in sales promotion and declining interest rates, which caused an increase in consumer volume.

With regard to the first factor, as sales promotion increased, so did consumer loan volume. The amount of this factor was developed by the marketing analytics team. For the second factor, the analytics team used industry sources to estimate the relationship between increased consumer loan volumes and lower interest rates.

These two estimates together accounted for a modest percentage of increased consumer loan volume. The remaining improvement was attributed to the consulting project.

This method is appropriate when the other factors are easily identified and the appropriate mechanisms are in place to calculate their impact on the improvement. In some cases it is just as difficult to estimate the impact of other factors as it is the impact of consulting, leaving this approach less advantageous. This process can be very credible if the method used to isolate the impact of other factors is credible.

Estimates from Credible Sources

If analytical approaches will not work, then the next set of approaches is estimates of the consulting project impact. A variety of different inputs can be used to provide estimates of how much of the improvement in a business measure is related to the consulting project. The challenge is to find the most credible sources to provide the data. The participants in a consulting project may be the most credible. Another possibility may be the managers of those participants, if they are active in the project, and still another is to use the senior management team, but only if they are familiar with all the factors that could affect the business performance measures. Finally, inputs from customers may be appropriate, but only if the customers can clearly see the factors that have caused them to purchase, open an account, or upgrade a purchase.

Participant's Estimate of Impact

An easily implemented method for isolating the impact of consulting is to obtain information directly from the participants in the consulting project. The effectiveness of this approach rests on the assumption that participants are capable of determining or estimating how much of a business performance improvement is related to the consulting project. Because their actions have produced the improvement, participants may have a credible input on the issue. They should know how much of the change was caused by implementing the consulting project. Although an estimate, this value will usually have considerable credibility with management because they know participants are at the center of the change or improvement. Participant estimation is obtained by asking participants the series of questions in the following list after describing the improvement. The credibility is enhanced with an error adjustment, obtained through a confidence estimate.

Questions for Participant Estimation

- Can you define the performance measure improved by the consulting project?
- How much improvement has been realized since the consulting project began?
- What other factors have contributed to this improvement in performance?
- What percentage of this improvement can be attributed to the consulting project?
- What is the basis for this estimation?

- What confidence do you have in this estimate, expressed as a percentage? (0% = No confidence; 100% = Complete confidence)
- What other individuals or groups could estimate this percentage?

The confidence percentage is actually a reflection of the error in the estimate. An 80 percent confidence level equates to a potential error range of 20 percent, which could be plus or minus. With this approach, the level of confidence is multiplied by the estimate using the lower side of the range. Table 12.1 shows this type of data collected from one participant in a consulting project. In the example, the participant allocates 40 percent of the improvement to the consulting project and is 80 percent confident in the estimate. The confidence percentage is multiplied by the estimate to develop a usable consulting factor value of 32 percent. This adjusted percentage is then multiplied by the actual amount of the improvement

Table 12.1   Example of a Participant's Estimation

Factor That Influenced Improvement	Percentage of Improvement Caused By	Confidence Expressed as a %	Adjusted % of Improvement Caused By
Consulting project	40%	80%	32%
System changes	20%	70%	14%
Environmental changes	10%	60%	6%
Compensation changes	30%	90%	27%
Other	__%	__%	__%
Total	**100%**		

(postproject minus preproject value) to isolate the portion attributed to consulting. The adjusted improvement is now ready for conversion to monetary values and, ultimately, use in the return on investment calculation.

Although an estimate, this approach does have considerable accuracy and credibility. Five adjustments are effectively applied to the participant estimation to reflect a conservative approach:

1. Participants who do not provide usable impact data are assumed to have experienced no improvements and are omitted from the analysis.

2. Extreme data and incomplete, unrealistic, and unsupported claims are omitted from the analysis, although they may be included in the intangible benefits.

3. For short-term consulting projects, it is assumed that no benefits from the consulting intervention are realized after the first year of implementation. For long-term projects, more than one year of consulting benefits is used in the analyses.

4. The improvement amount is adjusted by the amount directly related to the consulting project, expressed as a percentage.

5. The confidence level, expressed as a percentage, is multiplied by the improvement value to reduce the amount of the improvement by the potential error.

As an added enhancement to this method, the next level of management above the participants may be asked to review and approve the estimates from participants.

When presented to senior management, the result of an impact study is perceived to be an understatement of a project's success. The data and the process are considered to be credible and accurate.

An example will illustrate the process for participant estimates. A restaurant chain initiated a consulting project to improve store operations. The project was designed to improve the operating performance of the restaurant chain using a variety of tools to establish measurable goals for employees, provide performance feedback, measure progress toward goals, and take action to ensure that goals are met. As part of the project, each store manager developed an action plan for improvement. Managers also learned how to convert measurable improvements to monetary value for the restaurant if they were not already developed. The good news is that 95 percent of the measures that matter have been converted to money. Their action plans could focus on any improvement and converted the improvements to either cost savings or restaurant profits. Some of the improvement areas were inventory, food spoilage, cash shortages, employee turnover, absenteeism, and productivity.

As part of the follow-up evaluation, each action plan was thoroughly documented, showing results in quantitative terms, which were converted to monetary values. The annual monetary value for each improvement for each participant was calculated from action plans. Realizing that other factors could have influenced the improvement, managers were asked to estimate the percentage of the improvement that resulted directly from the consulting project (the contribution estimate).

Restaurant managers are aware of factors that influence specific business measures and usually know how much of an improvement is traceable to the project. Each manager was asked to be conservative and provide a confidence estimate for the above contribution estimate (100 percent = Certainty and 0 percent = No confidence). The results are shown in Table 12.2.

Estimation of the consulting impact can be calculated using the conservative approach of adjusting for the contribution of the project and adjusting for the error of the contribution estimate. For example, the $5,500 annual value for labor savings is adjusted to consider the consulting contribution ($5,500 × 60% = $3,300). Next, the value is adjusted for the confidence in this value ($3,300 × 80% = $2,640). The conservative approach yields an overall improvement of $68,386. Participant 5 did not submit a completed action plan and was discarded from the analysis, although the costs are still included in the ROI calculation, based on guiding principle #6 from Chapter 6.

Another interesting observation emerges from this type of analysis. When the average of the three largest improvements is compared with the average of the three smallest values, important information is revealed about the potential for return on investment. If all the participants in the consulting project had focused on high-impact improvements, a substantially higher ROI could have been achieved. This information can be helpful to the management group, whose support is often critical to the success of consulting. While an impressive ROI is refreshing, a potentially greater ROI is outstanding.

Table 12.2 Estimates of Consulting Project Impact from Participants

Participant	Total Annual Improvement (Dollar Value)	Basis-Measure	Contribution Estimate from Manager (Participants)	Confidence Estimate from Manager (Participants)	Conservative Value Reported
1	$5,500	Labor savings	60%	80%	$2,640
2	15,000	Employee turnover	50%	80%	6,000
3	9,300	Absenteeism	65%	80%	4,836
4	2,100	Daily shortages	90%	90%	1,701
5	0	—	—	—	—
6	29,000	Employee turnover	40%	75%	8,700
7	2,241	Inventory adjustments	70%	95%	1,490
8	3,621	Overtime	100%	80%	2,897
9	21,000	Employee turnover	75%	80%	12,600
10	1,500	Food spoilage	100%	100%	1,500
11	15,000	Labor savings	80%	85%	10,200
12	6,310	Accidents	70%	100%	4,417
13	14,500	Absenteeism	80%	70%	8,120
14	3,650	Productivity	100%	90%	3,285
Total	$128,722				$68,386

This process has some potential disadvantages. It is an estimate and, consequently, it may not have the accuracy desired by some consultants and clients. Also, the input data may be unreliable since some participants may be incapable of providing these types of estimates. They may not be aware of the factors that contributed to the results.

Several advantages make this technique attractive. It is a simple process, easily understood by most participants and by others who review evaluation data. It is inexpensive, takes very little time and analysis and, thus, results in an efficient addition to the evaluation process. Also, these estimates originate from a credible source—the individuals who produced the improvement, the consulting participants. There is a considerable amount of research that supports the accuracy and credibility of estimates. There is a wisdom in the crowds as detailed in the book *The Wisdom of Crowds* by James Surowiecki.[2]

The advantages of this approach seem to offset the disadvantages. Isolating the effects of a consulting project will never be precise, and this estimate may be accurate enough for most clients and management groups. The process is appropriate when the participants are managers, supervisors, team leaders, sales associates, engineers, and other professional or technical employees.

Manager's Estimate of Impact

In lieu of, or in addition to, participant estimates, the participants' manager may be asked to provide input as to the extent of the consultant's role in producing improved performance. In some settings, participants' managers may be more familiar with the other factors influencing performance. Consequently, they may be better equipped to provide estimates of impact. The recommended questions to ask managers are similar to those asked of participants.

Manager estimates should be analyzed in the same manner as participant estimates. To be more conservative, actual estimates are adjusted by the confidence percentage. When participants' estimates have also been collected, the decision of which estimate to use becomes an issue. If there is some compelling reason to think that one estimate is more credible than the other, then it should be used. If both are credible, the most conservative approach is to use the lowest value and include an appropriate explanation. This is guiding principle #4.

In some cases, upper management may estimate the percent of improvement that should be attributed to a project. After considering additional factors that could contribute to an improvement, such as technology, procedures, and process changes, management applies a subjective factor to represent the portion of the results that should be attributed to the consulting project. While this is quite subjective, the individuals who provide or approve funding for the consulting usually accept the input. Sometimes their comfort level with the process is the most important consideration.

This approach of using management estimates has the same disadvantages as relying on participant estimates. It is subjective and, consequently, may be viewed with skepticism by some. Also, managers may be reluctant to participate or may be incapable of providing accurate impact estimates. In some cases, they may not know about other factors that contributed to the improvement.

The advantages of this approach are similar to the advantages of participant estimation. It is simple, inexpensive, and enjoys an acceptable degree of credibility because it comes directly from the managers of individuals who are involved in the consulting project. When combined with participant estimation, the credibility is enhanced considerably. Also, when factored by the level of confidence, its value further increases.

Customer Estimates of Consulting Impact

Another helpful approach in some narrowly focused situations is to solicit input on the impact of consulting directly from customers. In these situations, customers are asked why they chose a particular product or service or to explain how their reaction to the product or service has been influenced by individuals or systems involved in the consulting project. This technique often focuses directly on what the consulting project is designed to improve. For example, after a customer service consulting project involving customer response was conducted with an electric utility, market research data showed that the percentage of customers who were dissatisfied with response time was reduced by 5 percent when compared to market survey data before the consulting project. Since response time was reduced by the consulting project and no other factor contributed to the reduction, the 5 percent reduction in dissatisfied customers was directly attributable to the consulting project.

Routine customer surveys provide an excellent opportunity to collect input directly from customers concerning their reaction to an assessment of a new or improved product, service, process, or procedure. Pre- and post-data can pinpoint the changes related to an improvement driven by a consulting project.

When collecting customer input, it is important to link it with the current data collection methods and avoid creating new surveys or feedback mechanisms if at all possible. This measurement process should not add to the data collection systems. Customer input could, perhaps, be the most powerful and convincing data if they are complete, accurate, and valid.

Expert Estimation of Consulting Impact

External or internal experts can sometimes estimate the portion of results that can be attributed to a consulting intervention. When using this technique, experts must be carefully selected based on their knowledge of the process, project, and situation. For example, an expert in quality might be able to provide estimates of how much change in a quality measure can be attributed to a consulting intervention and how much can be attributed to other factors.

An example will illustrate this process. Omega Consultants provides consulting services to the banking industry and implements sales consulting projects in a variety of settings. Utilizing control group arrangements, Omega determined that a typical project would generate a 30 percent increase in sales volume three months after implementation. Given this value, implementation should result in a 30 percent improvement in another financial institution with a similar target audience and a similar need. Although the situations may vary considerably, this is a very rough estimate that may be used in comparisons. If more than 30 percent was achieved, the additional amount could be due to factors other than the consulting. Experts, consultants, or researchers are usually available for almost any field. They bring their experience with similar situations into the analysis.

This approach does have disadvantages. It will be inaccurate unless the project and setting, in which the estimate is made, are quite similar to the project in question. Also, this approach may lose credibility because the estimates come from external sources and may not necessarily involve those who are close to the process.

This process has an advantage in that it is a quick source of input from a reputable expert or independent consultant. Sometimes top management will place more confidence in external experts than in its own internal staff.

Using the Techniques

With all the methods available to isolate the impact of consulting, selecting the most appropriate techniques for a specific project can be difficult. Some techniques are simple and inexpensive, while others are more time consuming and costly. When attempting to make the selection decision, the following factors should be considered:

- Feasibility of the technique
- Accuracy provided with the technique
- Credibility of the technique with the target audience
- Specific cost to implement the technique
- Amount of disruption in normal work activities as the technique is implemented
- Participant, staff, and management time needed for the particular technique

Multiple techniques or multiple sources for data input should be considered since two sources are usually better than one. When multiple sources are utilized, a conservative method is recommended for combining the inputs. A conservative approach builds credibility and acceptance. The target audience should always be provided with explanations of the process and the various subjective factors involved. Multiple sources allow an organization to experiment with different strategies and build confidence with a particular technique. For example, if management is concerned about the accuracy of participants' estimates, a combination of a control group arrangement and participants' estimates could be attempted to check the accuracy of the estimation process.

Final Thoughts

This chapter presents a variety of techniques for isolating the effects of consulting. The techniques represent the most effective approaches to address this issue and are used by some of the most progressive organizations. Too often, results are reported and linked with the consulting project without any attempt to isolate the portion that can be attributed to consulting. If consultants are committed to improving their image, as well as meeting their responsibility for obtaining results, this issue must be addressed early in the process for all major projects. The next chapter focuses on converting data to money, another challenge for consultants.

Converting Data to Money

If it's not a number that the client understands, does it mean much? Most of today's leading consultants are learning that the answer is "no." Money is something that a client clearly understands. Transforming or converting data into monetary values is an essential step in a consulting assignment. Many consulting projects stop with a tabulation of business results. While these results are important, it is more valuable to convert the positive outcomes into monetary values and weigh them against the cost of consulting to develop the ROI. This is the ultimate level in the five-level evaluation framework presented in Chapter 6. This chapter explains how leading consultants are moving beyond simply tabulating business results to developing monetary values used in calculating ROI.

Consulting project results include both tangible and intangible measures. Intangible measures are the benefits directly linked to a consulting project that cannot or should not be converted to monetary values. These measures are often monitored after the consulting project has been completed. Although they are not converted to monetary values, they are still an important part of the evaluation process.

Importance of Converting Data to Monetary Values

The answer to this question is not always clearly understood by some consultants. A consulting project could be labeled a success without converting to monetary values, just by using business impact data showing the amount of change directly attributed to the project. For example, an improvement in production, waste, cycle time, customer satisfaction, or employee engagement could represent significant improvements linked directly to consulting. For some projects this may be sufficient. However, if the client desires more insight into the impact data or return on investment calculation with the actual monetary benefits compared to the costs, then this extra step of converting data to monetary values will be necessary. Sometimes the monetary value has more impact on the client than just the change in the number itself. For example, consulting project success in terms of a reduction of 10 customer complaints per month may not seem to be significant. However, if the value of a customer complaint had been determined to be $3,000, this converts to an annual value of at least $36,000—a more impressive improvement.

The Five Key Steps to Convert Data to Money

Before describing specific techniques to convert both hard and soft data to monetary values, there are five general steps that should be completed for each data item.

1. **Focus on a unit of measure.** First, define a unit of measure. For output data, the unit of measure is one item produced, one service provided, one project

completed, or one sale consummated. Time measures might include one hour of cycle time, or one minute of customer-response time. The unit is usually expressed in minutes, hours, or days. Quality is a common measure, with a unit being defined as one error, one reject, one customer complaint, or one reworked item. Soft data measures vary, with a unit of improvement representing such things as one conflict, a one-point change in the customer satisfaction index, or one point on the employee engagement survey.

2. **Determine the value of each unit.** Place a value (V) on the unit identified in the first step. For measures of production, quality, cost, and time, the process is relatively easy. Most organizations maintain records or reports that can pinpoint the cost of one unit of production, or one defect. Soft data are more difficult to convert to money. For example, the value of one customer complaint or a one-point change in employee engagement is often difficult to determine. The techniques described in this chapter provide an array of approaches for making this conversion. When more than one value is available, the most credible or the lowest value is used in the calculation.

3. **Calculate the change in performance data.** Calculate the change in output data after the effects of the consulting project have been isolated from other influences. The change (Δ) is the performance improvement, measured as hard or soft data, which

is directly attributed to consulting. The value may represent the performance improvement for an individual, a team, a group of participants, or several groups of participants.

4. **Determine an annual amount for the change.** Annualize the Δ value to develop a total change in the performance data for at least one year (ΔP). Using annual values has become a standard approach for organizations seeking to capture the benefits of many consulting projects, although the benefits may not remain constant through the entire year. First year benefits are used even when the consulting project is considered to be short term. This approach is considered conservative. (Note: For long-term projects, multiple years would be used.)

5. **Calculate the annual value of the improvement.** Arrive at the total value of improvement by multiplying the annual performance change (ΔP) by the unit value (V) for the complete group in question. For example, if one group of participants is involved in a consulting project being evaluated, the total value will include total improvement for all participants in the group. This value for annual project benefits is then compared to the cost of consulting, usually with the ROI formula.

An example taken from a labor management consulting project at a manufacturing plant describes the five-step process of converting data to monetary values. This project was developed and implemented after the initial needs assessment and analysis revealed that a lack of teamwork was causing an excessive number of labor grievances. Thus, the actual number of grievances resolved at Step 2 in the four-step grievance process was selected as an output measure. Table 13.1 shows the steps taken in assigning a monetary value to the data, arriving at a total consulting impact of $546,000.

Table 13.1   An Example Illustrating the Steps for Converting Data to Monetary Values

Setting: Labor Management Consulting Project in a Manufacturing Plant	
Step 1	**Focus on a unit of measure.** One grievance reaching Step 2 in the four-step grievance resolution process
Step 2	**Determine the value of each unit.** Using internal experts (i.e., the labor relations staff), the cost of an average grievance was estimated to be $6,500, when time and direct costs were considered. ($V = \$6,500$)
Step 3	**Calculate the change in performance data, Δ.** Six months after the project was completed, total grievances per month reaching Step 2 declined by 10. Seven of the 10 reductions were related to the consulting project, as determined by first-level managers (isolating the effects of the consulting project).
Step 4	**Determine an annual amount for the change, ΔPV.** Using the six-month value of seven grievances per month yields an annual improvement of 84. ($\Delta P = 84$)
Step 5	**Calculate the annual value of the improvement, ΔPV.** Annual Value $= \Delta P \times V$ $= 84 \times \$6,500 = \$546,000$

Several strategies for converting data to monetary values are available. Some are appropriate for a specific type of data or data category, while others may be used with virtually any type of data. The consultant's challenge is to select the strategy that best suits the situation. These strategies are presented next, beginning with the most credible approach.

Standard Monetary Values

Most hard data items (output, quality, costs, and time) have standard values developed, because these are often the measures that matter to the organization. They reflect problems, and their conversion to monetary values shows their impact on the operational and financial well-being of the organization. For the past two decades, quality projects have typically focused only on the cost of quality. Organizations have been obsessed with placing a value on mistakes or the payoff from avoiding these mistakes. This assigned value—the standard cost of an item—is one of the critical outgrowths of the quality management movement.

A variety of process improvement projects—such as reengineering, reinventing the corporation, transformation, and continuous process improvement—have included a component in which the cost of a particular measure is determined. The development of a variety of cost control, cost containment, and cost management systems—such as activity-based costing—have forced organizations, departments, and divisions to place costs on activities and, in some cases, relate those costs directly to the revenues or profits of the organization. The following discussion describes how measures of output, quality, and time can be converted to standard values.

Converting Output Data to Money

When a consulting project produces a change in output, the value of the increased output can usually be determined from the organization's accounting or operating records. For organizations operating on a profit basis, this value is typically the marginal profit contribution of an additional unit of production or service provided. For example, an assembly team within a major appliance manufacturer is able to boost the production of small refrigerators after an operations consulting project. The unit of improvement is the operating margin of one refrigerator. For organizations that are nonprofit or in the public sector, this value is usually reflected in the savings accumulated when an additional unit of output is realized for the same input resources. For example, in the visa section of a government office, an additional visa application is processed at no additional cost in terms of resources. Thus, an increase in output translates into a cost savings equal to the unit cost of processing a visa application.

The formulas and calculations used to measure this contribution depend on the type of organization and the status of their record keeping. Most organizations have standard values readily available for performance monitoring and setting goals. A standard value is defined as value that has been previously developed and is accepted by the managers involved in the functional area where the consulting project is being eliminated.

The benefit of converting output data to money using standard values is that these calculations are already available for the most important data items. Perhaps no area has as much experience with standard values as the sales and marketing area. Table 13.2 shows a sampling of the sales and marketing measures that are often calculated and reported and standard values.[1]

Calculating the Standard Cost of Quality

Because many consulting projects are designed to increase quality, the consulting staff must find a value of the improvement in certain quality measures. Quality and the cost of quality are important issues in most manufacturing and service firms. In recent years it has worked its way into governments (the U.S. Department of Defense), nongovernment organizations (the United Nations), and nonprofits (American Cancer Society). The beginning point in these analyses is to calculate the cost of poor quality. For some quality measures, the task is easy. For example, if quality is measured with the defect rate, the value of the improvement is the cost to repair or replace the product. The most obvious cost of poor quality is the scrap or waste generated by mistakes. Defective products, spoiled raw materials, and discarded paperwork are all the result of poor quality. Scrap and waste translate directly into a monetary value. In a production environment, for example, the cost of a defective product is the total cost

Table 13.2 Examples of Standard Values in Sales and Marketing

Metric	Definition	Converting Issues
Sales	The sale of the product or service recorded in a variety of different ways: by product, by time period, by customer.	This data must be converted to monetary value by applying the profit margin for a particular sales category.
Profit Margin (%)	Price: cost/cost for the product, customer, time period	Factored to convert sales to monetary value-add to the organization
Unit Margin	Unit price less the unit cost	This shows the value of incremental sales.
Channel Margin	Channel profits as a percentage of channel selling price	This would be used to show the value of sales through a particular marketing channel.
Retention Rate	The ratio of customers retained to the number of customers at risk of leaving	The value is the saving of money necessary to acquire a replacement customer.
Churn Rate	The ratio of customers leaving compared to the number who are at risk of leaving	The value is the saving of money necessary to acquire a new customer.
Customer Profit	The difference between the revenues earned from and the cost associated with the customer relationship during the specified period	The monetary value added is the profit obtained from customers. It all goes to the bottom line.
Customer Value Lifetime	The present value of the future cash flows attributed to the customer relationship	Bottom line: as customer value increases, it adds directly to the profits. Also, as a new customer is added, the incremental value is the customer lifetime average.
Cannibalization Rate	The percentage of the new product sales taken from existing product lines	This is to be minimized, as it represents an adverse effect on existing products, with the value added being the loss of profits due to the sales loss.

(Continued)

Table 13.2 (*Continued*)

Metric	Definition	Converting Issues
Workload	Hours required to service clients and prospects	This includes the salaries, commissions, and benefits from the time the sales staff spends on the workload.
Inventories	The total amount of product or brand available for sale in a particular channel	Inventories are valued at the cost of carrying the inventory, space, handling, and the time value of money. Insufficient inventory is the cost of expediting the new inventory or loss of sales because of the inventory outage.
Market Share	Sales revenue as a percentage of total market sales	Actual sales are converted to money through the profit margins. This is a measure of competitiveness.

Source: Adapted from *Marketing Metrics: 50+ Metrics Every Executive Should Master* by Paul W. Farris, Neil T. Bendle, Phillip E. Pfeifer, and David J. Ribstein.

incurred to the point the mistake is identified, minus the salvage value.

Employee mistakes and errors can cause expensive rework. The most costly rework occurs when a product is delivered to a customer and must be returned for correction. The cost of rework includes both labor and direct costs. In some organizations, rework costs can be as much as 35 percent of operating expenses.

In one example, a consulting project focused on customer service provided by dispatchers in an oil company. The dispatchers processed orders and scheduled deliveries of fuel to service stations. A measure of quality that was considered excessive was the number of pullouts experienced. A pullout occurs when a delivery truck cannot fill an order for fuel at a service station. The truck must then return to the terminal for an adjustment to the order. This is essentially a rework item. The average cost of a pullout was previously developed by tabulating the cost from a sampling of actual pullouts. The elements in the tabulation included driver time, the cost of using the truck for adjusting the load, the cost of terminal use, and estimated administrative expenses. This value became the accepted standard to use in the consulting project.

Organizations have made great progress in developing standard values for the cost of quality. Quality costs can be grouped into six major categories: internal failure, penalties, external failure, analysis, prevention, and customer dissatisfaction.

1. **Internal failure** represents costs associated with problems detected prior to product shipment or service delivery. Typical costs are reworking, retesting, and redesigning.

2. **Penalty costs** are the fines and charges incurred as a result of unacceptable quality.

3. **External failure** refers to problems detected after product shipment or service delivery. Typical cost items are technical support, complaint investigation, remedial upgrades, and fixes.

4. **Analysis costs** are the expenses involved in determining the condition of a particular product

or service. Typical costs are testing and related activities, such as product-quality audits.

5. **Prevention costs** include actions to avoid unacceptable product or service quality. These efforts include service quality administration, inspections, process studies, and improvements.

6. **Customer dissatisfaction** is perhaps the costliest element of inadequate quality. In some cases, serious mistakes result in lost business. Customer dissatisfaction is difficult to quantify, and arriving at a monetary value may be impossible using direct methods. The judgment and expertise of sales, marketing, or quality managers are usually the best resources to draw upon in measuring the impact of dissatisfaction. More and more quality experts are measuring customer and client dissatisfaction with the use of market surveys. However, other strategies discussed in this chapter may be more appropriate for the task.

Converting Employee Time to Money Using Compensation

Decreasing the workforce or employee time is a common objective for consulting projects. In a team environment, a project may enable the team to complete tasks in less time or with fewer people. A major consulting project could effect a reduction of several hundred employees. On an individual basis, consulting may be designed to help professional, sales, supervisory, and managerial employees save time in performing daily tasks. The value of the time saved is an important measure, and determining the monetary value is a relatively easy process.

The most obvious time savings are from reduced labor costs for performing the same amount of work. The monetary savings are found by multiplying the hours saved by the labor cost per hour. For example, after participating in personal time-management consulting, participants estimated that they saved an average of 74 minutes per day, worth $31.25 per day or $7,500 per year. The time savings were based on the average salary plus benefits for the typical participant. This is a benefit only if the time saved is used in other productive ways.

The average wage, with a percent added for employee benefits, will suffice for most calculations. However, employee time may be worth more. For example, additional costs in maintaining an employee (office space, furniture, telephones, utilities, computers, secretarial support, and other overhead expenses) could be included in calculating the average labor cost. Thus, the average wage rate may escalate quickly. In a large-scale employee reduction effort, calculating additional employee costs may be more appropriate for showing the value. However, for most projects the conservative approach of using salary plus employee benefits is recommended.

Beyond reducing the labor cost per hour, time savings can produce benefits such as improved service, avoidance of penalties for late projects, and additional profit opportunities. These values can be estimated using other methods discussed in this chapter.

A word of caution is in order when developing time savings. Savings are only realized when the amount of time saved translates into a cost reduction or profit contribution. Even if a consulting project produces savings in manager time, a monetary value is not realized unless the manager puts the additional time to productive use. Having managers estimate the percentage of time saved that is devoted to productive work may be helpful, if it is followed up with a request for examples of how the extra time was used. If a team-based project sparks a new process that eliminates several hours of work each day, the actual savings will be based on a reduction in staff or overtime pay. Therefore, an important preliminary step in developing time savings is determining whether the expected savings will be genuine.

Finding Standard Values

Standard values are available for all types of data. Virtually every major department will develop standard values that are monitored for that area. Typical functions in a major organization where standard values are tracked include these:

- Finance and accounting
- Production
- Operations
- Engineering
- IT
- Administration
- Sales and marketing
- Customer service and support
- Procurement
- Logistics

- Compliance
- Research and development
- HR

Thanks to organization-wide systems software, standard values are commonly integrated and made available for access by a variety of people. In some cases, access may need to be addressed to ensure that the data can be obtained by those who require them.

When Standard Values Are Not Available

When standard values are not available, several alternative strategies for converting data to monetary values are available. Some are appropriate for a specific type of data or data category, while others may be used with virtually any type of data. The challenge is to select the strategy that best suits the situation.

Calculating the Value Using Historical Costs from Records

Sometimes historical records contain the value of a measure and reflect the cost (or value) of a unit of improvement. This strategy relies on identifying the appropriate records and tabulating the actual cost components for the item in question. For example, a large construction firm initiated a consulting project to improve safety. The consulting project improved several safety-related performance measures, ranging from government fines to total worker's compensation costs. By examining the company's records using one year of data, the average cost for each safety measure was obtained. This value included the direct costs of medical payments, insurance payments and premiums, investigation services, and lost-time payments to employees, as well as payments for legal expenses, fines, and other direct services. The amount of time to investigate, resolve, and correct the issues was also factored. This time involved not only the health and safety staff but other personnel as well. In addition, the costs of lost productivity, disruption of services, morale, and dissatisfaction were estimated to obtain a full cost. The corresponding costs for each item were then developed.

Managers often use marginal cost statements and sensitivity analyses to pinpoint values associated with changes in output. If the data are not available, the consulting staff may have to develop or coordinate the development of appropriate values. Historical cost data are usually available for most hard data. Unfortunately, this is generally not true for soft data, so other techniques explained in this chapter must be employed to convert the data to monetary values.

Calculating monetary value using historical data should be done with caution and only when these two conditions exist:

1. The sponsor has approved the use of additional time, effort, and money to develop a monetary value from the current records and reports.
2. The measure is simple and can be found by searching only a few records.

Otherwise, an alternative method is preferred.

Using Expert Input

When converting data items for which historical cost data are not available, it might be feasible to consider input from experts on the processes. Internal experts provide the cost (or value) of one unit of improvement. Individuals with knowledge of the situation and the respect of management are often the best prospects for expert input. They must understand the processes and be willing to provide estimates—as well as the assumptions made in arriving at the estimates. Most experts have their own methodology for developing these values. So when requesting their input, it is important to explain the full scope of what is needed, providing as many specifics as possible. Internal experts are everywhere. They may be in the obvious department (quality), the section or unit that sends the report (human resources), or in job title (customer complaint coordinator). The key is to find them. Asking may help.

In the example described earlier of the team building intervention designed to reduce grievances, other than actual settlement costs and direct external expenses the company had no records reflecting the total cost of grievances (i.e., there were no data for the time required to resolve a grievance). Therefore, an estimate was needed. The manager of labor relations, who had credibility with senior management and thorough knowledge of the grievance process, provided a cost estimate. He based it on the average settlement when a grievance was lost, the direct costs related to the grievances (arbitration, legal fees, printing, research), the estimated amount of supervisor and employee time expended, and a factor for reduced morale. This internal estimate, although not a precise figure, was appropriate for the analysis and had credibility with management.

If internal experts have a strong bias regarding the measure or are not available, external experts are sought. External experts should be selected based on their experience with the unit of measure. Fortunately, many experts are available who work directly with important measures, such as employee attitudes, customer satisfaction, turnover, absenteeism, and grievances. They are often willing to provide estimates of the costs (or value) of these intangibles.

External experts—including consultants, professionals, or suppliers in a particular area—can also be found in obvious places. For example, the costs of accidents can be estimated by the worker's compensation carrier, or the costs of a grievance may be estimated by the labor attorney defending the company in grievance transactions. The process of locating an external expert is similar to the external database search, which is described later.

The credibility of the expert, whether internal or external, is a critical issue if the monetary value on a measure is to be reliable. Foremost among the factors behind an expert's credibility is the individual's experience with the process or measure at hand. Ideally, he or she would work with this measure routinely. Also, the person must be unbiased. Experts should be neutral in connection with the measure's value and should have no personal or professional interest in it.

In addition, the credentials of external experts—published works, degrees, and other honors or awards—are important in validating their expertise. Many of these people are tapped often, and their track records can and should be checked. If their estimate has been validated in more detailed studies and was found to be consistent, this can serve as a confirmation of their qualifications in providing such data.

Using Values from External Databases

For some soft data, it may be appropriate to use cost (or value) estimates based on the research of others. This technique taps external databases that contain studies and research projects focusing on the cost of data items. Fortunately, there are many databases that include cost studies of many data items related to consulting projects, and most are accessible through the Internet. Data are available on the cost of turnover, absenteeism, grievances, accidents, and even customer satisfaction. The difficulty is in finding a database with studies or research appropriate to the current intervention. Ideally, the data should come from a similar setting in the same industry, but that is not always possible. Sometimes data on all industries or organizations are sufficient, perhaps with some adjustments to suit the project at hand.

An example illustrates the use of this process. A consulting project was designed to reduce turnover of branch managers in a financial services company. To complete the evaluation and calculate the ROI, the cost of turnover was needed. To develop the turnover value internally, several costs were identified, including the expense of recruiting, employment processing, orientation, training new managers, lost productivity while training new managers, quality problems, scheduling difficulties, and customer satisfaction problems. Additional costs include the time regional managers spend working with turnover issues and, in some cases, the costs of litigation, severance, and unemployment. Obviously, these expenses are significant. Most consultants do not have time to calculate the cost of turnover, particularly if it is needed for a one-time event, such as evaluating a consulting project. In this example, turnover cost studies in the same industry for the same job group placed the value at about one and a half times the average annual salary of employees. Most turnover cost studies report the cost of turnover as a multiple of annual base salaries. In this example, management decided to be conservative and adjust the value downward to equal the average base salary of branch managers.

An example will illustrate the power of an external database. Employee turnover is very costly and difficult to capture on a precise basis, especially considering the indirect and direct cost of turnover. One excellent database for finding studies on a fully loaded cost of turnover is a database called ERIC, Educational Resources Information Center, which is available at www.eric.ed.gov or any public or university library.

Table 13.3 shows selected turnover cost data captured from dozens of impact studies arranged by job category, ranging from entry-level, nonskilled jobs to

Table 13.3 Turnover Costs Summary

Job Type/Category	Turnover Cost Ranges as a Percentage of Annual Wage/Salary
Entry Level: Hourly, Nonskilled (e.g., Fast-Food Worker)	30–50
Service/Production Workers: Hourly (e.g., Courier)	40–70
Skilled Hourly (e.g., Machinist)	75–100
Clerical/Administrative (e.g., Scheduler)	50–80
Professional (e.g., Sales Representative, Nurse, Accountant)	75–125
Technical (e.g., Computer Technician)	100–150
Engineers (e.g., Chemical Engineer)	200–300
Specialists (e.g., Computer Software Designer)	200–400
Supervisors/Team Leaders (e.g., Section Supervisor)	100–150
Middle Managers (e.g., Department Manager)	125–200

Note: Percentages are rounded to reflect the general range of costs from studies. Costs are fully loaded to include all of the costs of replacing an employee and bringing him or her to the level of productivity and efficiency of the former employee.

middle managers. The cost of turnover is shown as a percentage of base pay of the job group. The ranges are rounded off. The costs include exit cost of departing employees, recruiting, selection, orientation, initial training, wages and salaries while in training, lost productivity, quality problems, customer dissatisfaction, loss of expertise/knowledge, supervisor's time for turnover, and temporary replacement costs. The sources for these studies follow these general categories:

- Industry and trade magazines where the costs have been reported for a specific job within the industry

- Practitioner publications in general management, human resource management, human resources development, and performance improvement
- Academic and research journals where professors, consultants, and researchers publish the results of their work on retention
- Independent studies conducted by organizations and not reported in the literature, but often available on a website or through membership arrangements. These are research-based groups supported by professional and management associations.
- In addition, a few consulting teams develop and report on cost impact studies.

This list is not intended to be all-inclusive but illustrates the availability of current studies and the tremendous cost associated with turnover. Unfortunately, finding a study in a specific field is sometimes difficult and can tax the search skills of even the most adept Internet browser.

Linking with Other Measures

When standard values, records, experts, and external studies are not available, a feasible approach might be developing or finding a relationship between the measure in question and some other measure that may be easily converted to a monetary value. This involves identifying existing relationships already developed, if possible, that show a strong correlation between one measure and another with a standard value.

For example, a project is designed to improve customer satisfaction. The search is on to find a relationship to another measure that can easily be converted to a monetary value. Figure 13.1 shows a relationship between customer satisfaction and customer loyalty. Many organizations are able to show a strong connection between these two measures. Furthermore, there is often a strong correlation between customer loyalty—which may be defined in terms of customer retention or defection—and the actual profit per customer. By connecting these two variables, it becomes possible to estimate the actual value of customer satisfaction by linking it to other measures.

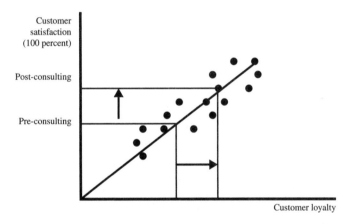

FIGURE 13.1 The Relationship between Customer Satisfaction and Loyalty

In another example, a project is designed to improve employee engagement. A classical relationship is found, as depicted in Figure 13.2, which shows a correlation between job engagement and employee turnover. In a consulting project designed to improve engagement,

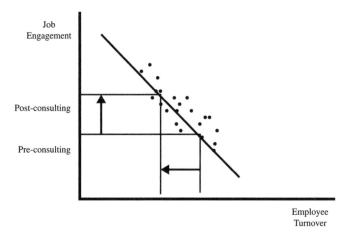

FIGURE 13.2 Relationship between Job Engagement and Employee Turnover

a value is needed for changes in the job engagement index. The predetermined relationship showing the correlation between improvements in job engagement and reductions in turnover can link the changes directly to turnover. Using standard data or external studies, the cost of turnover can easily be developed, as described earlier. Thus, a change in job engagement is converted to a monetary value or, at least, an approximate value. It is not always exact because of the potential for error and other factors, but the estimate is sufficient for converting the data to monetary values.

A word of caution is in order. The key is find the relationships developed. It may take too many resources for the consulting team to do this, especially when there is a need to show the connection between two or more variables.

Using Estimates from Participants

In some cases, participants in the consulting project should estimate the value of soft data improvement. This technique is appropriate when participants are capable of providing estimates of the cost (or value) of the unit of measure improved through consulting solutions. When using this approach, participants should be provided clear instructions, along with examples of the type of information needed. The advantage of this approach is that the individuals closest to the improvement are often capable of providing the most reliable estimates of its value.

An example illustrates this process. A group of supervisors was involved in a major absenteeism reduction project. Successful application of the project should produce a reduction in absenteeism. To calculate the ROI for the project, it was necessary to determine the average value of one absence in the company. As is the case with most organizations, historical records for the cost of absenteeism were not available. Experts were not available, and external studies were sparse for this particular industry. Consequently, supervisors (consulting participants) were asked to estimate the cost of an absence. In a focus group format, each participant was asked to recall the last time an employee in his or her work group was unexpectedly absent and describe what was necessary to adjust to the absence. Because the impact of an absence varies considerably from one employee to another within the same work unit, the group listened to all explanations.

After reflecting on what actions to take when an employee is absent, each supervisor was asked to provide an estimate of the average cost of an absence in the company.

Although some supervisors are reluctant to provide estimates, with prodding and encouragement they usually will. The group's values can be averaged, and the result is the cost of an absence that may be used in evaluating the project. Although this is an estimate, it is probably more accurate than data from external studies, calculations using internal records, or estimates from experts. And, because it comes from supervisors who wrestle with the issue daily, it will carry weight with senior management.

Using Estimates from the Management Team

In some situations, participants in a consulting project may be incapable of placing a value on the improvement. Their work may be so far removed from the output of the process that they cannot reliably provide estimates. In these cases, the team leaders, supervisors, or managers of participants may be capable of providing estimates. Consequently, they may be asked to provide a value for a unit of improvement linked to the intervention.

For example, a consulting project involving customer service representatives was designed to reduce customer complaints. While the project resulted in a reduction of complaints, the value of a single customer complaint was still needed to determine the value of improvement. Although customer service representatives had knowledge of some issues surrounding customer complaints, they could not gauge the full impact, so their managers were asked to provide a value. In other situations, managers are asked to review and approve participants' estimates and confirm, adjust, or discard the values.

In some cases, senior management provides estimates of the value of data. With this approach, senior managers interested in the consulting project are asked to place a value on the improvement based on their perception of its worth. This approach is used when it is difficult to calculate the value or when other sources of estimation are unavailable or unreliable.

When Conversion Should Not Be Pursued: The Intangible Benefits

Consulting project results include both tangible and intangible measures. Intangible measures are the benefits directly linked to a consulting project that cannot or should not be converted to monetary values. These measures are often monitored after the consulting project has been completed. Although they are not converted to monetary values, they are still an important part of the evaluation process. The range of intangible measures is almost limitless, and the following list presents common examples of these measures. This list is not meant to imply that these measures cannot be converted to monetary values. In one study or another, each item has been monetarily quantified. However, in typical impact studies, these variables are considered intangible benefits.

Typical Intangible Measures Linked with Programs

- Job Satisfaction
- Organizational commitment
- Climate
- Engagement
- Employee complaints
- Recruiting image
- Brand awareness
- Stress
- Leadership effectiveness
- Resilience
- Caring
- Career-minded
- Customer satisfaction
- Customer complaints
- Customer response time
- Teamwork
- Cooperation
- Conflict
- Decisiveness
- Communication

Not all measures can or should be converted to monetary values. By design, some are captured and reported as intangibles. Although they may not be perceived as being as valuable as the quantifiable measures, intangibles are critical to the overall evaluation process. In some consulting projects, teamwork, job engagement, commu-nications, image, and customer satisfaction may be more important than monetary measures. Consequently, these measures should be monitored and reported as part of the overall evaluation. In practice, every project, regardless of its nature, scope, and content, will produce intangible measures. The challenge is to identify them effectively and report them appropriately.

Where Do They Come From?

Intangible measures can be taken from different sources and at different times in the process, as depicted in Figure 13.3. They can be uncovered early in the process, during the needs assessment, and planned for collection as part of the overall data collection strategy. For example, one consulting project has several hard data measures linked to the project. An intangible measure, employee satisfaction, is identified and monitored with no plans to convert it to a monetary value. Thus, from the beginning,

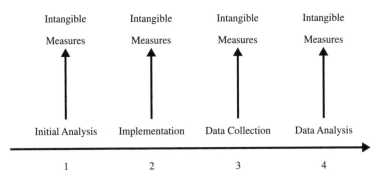

FIGURE 13.3 When Intangibles Are Identified

this measure is destined to be a nonmonetary benefit reported along with the ROI results.

A second opportunity to identify intangible benefits is to discuss the issue with clients or sponsors of the consulting project. Clients can usually identify the intangible measures they expect to be influenced by the project. For example, an environmental consulting project was conducted for a large multinational company and an ROI analysis was planned. Consultants, participants, participants' managers, and senior executives identified potential intangible measures that were perceived to be influenced by the project, including corporate social responsibility image, reputation, brand awareness, and eco-friendly organization.

The third opportunity to identify intangible measures presents itself during data collection. Although the measure is not anticipated in the initial project design, it may surface on a questionnaire, in an interview, or during a focus group. Questions are often asked about other improvements linked to a consulting project, and participants usually provide several intangible measures for which there are no plans to assign a value. For example, in the evaluation of a new technology consulting project, participants (financial advisors) were asked what specifically had improved about their work area and relationships with customers as a result of the project. Participants provided more than a dozen intangible measures that managers attributed to the project.

The fourth opportunity to identify intangible measures is during data analysis and reporting, while attempting to convert data to monetary values. If the conversion loses credibility, the measure should be reported as an intangible benefit. For example, in a project to standardize procedures in a large nongovernmental organization, time savings was identified early in the process as a measure of the consulting success. A conversion to monetary values was attempted, but it lacked the accuracy and credibility needed. Consequently, time savings were reported as an intangible benefit.

How Are Intangibles Analyzed?

For each intangible measure identified there must be some evidence of its connection to the consulting project. However, in many cases no specific analysis is planned beyond tabulating responses. Early attempts to quantify intangible data sometimes result in aborting the entire process; thus, no further data analysis is conducted. In some cases, isolating the effects of the consulting project may be undertaken using one or more of the methods outlined in Chapter 12. This step is necessary when there is a need to know the specific amount of change in the intangible measure linked to the project. Intangible data often reflect improvement. However, neither the precise amount of improvement nor the amount of improvement directly related to consulting is usually identified. Since the value of this data is not included in the ROI calculation, intangible measures are not normally used to justify additional consulting or continuing an existing project. A detailed analysis is not necessary. Intangible benefits are viewed as additional evidence of the consulting success and are presented as supportive qualitative data.

Selecting the Techniques and Finalizing the Values

With so many techniques available to convert data to money, the challenge is selecting one or more strategies appropriate for the situation and available resources. It may be helpful to develop a table or list of values or techniques appropriate for the situation.

Selection Guidelines

The following guidelines may help determine the proper selection and finalize the values.

- **Use the technique appropriate for the type of data.** Some strategies are designed specifically for hard data, while others are more appropriate for soft data. Consequently, the type of data often dictates the strategy. Hard data, while always preferred, are not always available. Soft data are often required and, thus, must be addressed using appropriate strategies.

- **Move from most accurate to least accurate.** The strategies are presented in order of accuracy, beginning with the most accurate. Working down the list, each strategy should be considered for its feasibility in the situation. The strategy with the most accuracy is always recommended if it is feasible in the situation.

- **Consider availability and convenience.** Sometimes the availability of a particular source of data will drive the selection. In other situations, the convenience of a technique may be an important selection factor.

- **When estimates are sought, use the source with the broadest perspective on the issue.** The individual providing the estimate must be knowledgeable of the processes and the issues surrounding the value of the data.

- **Use multiple techniques when feasible.** Sometimes it is helpful to have more than one technique for obtaining values for the data. When multiple sources are feasible, they should be used to serve as comparisons or to provide additional perspectives. The data must be integrated using a convenient decision rule, such as the lowest value (guiding principle #4 from Chapter 6). A conservative approach must be taken.

- **Minimize the amount of time to use a technique.** As with other processes, it is important to keep the time invested in this phase to a minimum so that the total effort for the ROI study does not become excessive. Some techniques can be implemented in less time than others. Too much time on this step may dampen otherwise enthusiastic attitudes about the process.

Apply the Credibility Test

The techniques presented in this chapter assume that each data item collected and linked with consulting projects can be converted to a monetary value. Although estimates can be developed using one or more strategies, the process of converting data to monetary values may lose credibility with the target audience, which may question its use in analysis. Highly subjective data, such as changes in employee attitudes or a reduction in the number of employee conflicts, are difficult to convert. The key question in making this determination is' "Could these results be presented to senior management with confidence?" If the process does not meet this credibility test, the data should not be converted to monetary values but, rather, listed as intangibles. Other data, particularly hard data items, may be used in the ROI calculation, leaving the highly subjective data expressed in intangible terms.

Review the Client's Needs

The accuracy of data and the credibility of the conversion process are important concerns. Consultants sometimes avoid converting data because of these issues. They are more comfortable reporting that an intervention reduced absenteeism from 6 percent to 4 percent, without attempting to place a value on the improvement. They may assume that the client will place a value on the absenteeism reduction. Unfortunately, the target audience may know little about the cost of absenteeism and will usually underestimate the actual value of the improvement. Consequently, there should be some attempt to include this conversion in the ROI analysis.

Consider a Potential Management Adjustment

In organizations where soft data are used and values are derived with imprecise methods, senior management is sometimes offered the opportunity to review and approve the data. Because of the subjective nature of this process, management may factor (reduce) the data so that the final results are more credible. In one example, senior managers at Litton Industries adjusted the value for the benefits derived from implementing self-directed teams.

Consider an Adjustment for the Time Value of Money

Since an intervention investment is made in one time period, and the return is realized at a later time, some organizations adjust consulting benefits to reflect the time value of money using discounted cash-flow techniques. The actual monetary benefits of the consulting project are adjusted for this time period. The amount of adjustment, however, is usually small when compared with the typical benefits of consulting projects.

Final Thoughts

In consulting, money is an important value, but so are intangibles, which are crucial in reflecting the success of a consulting project. Consultants are striving to be more aggressive in defining the monetary benefits of a consulting project. Progressive consultants are no longer satisfied to simply report the business performance results from projects. Instead, they are taking additional steps to convert impact data to monetary values and weigh them against the consulting cost. In doing so, they achieve the ultimate level of evaluation: the return on investment.

Additionally, consultants are concentrating on intangible measures because they add a unique dimension to the consulting report since most, if not all, projects involve intangible variables. This chapter presents several strategies used to convert business results to monetary values, offering an array of techniques to fit any situation and consulting projects as well as exploring some of the most common intangible measures. The next chapter explores costs and ROI.

Tabulating Project Costs and Calculating ROI

When the monetary benefits from Chapter 13 are combined with consulting project costs, the ROI can be developed. This chapter outlines the specific costs that should be captured and economical ways in which they can be developed. One of the important challenges addressed in this chapter is deciding which costs should be tabulated and which should be estimated. In consulting, some costs are hidden and never counted. The conservative philosophy presented here is to account for all costs, direct and indirect. Several checklists and guidelines are also included in the chapter. The different ways to calculate ROI are presented with examples and interpretation.

The Importance of Costs and ROI

Monitoring the consulting costs is an essential step in developing the ROI calculation since it represents the denominator in the ROI formula. It is just as important to focus on costs as benefits. In practice, however, costs are often more easily captured than benefits. Costs should be monitored in an ongoing effort to control expenditures and keep the project within budget. Monitoring cost activities not only reveals the status of expenditures, but also gives visibility to expenditures and influences the entire project team to spend wisely. And of course, monitoring consulting project costs in an ongoing fashion is much easier, more accurate, and more efficient than trying to reconstruct events to capture costs retrospectively.

As discussed in earlier parts of the book, ROI is becoming a critical measure demanded by many stakeholders, including clients and senior executives. It is the ultimate level of evaluation showing the actual payoff of the consulting project, expressed as a ratio or percentage and based on the same formula as the evaluation for other types of investment. Because of its perceived value and familiarity with senior management, it is now becoming a common requirement for consulting projects. When ROI is required or needed, ROI must be developed; otherwise it may be optional unless there is some compelling reason to take the evaluation to this level.

Developing Costs

The first step in monitoring consulting project costs is to define costs and explore critical issues about costs and their use. Several concerns about a cost-monitoring system are examined next. A good understanding about these issues can prevent problems later.

Costs Are Credible

Capturing costs is challenging because the numbers must be reliable and realistic. Although most organizations develop costs with much more ease than the monetary value of the benefits, the true cost of consulting projects is often an elusive figure even in some of the easiest projects. While the direct charges are usually easily developed and are part of the problem, it is more difficult to determine the indirect costs of a project. While the major costs are known up front, the hidden costs to the organization that are linked to the project are not usually detailed. To develop a realistic ROI, costs must be complete and credible. Otherwise, the painstaking difficulty and attention to the monetary benefits will be wasted because of inadequate or inaccurate costs.

Fully Loaded

Today, there is more pressure than ever before to report all consulting costs, or what is referred to as *fully loaded costs*. This takes the cost profile beyond the direct cost of consulting fees and expenses and includes the time that others are involved in the project, including their benefits and other overhead. For years, management has realized that there are many indirect costs of consulting. Now they are asking for an accounting of these costs.

With this approach, all costs that can be identified and linked to a particular consulting assignment are included. The philosophy is simple: For the denominator of the ROI equation, when in doubt, include it (i.e., if it is questionable whether a cost be included, it is recommended that it be included, even if the cost guidelines for the organization do not require it). When an ROI is calculated and reported to target audiences, the process should withstand even the closest scrutiny in terms of its completeness and credibility. The only way to meet this test is to ensure that all costs are included. Of course, from a realistic viewpoint, if the finance department or executive client insists on not using certain costs, then it is best to leave them out.

The Danger of Reporting Costs without the Benefits

It is dangerous to communicate the fully loaded costs of a consulting project without presenting benefits. Unfortunately, many organizations have fallen into this trap for years. Because costs can easily be collected, they are presented to management in ingenious ways, such as cost of the project, cost per employee involved, and cost per unit of product or service. While these may be helpful for efficiency comparisons, it may be troublesome to present them without benefits. When most executives review consulting costs, a logical question comes to mind: What benefit was received from the project? This is a typical management reaction, particularly when costs are perceived to be high.

In one organization, all of the costs associated with a major transformation consulting project were tabulated and reported to the senior management team at their request. The total figure exceeded the perceived value of the project, and the executive group's immediate reaction was to request a summary of (monetary and nonmonetary) benefits derived from the complete trans-formation. The conclusion was that there were few, if any, economic benefits from the project. Consequently, future consulting projects were drastically reduced. While this may be an extreme example, it shows the danger of presenting only half of the equation. Because of this, some organizations have developed a policy of not communicating consulting cost data unless the benefits can be captured and presented along with the costs (or at least have a plan for it). Even if the benefits are subjective and intangible, they are included with the cost data. This helps to maintain a balance between the two issues.

Developing and Using Cost Guidelines

For some consulting groups, it may be helpful to detail the philosophy and policy on costs in guidelines for the consultants or others who monitor and report costs. Cost guidelines detail specifically which cost categories are included with consulting projects and how the data are captured, analyzed, and reported. Standards, unit cost guiding principles, and generally accepted values are included in the guidelines. Cost guidelines can range from a one-page brief to a hundred-page document in a large, complex organization. The simpler approach is better. When fully developed, cost guidelines should be reviewed and approved by the finance and accounting staff. The final document serves as the guiding force in collecting, monitoring, and reporting costs. When the ROI is calculated and reported, costs are included in a summary form or table, and the cost guidelines are referenced in a footnote or attached as an appendix.

Cost Tracking Issues

The most important task is to define which specific costs are included in consulting project costs. This task involves decisions that will be made by consultants and usually approved by the client. If appropriate, the client's finance and accounting staff may need to approve the list.

Sources of Costs

It is sometimes helpful to first consider the sources of consulting cost. There are three major categories of sources as illustrated in Table 14.1. The charges and expenses from the external consulting team will usually represent the latest segment of costs and may be transferred directly to the client for payment. Internal consulting groups with charge-back arrangements would also transfer their expenses. These are often placed in categories under fees and expenses. The second major cost category is those related expenses absorbed by the client organization—both direct and indirect. In many consulting projects, these costs are not identified but nevertheless reflect the cost of the consulting project. The third cost is the cost of payments made to other organizations as a result of the consulting project. These include payments directly to suppliers for equipment and other services prescribed in the consulting project. The finance and accounting records should be able to track and reflect the costs from these three different sources, and

Table 14.1   Sources of Costs

Source of Costs	Cost Reporting Issues
1. Consulting team: Fees/costs and expenses	A Costs are usually accurate.
	B Variable expenses may be underestimated.
2. Client expenses: direct and indirect	A Direct expenses are usually not fully loaded.
	B Indirect expenses are rarely included in costs.
3. Other expenses, such as equipment and services	A Sometimes understated.
	B May lack accountability.

the process presented in this chapter has the capability of tracking these costs as well.

Consulting Process Steps and Cost

Another way to consider consulting costs is in the characteristics of how the project unfolds. Figure 14.1 shows the specific functions of a complex consulting assignment, beginning with the initial analysis and assessment and migrating to the evaluation and the reporting of the results. These are the functional process steps that were outlined earlier in the book and later in this chapter.

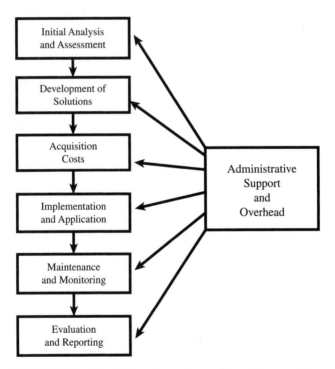

FIGURE 14.1 Costs Based on Consulting Process Steps

They represent the typical flow of work. As a problem is addressed, a solution is developed or acquired and implemented in the organization. There are maintenance and monitoring processes usually put in place that will result in ongoing costs. The entire process is routinely reported to the client and evaluation is undertaken to show the success of the project. There is also a group of costs that will support the process primarily from the client perspective, as these represent important administrative support and overhead costs. To be fair, the consulting project should be analyzed in these different categories, as will be described later in the chapter.

This may be a bit complex for some consulting processes, which are small in scope and involve only a few consultants—in some cases maybe only one consultant. In these situations a more simplistic approach is taken following a simplified process flow described in Figure 14.2, which represents the consulting process reflected in fees, the direct cost of the expenses, and the client cost. These occur as the consultant allocates time, generates costs, and the client has some recurring or ongoing costs in the project. The important point is to

FIGURE 14.2 Simplified Fully Loaded Costs

consider costs as they occur naturally and systematically in the consulting intervention.

Prorated versus Direct Costs

Usually all costs related to a consulting project are captured and allocated to that project. However, some costs are prorated over a longer period of time. Equipment purchases, software development and acquisition, and the construction of facilities are all significant costs with a useful life that may extend beyond a specific consulting project. Consequently, a portion of these costs should be prorated to the consulting project. Using a conservative approach, the expected life of the consulting project is fixed. Some organizations will consider one year of operation for a simple project. Others may consider three to seven years. If there is some question about the specific time period to be used in the proration formula, the finance and accounting staff should be consulted, or appropriate guidelines should be developed and followed.

Employee Benefits Factor

Employee time is valuable, and when time is required on a consulting project, the costs must be fully loaded, representing total compensation. This means that the employee benefits factor should be included. This number is usually well known in the organization and is used in other costing formulas. It represents the cost of all employee benefits expressed as a percentage of payroll. In some organizations this value is as high as 50–60 percent.

In others, it may be as low as 25–30 percent. The average in the United States is about 38 percent.

Major Cost Categories

Table 14.2 shows the recommended cost categories for a fully loaded, conservative approach to estimating costs. In this table, there are four categories. The first is the cost that could be prorated from one consulting project to another. There are not many of these, but sometimes an

Table 14.2 Consulting Cost Categories

	Cost Item	Prorated	Expensed*	Consulting Proposal	Client Expenses
A	Initial analysis and assessment		✓		✓
B	Design development of project	✓	✓	✓	
C	Acquisition costs	✓	✓	✓	
D	Capital expenditures	✓			✓
E	Implementation and application				
	Salaries/benefits for consultant time		✓	✓	
	Salaries/benefits for coordination time		✓		✓
	Salaries/benefits for participant time		✓		✓
	Consulting materials and supplies		✓	✓	
	Travel/lodging/meals		✓	✓	✓
	Use of facilities		✓		✓
F	Maintenance and monitoring		✓	✓	✓
G	Administrative support and overhead	✓			✓
H	Evaluation and reporting		✓	✓	✓

*For external consultants (with various other approaches for internal consultants)

item is purchased or equipment is acquired that will serve other purposes rather than just this consulting project. These would be prorated to other initiatives as well. The second column would be the direct charges to the consulting project, and these are the substantial costs, which are, by far, the largest costs for most projects. The third column is the expense absorbed by the consulting team. These costs would be in the proposal, agreed to at the beginning of the project, and these are traditional costs of consulting. However, they may be less than the other costs. The last column is the cost to the client. For any consulting project, the client does have some involvement and some expense. In some cases, they may be significant, and this table is an attempt to sort this out. The important part is to think of each project as its own, considering all possible costs.

Initial Analysis and Assessment

One of the most underestimated items is the cost of conducting the initial analysis and assessment. In a comprehensive project, this involves data collection, problem solving, assessment, and analysis. In some consulting projects, this cost is near zero because the project is launched without an appropriate assessment of need. However, as more consultants and clients place increased attention on needs assessment and analysis, this item will become a significant cost in the future. All costs associated with the analysis and assessment should be captured to the fullest extent possible. These costs include consulting time, direct expenses, and internal services and supplies used in the analysis.

Design and Development of the Project

One of the more significant items is the cost of designing and developing the solutions for a consulting project of the project itself. These costs include consulting time in both design and development and the purchase of supplies, technology, and other materials directly related to the project or solutions. As with needs assessment costs, design and development costs are usually fully charged to the project. However, in some situations, major expenditures may be prorated over several projects.

Acquisition Costs

In lieu of development costs, many organizations purchase hardware, software, equipment, or facility from other sources to use directly or in a modified format. The acquisition costs for these projects include the purchase price, support materials, and licensing agreements. Many consulting projects have both acquisition costs and design and development costs.

Capital Expenditures

For expenses that represent significant investments, such as in a major remodeling of facilities, the purchase of a building, and purchases of major equipment, the expenses should be recorded as capital expenditures and allocated over a period of time. If the equipment, building, or facility is used for other projects, then the costs should be allocated over the different projects and only a portion captured for a particular assignment.

Application and Implementation Costs

Usually the largest cost segment in a consulting project is associated with delivery and implementation. Six major categories are reviewed below:

1. **Salaries and benefits for consulting time.** This includes all of the charges for consultants assigned directly to the staff. This cost represents specific fees for the time they are involved in the project. These are direct charges only and are usually charges allocated directly from the consulting organization.

2. **Salaries and benefits for coordinators and organizers.** The salaries of those who implement the consulting project should be included. These are usually client staff members. If a coordinator is involved in more than one project, the time should be allocated to the specific project under review. If external facilitators are used, all expenses should be included in the project. The important issue is to capture all of the time of internal employees or external providers who work directly with the consulting project. The benefits factor should be included each time direct labor costs are involved. This factor is a widely accepted value, usually generated by the finance and accounting staff and in the 30–50% range.

3. **Participants' salaries and benefits.** The salaries plus employee benefits of consulting participants represent an expense that should be included. These client costs are significant and can be estimated using average or midpoint values for salaries in typical job classifications.

4. **Consulting materials and supplies.** Consulting materials and supplies, such as field journals, instructions, reference guides, case studies, job aids, and participant workbooks should be included in the delivery costs, along with license fees, user fees, and royalty payments. CD ROMs and supplies are also included in this category.

5. **Travel, lodging, and meals.** Direct travel and lodge costs for consultants, consulting participants, facilitators, coordinators, and managers are included. Entertainment and refreshments during the intervention are included as well.

6. **Use of facilities.** The direct cost for the use of facilities for the consulting project should be included. For external meetings, this is the direct charge from the conference center, hotel, or motel. If the meetings are conducted in-house, the conference room represents a cost for the organization, and the cost should be estimated and included—even if it is uncommon to include facilities costs in other reports. A common-sense approach should be taken with this issue. Charging excessively for space or

charging for small intervals may be unreasonable, underscoring the need for formal guidelines.

Maintenance and Monitoring

Maintenance and monitoring involves routine expenses to maintain and operate a system process, procedure, or solution implemented as part of the consulting project. Although not always present, these represent ongoing expenses to make the new solution continue to work. These may involve staff members, additional expenses, and may be significant for some projects.

Administrative Support and Overhead

Another charge is the cost of support and overhead, the additional costs of consulting not directly related to a particular project. The overhead category represents any consulting cost not considered in the above calculations. Typical items include the cost of administrative support, telecommunication expenses, office expenses, salaries of client managers, and other fixed costs. A rough estimate will usually suffice.

Evaluation and Reporting

Usually the total evaluation cost is included in consulting costs to compute the fully loaded cost. This category includes the cost of developing the evaluation strategy, designing instruments, collecting data, data analysis, report preparation and distribution, and communication of results. Cost categories include time, materials, purchased instruments, or surveys.

Basic ROI Issues

Before presenting the formulas for calculating the ROI, a few basic issues are described and explored. Because of the myths and mysteries about ROI, an adequate understanding of these issues is necessary to address the concerns.

Definitions

The term *return on investment* is occasionally misused, sometimes intentionally. In these situations, a very broad definition for ROI is offered to include any benefit from the consulting project. ROI is thus defined as a vague concept in which even subjective data linked to a project are included in the concept. In this book, the return on investment is more precise and is meant to represent an actual value by comparing consulting costs to monetary benefits. The two most common measures are the benefit/cost ratio and the ROI formula. Both are presented along with other approaches to calculate the return or payback.

For many years, consultants sought to calculate the actual return on investment for a consulting intervention. If the consulting intervention is considered an investment, not an expense, then it is appropriate to place consulting in the same funding process as other investments, such as the investment in equipment and facilities. Although the other investments are quite different, management often views them in the same way. Thus, it is critical to the success of the consulting intervention to develop specific values that reflect the return on the investment.

Annualized Values: A Fundamental Concept

All of the formulas presented in this chapter use annualized values so that the first-year impact of the consulting project investment can be calculated. Using annualized values is becoming a generally accepted practice for developing the ROI in many organizations' projects (guiding principle #9). This approach is a conservative way to develop the ROI, since many short-term consulting projects have added value in the second or third year. For long-term consulting projects, first-year values are inappropriate and longer time frames need to be used. For example, in an ROI analysis of a technology consulting project involving software implementation at a hospital, a three-year time frame was used. However, for most short-term consulting projects that last only a few weeks, first-year values are appropriate.

ROI Measures

When selecting the approach to measure ROI, it is important to communicate to the target audience the formula used and the assumptions made in arriving at the decision to use it. This helps avoid misunderstandings and confusion surrounding how the ROI value was actually developed. Although several approaches are described in this chapter, two stand out as the preferred methods: the benefit/cost ratio and the basic ROI formula. These two approaches are described next, along with brief coverage of the other approaches.

Benefits/Costs Ratio

One of the earliest methods for evaluating a consulting project is the benefits/cost ratio. This method compares the monetary benefits of consulting intervention to the costs, using a ratio. In formula form, the ratio is this:

$$BCR = \frac{\text{Consulting Project Monetary Benefits}}{\text{Consulting Project Costs}}$$

In simple terms, the BCR compares the annual economic benefits of the consulting project to the cost of the consulting project. A BCR of 1 means that the benefits equal the costs. A BCR of 2, usually written as 2:1, indicates that for each dollar spent on consulting, two dollars are returned in benefits.

The following example will illustrate the use of the benefits/cost ratio. A consulting project designed to improve the efficiency of procurement was implemented at a nonprofit. In a follow-up evaluation, direct cost savings and time savings were captured. The first-year payoff for the project was $439,480. The total fully loaded implementation cost was $141,000. Thus, the ratio was:

$$BCR = \$439,480/\$141,500 = 3.1 : 1$$

For every dollar invested in consulting, 3.1 dollars in benefits were returned. There are no standards that constitute an acceptable benefits/cost ratio from the client perspective. A standard should be established within the organization, perhaps even for a specific type of consulting intervention. A 1:1 ratio (breakeven status) is unacceptable for many consulting projects. In others, a 1.25:1 ratio is required, where the benefits are 1.25 times the cost of the consulting.

ROI Formula

Perhaps the most appropriate formula for evaluating consulting investments is net project benefits divided by cost. The ratio is usually expressed as a percentage when the fractional values are multiplied by 100. In formula form, the ROI becomes this:

$$\text{ROI}(\%) = \frac{\text{Net Consulting Project Monetary Benefits}}{\text{Consulting Project Costs}} \times 100$$

Net benefits are consulting benefits minus costs. The ROI value is related to the BCR by a factor of one. For example, a BCR of 2.45 is the same as an ROI value of 145 percent ($1.45 \times 100\%$). This formula is essentially the same as the ROI in other types of investments. When an organization builds a new plant, the ROI is developed by dividing annual earnings by the investment. The annual earnings are comparable to net benefits (annual benefits minus the cost). The investment is comparable to fully loaded consulting project intervention costs, which represent the investment in consulting.

An ROI on a consulting project of 50 percent means that the costs are recovered and an additional 50 percent of the costs are reported as "earnings." A consulting ROI of 150 percent indicates that the costs have been recovered and an additional 1.5 times the costs is captured as "earnings." An example illustrates the ROI calculation. A quality improvement–consulting project was implemented in a small manufacturing company in Italy. The results of the project were impressive. Quality improvements alone yielded an annual value of €243,340. The total fully loaded costs for the project were €79,400. Thus, the return on investment becomes this:

$$\text{ROI}(\%) = \frac{€243,340 - €79,400}{€79,400} \times 100 = 206\%$$

For each euro invested, this company received €2.06 in return after the costs of the consulting project had been recovered. Using the ROI formula essentially places consulting investments on a level playing field with other investments using the same formula and similar concepts. Key management and financial executives who regularly use ROI with other investments easily understand the ROI calculation.

While there are no generally accepted standards, some organizations establish a minimum requirement or objective for the ROI. This objective could be based on the accepted ROI for other investments, which is determined by the cost of capital and other factors. When there is low inflation in a country, this value may be in the range of 10–15 percent. An ROI objective of 25 percent is set by many organizations in North America, Western

Europe, and the Asia Pacific regions. This target value is usually greater than the percentage required for other types of investments. The rationale? The ROI process for consulting is still relatively new and sometimes involves subjective input, including estimations. Because of that, a higher standard is required or suggested, with 25 percent being the desired figure for most organizations. Sometimes it is helpful to let the client set the ROI objective with the caution of keeping it reasonable.

Other ROI Measures

In addition to the traditional ROI formula described earlier, several other measures are occasionally used under the general heading of return on investment. These measures are designed primarily for evaluating other types of projects but sometimes work their way into consulting intervention evaluations.

Payback Period

The payback period is a common method for evaluating capital expenditures. With this approach, the annual cash proceeds (savings) produced by an investment are equated to the original cash outlay required by the investment to arrive at some multiple of cash proceeds equal to the original investment. Measurement is usually in terms of years and months. For example, if the cost savings generated from a consulting project are constant each year, the payback period is determined by dividing the total original cash investment (development costs, expenses, etc.) by the amount of the expected annual or actual savings. The savings represent the net savings after the project expenses are subtracted.

To illustrate this calculation, assume that an initial project cost is $100,000 with a three-year life. The annual net savings from the project is expected to be $40,000. Thus, the payback period becomes this:

$$\text{Payback period} = \frac{\text{Total Investment}}{\text{Annual Savings}} = \frac{\$100,000}{40,000} = 2.5 \text{ years}$$

The project will "pay back" the original investment in 2.5 years. The payback period is simple to use but has the limitation of ignoring the time value of money. It has not enjoyed widespread use in evaluating consulting investments.

Discounted Cash Flow

Discounted cash flow is a method of evaluating investment opportunities in which certain values are assigned to the timing of the proceeds from the investment. The assumption, based on interest rates, is that money earned today is more valuable than money earned a year from now.

There are several ways of using the discounted cash flow concept to evaluate the consulting investment. The most common approach is the net present value of an investment. This approach compares the savings, year by year, with the outflow of cash required by the investment. The expected savings received each year is discounted by selected interest rates. The outflow of cash is also discounted by the same interest rate. If the present value of the savings should exceed the present value of the outlays after discounting at a common interest rate, the investment is usually considered acceptable by management. The discounted cash flow method has the advantage of ranking investments, but it becomes difficult to calculate.

Internal Rate of Return

The internal rate of return (IRR) method determines the interest rate required to make the present value of the cash flow equal to zero. It represents the maximum rate of interest that could be paid if all project funds were borrowed and the organization had to break even on the projects. The IRR considers the time value of money and is unaffected by the scale of the project. It can be used to rank alternatives and can be used to accept/reject decisions when a minimum rate of return is specified. A major weakness of the IRR method is that it assumes all returns are reinvested at the same internal rate of return. This can make an investment alternative with a high rate of return look even better than it really is and a project with a low rate of return look even worse. In practice, the IRR is rarely used to evaluate consulting investments.

Benefits of the ROI Process

Although the benefits of adopting the ROI evaluation may appear to be obvious, several important benefits can be derived from the implementation of ROI for consulting.

Here is a brief summary of the advantages of the ROI process.

Measures the Contribution

With this, methodology consultants will know the contribution of a specific consulting project. The mystery of the success and contribution of consulting is removed. The ROI will show how the benefits, expressed in monetary values, compare to costs. It will determine if the project made a business contribution to the organization and if it was a good investment.

Develops Priorities for Consulting Projects

Sometimes there is a need to identify which projects are adding the most value. Calculating the ROI for different types of consulting projects will determine which projects contribute the most to the organization, allowing priorities to be established for high-impact projects.

Improves the Consulting Process

As with any evaluation system, an ROI study provides a variety of data to make adjustments and changes to the consulting process. Barriers and enablers to success are identified and used as a basis for changes and improvement. Because different data are collected at different levels, from different sources, the opportunity for improvement is significant. This allows for a complete analysis.

Focuses on Results

The ROI methodology is a results-based process that focuses on outcomes from all consulting projects, even for those not targeted for an ROI calculation. The process enhances business alignment in the beginning and requires consultants and support teams to concentrate on measurable objectives (i.e. what the consulting is designed to accomplish). In short, the use of ROI drives results. Expectations are created with stakeholders. Key managers, who make the project successful, are involved in the project.

Builds Management Support for the Consulting Process

The ROI methodology, when applied consistently and comprehensively, can convince the management group that consulting is an investment and not an expense. Managers will see consulting as making a viable contribution to their objectives, thus increasing the respect and support for the process. ROI use is an important step in building a partnership with senior management and increasing the commitment to consulting.

Alters Perceptions of Consulting

Routine ROI impact data, when communicated to a variety of target audiences, will alter perceptions of the value of consulting. Consulting participants, their leaders, and other client staff will view consulting as a legitimate function in the organization, adding value to work units, departments, and divisions. They will have a better understanding of the connection between consulting and results.

Simplifies a Complex Issue

As discussed in Chapter 6, developing the return on investment for consulting appears to be a complex issue. The approach presented in this book is to take a task that seems complex and simplify it by breaking it into small steps, so it is understandable and acceptable to a variety of audiences. When each step is taken separately and issues are addressed for a particular topic, the decisions are made incrementally all the way through the process. This helps reduce the process to a simplified and managable effort.

Final Thoughts

With the monetary benefits from Chapter 13, this chapter focuses on the costs of the consulting project and shows how costs and benefits come together to calculate ROI. This chapter presents the two basic approaches for calculating the return—the ROI formula and the benefit/costs ratio. Each has its own advantages and disadvantages. Costs should be fully loaded in the ROI calculation, but from a practical standpoint, some costs may be optional based on the organization's guidelines and philosophy.

However, because of the scrutiny involved in ROI calculations, it is recommended that all costs be included, even if this goes beyond the requirements of the policy. The reporting or charging back for these project costs to the client would be dependent upon local company policy; however, a true ROI calculation should include all components of this methodology. The next chapter focuses on reporting results.

Reporting Results to Key Audiences

With data in hand, what's next? Should the data be used to modify the project, change the process, show the contribution, justify new projects, gain additional support, or build goodwill? How should the data be presented? The worst course of action is to do nothing. Communicating results is as important as achieving results. Achieving results without communicating them is like planting seeds and failing to fertilize and cultivate the seedlings—the yield simply won't be as great. This chapter provides useful information to help present evaluation data to the various audiences using a variety of reporting methods.

Communicating Results: Key Issues

Communicating results is a critical issue in consulting. While it is important to communicate achieved results to interested stakeholders when the project is complete, it is also important to communicate throughout the consulting project. Routine communication ensures that information is flowing so that adjustments can be made and so that all stakeholders are aware of the success and issues surrounding the consulting project.

Communication Is Necessary to Explain Contributions

The contribution of the consulting project involves the six major types of outcome measures, a confusing issue at best. The varied target audiences will need a thorough explanation of the results. A communication strategy including techniques, media, and the overall process will determine the extent to which they understand the contribution. Communicating results, particularly with business impact and ROI, can quickly become confusing for even the most sophisticated target audiences. Communication must be planned and implemented with the goal of making sure the audiences understand the full contribution.

Communication Is Necessary to Make Improvements

Because information is collected at different points during the process, the communication or feedback to the various groups that will take action is the only way adjustments can be made. Thus, the quality and timeliness of communication become critical issues for making necessary adjustments or improvements. Even after the project is completed, communication is necessary to ensure the target audience fully understands the results achieved and how the results could be enhanced in either future projects or in the current project, if it is still operational. Communication is the key to making these important adjustments at all phases of the project.

Communication Is a Sensitive Issue

Communication is one of those important issues that can cause major problems. Because the results of an intervention can be closely linked to the political issues in an organization, communication can upset some individuals while pleasing others. If certain individuals do not receive the information, or it is delivered inconsistently from one group to another, problems can quickly surface. Not only is it an understanding issue, it is also a fairness, quality, and political correctness issue to make sure communication is properly constructed and effectively delivered to all key individuals who need the information.

A Variety of Target Audiences Need Different Information

Because there are so many potential target audiences for receiving communication on the success of a consulting project, it is important for the communication to be tailored directly to their needs. A varied audience will command varied needs. Planning and effort are necessary to make sure the audience receives all of the information it needs, in the proper format, and at the proper time. A single report for all audiences may not be appropriate. The scope, size, media, and even the actual information of different types and different levels will vary significantly from one group to another, making the target audience the key to determining the appropriate communication process.

Communication Must Be Timely and Consistent

Usually, consulting results should be communicated as soon as they are known. From a practical standpoint, it may be best to delay the communication until a convenient time, such as the publication of the next client newsletter or the next general management meeting.

Questions about timing must be answered. Is the audience ready for the results in light of other things that may have happened? Is it expecting results? When is the best time for having the maximum effect on the audience? Are there circumstances that dictate a change in the timing of the communication? The timing and content of the communication should be consistent with past practices. A special communication at an unusual time during the consulting intervention may provoke suspicion. Also, if a particular group, such as top management, regularly receives communication on consulting outcomes, it should continue receiving communication—even if the results are not positive. If some results are omitted, it might leave the impression that only positive results are reported.

Communication Should Be Unbiased and Modest

It is important to separate fact from fiction and accurate statements from opinions. Various audiences may accept communication from consultants with skepticism, anticipating biased opinions. Boastful statements sometimes turn off recipients, and most of the content is lost. Observable, believable facts carry far more weight than extreme or sensational claims. Although such claims may get audience attention, they often detract from the importance of the results.

Collectively, these reasons make communication a critical issue, although it is often overlooked or underestimated in consulting interventions. This chapter builds on this important issue and shows a variety of techniques for accomplishing all types of communication for various target audiences.

Analyzing the Need for Communication

Because there may be many reasons for communicating results, the rationale should be tailored to the organization on the specific project, the setting, and the unique needs. The results communicate are in three broad categories: projected results, early feedback, and complete results. Here are the eleven most common reasons.

1. **To secure approval for the consulting project and allocate resources of time and money.** The initial communication is in the proposal, where the anticipated results, projected ROI, or value proposition are reported to secure project approval. This communication may not have very much data but rather anticipates what is to come.

2. **To stimulate desire in participants to be involved in the project.** Ideally, consulting participants want to be involved in the consulting project if they have an option. Projected results will pique their interest in the project and the assignment, and show them the importance of the project.

3. **To gain support for the project and its objectives.** Project support is needed from a variety of groups.

Projected results and early feedback is needed to build the necessary support to make the project work successfully.

4. **To prepare participants for the consulting project.** It is necessary for those most directly involved in the project, the consulting participants, to be prepared for assignments, roles, and responsibilities that will be required of them as they bring success to the project.

5. **To secure agreement on the issues, solutions, and resources.** As the project begins, it is important for all those directly involved to have some agreement and understanding of the important elements and requirements surrounding the project. Projected results and early feedback may help with this issue.

6. **To enhance results throughout the project and the quality of future feedback.** Early feedback is designed to show the status of the project and to influence decisions, seek support, or communicate events and expectations to the key stakeholders. In addition, it will enhance both the quality and quantity of information as stakeholders see the feedback cycle in action.

7. **To drive action for improvement in the consulting project.** Early feedback is designed as a process improvement tool to effect changes and improvements as the needs are uncovered and project stakeholders make suggestions. Complete results will be used to make improvements going forward and for similar projects in the future.

8. **To underscore the importance of measuring results**. Some individuals need to understand the importance of measurement and evaluation and see the need for having important data on different measures. Early feedback and complete results will help with this issue.

9. **To show the complete results of consulting and the approach used to measure it**. Perhaps the most important communication is the results: All six types of measures are communicated to the client and other appropriate individuals, so they have a full understanding of the success or shortcomings of the project. Several individuals on the client team and support staff need to understand the techniques used in measuring results. In some cases, these techniques may be transferred internally to use with other projects. In short, these individuals need to understand the soundness and theoretical framework of the process used.

10. **To demonstrate accountability for client expenditures**. For those individuals who fund projects, there is the need for accountability. These ultimate clients must understand the approach of the consultant or the consulting team to show value. This ensures accountability for expenditures on the project.

11. **To build credibility for the consulting team, its techniques, and the finished products**. Communicating a balanced set of data with recommendations will enhance the reputation of the consulting team, based on the approach taken and the results achieved.

If the reasons for communicating results are plentiful because there may be other reasons for communicating results, the list should be tailored to the project and situation.

Planning the Communication

Any successful activity must be carefully planned for it to produce the maximum results. This is certainly true when communicating the results of consulting projects. Planning is necessary to ensure that each audience receives the proper information at the right time and that appropriate actions are taken. Several issues are important in planning the communication of results.

Communication Policy Issues

Client and consulting team policy issues will influence the content medium, duration, and timing of communication. Some policies may exist; others may need to be developed. Internally, the client may have policies for communicating results as part of an overall policy on consulting projects. The consulting team may have a policy as part of the results-based approach to consulting. Seven different areas will need some attention as the policies are developed or followed.

1. **What will actually be communicated?** The types of information communicated throughout the consulting project must be detailed—not only the six

types of data from the ROI process model, but the overall progress with consulting may be a topic of communications as well.

2. **When will the data be communicated?** With communications, timing is critical. If adjustments in the project need to be made, the information should be communicated quickly so that swift actions can be taken.

3. **How will the information be communicated?** Preferences for specific types of communication media may exist. For example, some organizations prefer to have written documents sent out as reports, while others prefer face-to-face meetings, and still others want electronic communications used as much as possible.

4. **Where is the location for communication?** Some prefer that the communication take place close to the consulting project, others prefer client's offices, and still others prefer the consulting team's facilities. The location can be an important issue in terms of convenience and perception.

5. **Who will communicate the information?** Will the consultants, an independent person, or an individual on the client team communicate the information? The person communicating must have credibility so that the information is believable.

6. **Who is the target audience?** Identify specific target audiences that should always receive information and others that will receive information when appropriate.

7. **What specific actions are required or desired?**
   When information is presented, in some cases no action is needed; in others, changes are desired and sometimes even required.

Collectively, these seven issues will frame the policy for communication as a whole. If a policy does not exist, perhaps it should be created.

Planning the Communication for the Entire Project

When a project is approved, the communication plan is usually developed. This details how specific information is developed and communicated to various groups and the expected actions. In addition, this plan details how the overall results will be communicated, the time frames for communication, and the appropriate groups to receive information. The client and consultant need to agree on the extent of detail in the plan. Additional information on this type of planning is provided later.

Communicating the Complete Results

The third type of plan is aimed at presenting the results of an impact study. This occurs when a major consulting project is completed, and the detailed and compete results are known. One of the major decisions is to determine who should receive the results and in what form. This is more specialized than the plan for the entire project because it involves the final study from the project. Table 15.1 shows the communication plan

Table 15.1 Consulting Project Communication Plan

Communication Document	Communication Target(s)	Distribution Method
Complete report with appendices (75 pages)	• Client team • Consulting team • Intact team manager	Distribute and discuss in a special meeting
Executive Summary (8 pages)	• Senior management in the business units • Senior corporate management	Distribute and discuss in routine meeting
General interest overview and summary without the actual ROI calculation (10 pages)	• Participants	Mail with letter
General interest article (1 page)	• All employees	Publish in company publication
Brochure highlighting project, objectives, and specific results	• Other team leaders with an interest in the project • Other clients	Include with other marketing materials

for a consulting project for stress reduction. Teams were experiencing high levels of stress and, through a variety of activities and job changes, stress began to diminish among the teams. The same process was made available to other teams who were experiencing similar symptoms.

Five different communication pieces were developed for different audiences. The complete report was an ROI impact study, a 75-page report that served as the historical document for the project, distributed after a live meeting with the ultimate client. It went to the client, the consulting team, and the managers of each of the teams involved in the studies. An executive summary, a much smaller document, went to some of the higher-level executives. A general interest overview and summary without the ROI calculation went to the participants. A general-interest article was developed for company publications, and a brochure was developed to show the success of the consulting project. That brochure was used in marketing the same process internally to other teams and served as additional marketing material for the consulting team. This detailed plan may be part of the overall plan for the consulting assignment but may be fine-tuned during the actual consulting process.

Selecting the Audience for Communications

The potential target audiences to receive information on consulting results are varied in terms of job levels and responsibilities. Determining which groups will receive a particular communication piece deserves careful thought, as problems can arise when a particular group receives inappropriate information or when another is omitted altogether.

Understanding the Potential Audience

When approaching a particular audience, the following questions should be asked about each potential group:

- Are they interested in the project?
- Do they really want to receive the information?
- Has someone already made a commitment to provide information?

- Is the timing right for this audience?
- Are they familiar with the project?
- How do they prefer to have results communicated?
- Do they know the consultants? The consulting team?
- Are they likely to find the results threatening?
- Which medium will be most convincing to this group?

For each target audience, three actions are needed. First, the consultants should get to know and understand the target audience. Next, the consultants should find out what information is needed and why. Each group will have its own needs relative to the information desired. Some will want detailed information while others want brief information. Rely on the input from others to determine audience needs. Finally, the consultants should try to understand audience bias. Each will have a particular bias or opinion. Some will quickly support the results, whereas others may be against them or be neutral. The staff should be empathetic and try to understand differing views. With this understanding, communications can be tailored to each group. This is especially critical when the potential exists for the audience to react negatively to the results.

Basis for Selecting the Audience

A sound basis for proper audience selection is to analyze the reason for communication, as discussed in an earlier section. Table 15.2 shows common target audiences and the basis for selecting the audience.

Table 15.2   Common Target Audiences

Reason for Communication	Primary Target Audiences
To Secure Approval for the Project	Client, Top Executives
To Gain Support for the Project	Immediate Managers, Team Leaders
To Secure Agreement with the Issues	Participants, Team Leaders
To Build Credibility for the Consulting Team	Top Executives
To Enhance Reinforcement of the Processes	Immediate Managers
To Drive Action for Improvement	Consultants
To Prepare Participants for the Project	Team Leaders
To Enhance Results and Quality of Future Feedback	Participants
To Show the Complete Results of the Project	Client Team
To Underscore the Importance of Measuring Results	Client, Consultants
To Explain Techniques Used to Measure Results	Client, Support Staff
To Create Desire for a Participant to Be Involved	Team Leaders
To Stimulate Interest in the Consulting Firm's Products	Top Executives
To Demonstrate Accountability for Client Expenditures	All Employees
To Market Future Consulting Projects	Prospective Clients

Perhaps the most important audience is the client or client team. This group (or individual) initiates the project, reviews data, selects the consultant, and weighs the final assessment of the effectiveness of the project. Another important target audience is the top management group. This group is responsible for allocating resources to the consulting intervention and needs information to help justify expenditures and gauge the effectiveness of the efforts.

Selected groups of managers (or all managers) are also important target audiences. The support and involvement of management in the consulting process and the department's credibility are important to success. Effectively communicating project results to management can increase both support and credibility.

Communicating with the participants' team leaders or immediate managers is essential. In many cases, they must encourage participants to implement the project. Also, they often support and reinforce the objectives of the project. An appropriate return on investment improves the commitment to consulting and provides credibility for consultants.

Consulting participants need feedback on the overall success of the effort. Some individuals may not have been as successful as others in achieving the desired results. Communicating the results adds additional pressure to effectively implement the project and improve results for the future. For those achieving excellent results, the communication will serve as a reinforcement of the consulting. Communicating results to project participants is often overlooked, with the assumption that since the project is over, they do not need to be informed of its success.

Occasionally, results are communicated to encourage participation in the project. This is especially true for those projects where the participants are involved on a volunteer basis. The potential participants are important targets for communicating results.

The consulting team must receive information about project results. Whether for small projects where consultants receive a project update, or for larger projects where a complete team is involved, those who design, develop, facilitate, and implement the project must be given information on the project's effectiveness. Evaluation information is necessary, so adjustments can be made if the project is not as effective as it could be.

The support staff should receive detailed information about the process to measure results. This group provides support services to the consulting team, usually in the department where the project is conducted.

Company employees and stockholders may be less likely targets. General-interest news stories may increase employee respect. On the one hand, Goodwill and positive attitudes toward the organization may also be byproducts of communicating project results. Stockholders, on the other hand, are more interested in the return on their investment.

While Table 15.2 shows the most common target audiences, there can be others in a particular organization. For instance, management or employees could be subdivided into different departments, divisions, or even subsidiaries of the organization. The number of audiences can be large in a complex organization. At a minimum, four target audiences are always recommended: a senior management group, the consulting participants, the consulting participants' immediate manager or team leader, and the consulting team.

Developing the Information: The Impact Study

The type of formal evaluation report depends on the extent of detailed information presented to the various target audiences. Brief summaries of project results with appropriate charts may be sufficient for some communication efforts. In other situations, particularly with significant consulting projects requiring extensive funding, the amount of detail in the evaluation report is more crucial. A complete and comprehensive impact study report may be necessary. This report can then be used as the basis of information for specific audiences and various media. The report may contain the following sections.

Management/Executive Summary

The management summary is a brief overview of the entire report, explaining the basis for the evaluation and the significant conclusions and recommendations. It is designed for individuals who are too busy to read a detailed report. It is usually written last but appears first in the report for easy access.

Background Information

The background information provides a general description of the project. If applicable, the needs assessment that led to the need for the project is summarized. The project is fully described, including the events that led to the consulting project. Other specific items necessary to provide a full description of the project are included. The extent of detailed information depends on the amount of information the audience needs.

Objectives

The objectives for the project are outlined so that the reader clearly understands desired accomplishments for the project. These are the objectives from which the different types or levels of data were collected.

Evaluation Strategy/Methodology

The evaluation strategy outlines all of the components that make up the total evaluation process. Several components of the results-based approach and the ROI methodology presented in this book are discussed in this section of the report. The specific purposes of evaluation are outlined, and the evaluation design and methodology are explained. The instruments used in data collection are also described and presented as exhibits. Any unusual issues in the evaluation design are discussed. Finally, other useful information related to the design, timing, and execution of the evaluation is included.

Data Collection, Integration, and Analysis

This section explains the methods used to collect data as outlined in earlier chapters of this book. The data collected are usually presented in the report in summary form. A section, showing how the data are integrated along different levels, is usually presented. The methods of data analysis are briefly described.

Reaction

This section details the data collected from key stakeholders, particularly the participants involved in the process, to measure the reaction to the consulting project and a level of satisfaction with various issues and parts of the process. Other input from the client group is also included to show the level of satisfaction.

Learning

This section shows a brief summary of the formal and informal measures of learning. It explains what participants have learned in the terms of new processes, skills, tasks, procedures, and practices needed to make the consulting project successful.

Application and Implementation

This section shows the success with the application of new skills and knowledge. Implementation success is addressed, including progress and/or lack of progress.

Business Impact

This section shows the business impact measures representing the business needs that initially drove the project. This shows the extent to which business performance has changed during the implementation of the consulting project.

Project Costs

Project costs are presented in this section. A summary of the costs by category is included. For example, analysis, development, implementation, and evaluation costs are recommended categories for cost presentation. The assumptions made in developing and classifying costs are discussed in this section of the report.

Return on Investment

This section shows the ROI calculation along with the benefits/cost ratio. It compares the value to what was acceptable (objective) and provides an interpretation of the calculation.

Intangible Measures

This section shows the various intangible measures directly linked to the consulting project. Intangibles are those measures not converted to monetary values and not included in the ROI calculation.

Barriers and Enablers

The various problems and obstacles affecting the success of the project are detailed and presented as barriers to implementation. Also, those factors or influences that had a positive effect on the project are included as enablers. Together, they provide insight into what can inhibit or enhance projects in the future.

Conclusions and Recommendations

This section presents conclusions based on all of the results. If appropriate, brief explanations are presented on how each conclusion was reached. A list of recommendations or changes in the project, if appropriate, is provided with brief explanations for each recommendation. It is important that the conclusions and recommendations are consistent with one another and with the findings described in the previous section.

Collectively, these components make up the major parts of a complete evaluation report, an all-important document that reflects the complete project for those individuals who need much detail. Also, it's an excellent document for knowledge sharing and management for both the client and consultant.

Organization of the Report

Table 15.3 shows the contents from a typical evaluation report for an ROI study on consulting. This specific study was conducted for a large financial institution and involved an ROI analysis on a consulting project for commercial banking. The typical report provides background information, explains the processes used, and most important, presents the results.

While this report is an effective, professional way to present ROI data, several cautions need to be followed. Since this document reports the success of a consulting project involving a group of employees, complete credit for the success must go to the participants and their immediate leaders. Their performance generated the success. Another important caution is to avoid boasting about results. Although the ROI methodology is accurate and

Table 15.3   Format of an Impact/ROI Study Report

- General Information
  - Background
  - Objectives of the Study
- Methodology for Impact Study
  - Levels of Evaluation
  - ROI Process
  - Collecting Data
  - Isolating the Effects of Consulting
  - Converting Data to Monetary Values
- Data Issues
- Results: General Information
  - Response Profile
  - Success with Objectives
- Results: Reaction and Satisfaction
  - Data Sources
  - Data Summary
  - Key Issues
- Results: Learning
  - Data Sources
  - Data Summary
  - Key Issues
- Results: Application and Implementation
  - Data Sources
  - Data Summary
  - Key Issues
- Results: Business Impact
  - General Comments
  - Linkage with Business Measures
  - Key Issues
- Data Issues
- Results: ROI and Its Meaning
- Results: Intangible Measures

Table 15.3 (*Continued*)

- Barriers and Enablers
  - Barriers
  - Enablers
- Conclusions and Recommendations
  - Conclusions
  - Recommendations
- Exhibits

---

credible, all executives do not necessarily understand it. Huge claims of success can quickly turn off an audience and interfere with the delivery of the desired message.

A final caution concerns the structure of the report. The methodology should be clearly explained, along with assumptions made in the analysis. The reader should readily see how the values were developed and how the specific steps were followed to make the process more conservative, credible, and accurate. Detailed statistical analyses should be placed in the appendix.

Selecting the Communication Media

There are many options available to communicate project results. In addition to the impact study report, the most frequently used media are meetings, interim and progress reports, routine communication tools, electronic media, brochures and pamphlets, and case studies.

Meetings

Meetings are fertile opportunities for communicating project results, if used properly. All organizations have a variety of meetings and, in each, the proper context and consulting results are an important part. A few examples illustrate the variety of meetings.

Regular meetings with the first-level management group are quite common. These meetings can be an excellent forum for discussing the results achieved in a consulting project when the project relates to the group's activities. A discussion of results can be integrated into the regular meeting format.

A few organizations have initiated a periodic meeting for all members of management, in which the CEO reviews progress and discusses plans for the coming year. A few highlights of consulting project results can be integrated into the CEO's speech, showing top executive interest, commitment, and support. Consulting results are mentioned along with operating profit, new facilities and equipment, new company acquisitions, and next year's sales forecast.

Whenever a management group convenes in significant numbers, evaluate the appropriateness of communicating consulting project results.

Interim and Progress Reports

Although usually limited to large projects, a highly visible way to communicate results is through interim and routine memos and reports. Published or disseminated through e-mail on a periodic basis, they usually have several purposes:

- To inform management about the status of the project
- To communicate the interim results achieved in the consulting project
- To activate needed changes and improvements

A more subtle reason for the report is to gain additional support and commitment from the management group and to keep the project intact. This report is produced by the consulting staff and distributed to a select group of managers in the organization. Format and scope vary considerably. Common topics are as follows:

- A schedule of planned steps/activities should be an integral part of this report.
- A brief summary of reaction evaluations may be appropriate to report initial success.
- The results achieved from the consulting project should be presented in an easily understood format.
- A section that features a key support team member can be very useful, highlighting the member's efforts and involvement in consulting.
- It is important to communicate changes in people involved in planning, developing, implementing, or evaluating the project.
- A section that highlights a member of the client team can focus additional attention on results.

While the list may not be suited for every report, it represents topics that should be presented to the management group. When produced in a professional manner, the report can improve management support and commitment to the effort.

Routine Communication Tools

To reach a wide audience, consultants can use in-house publications. Whether a newsletter, magazine, newspaper, or electronic files, these types of media usually reach all employees. The information can be quite effective if communicated appropriately. The scope should be limited to general interest articles, announcements, and interviews.

Results communicated through these types of media must be significant enough to arouse general interest. For example, a story with the headline "Safety project helps produce 1 million hours without a lost-time accident" will catch the attention of many people because they may have participated in the project and can appreciate the significance of the results. Reports on the accomplishments of a group of participants may not create interest unless the audience relates to the accomplishments.

For many consulting projects, results are achieved weeks or even months after the project is completed. Participants need reinforcement from many sources. If results are communicated to a general audience, including the participant's subordinates or peers, there is additional pressure to continue the project or pursue similar ones in the future.

Stories about participants involved in consulting projects and the results they achieve create a favorable image. Employees are made aware that the company is investing time and money to improve performance and prepare for the future. This type of story provides information about projects that employees otherwise may not have known about and sometimes creates a desire to participate if given the opportunity.

General audience communication can bring recognition to project participants, particularly those who excel in some aspect of the project. When participants deliver unusual performance, public recognition can enhance their self-esteem. Many human-interest stories can come out of consulting projects. A rigorous project with difficult requirements can provide the basis for an interesting story on participants who implement the project.

In one organization, the editor of the company newsletter participated in a very demanding consulting project and wrote a stimulating article about what it was like to be a participant. The article gave the reader a tour of the entire project and its effectiveness in terms of the results achieved. It was an interesting and effective way to communicate about a challenging activity.

The benefits are many and the opportunities endless for consultants to utilize in-house publications and company-wide intranets to let others know about the success of projects.

E-mail and Electronic Media

Internal and external web pages on the Internet, company-wide intranets, and e-mail are excellent vehicles for releasing results, promoting ideas, and informing employees and other target groups of consulting results.

E-mail, in particular, provides a virtually instantaneous means by which to communicate and solicit response from large numbers of people.

Project Brochures and Pamphlets

A brochure might be appropriate for projects conducted on a continuing basis, where participants have produced excellent results. It should be attractive and present a complete description of the project, with a major section devoted to results obtained with previous participants, if available. Measurable results and reactions from participants, or even direct quotes from individuals, could add spice to an otherwise dull brochure.

Case Studies

Case studies represent an effective way to communicate the results of a consulting project. Consequently, it is recommended that a few projects be developed in a case format. A typical case study describes the situation, provides appropriate background information (including the events that led to the intervention), presents the techniques and strategies used to develop the study, and highlights the key issues in the project. Case studies tell an interesting story of how the evaluation was developed and the problems and concerns identified along the way.

Case studies have many useful applications in an organization. First, they can be used in group discussions, where interested individuals can react to the material, offer different perspectives, and draw conclusions about approaches or techniques. Second, the case study can serve as a self-teaching guide for individuals trying to understand how evaluations are developed and utilized in the organization. Finally, case studies provide appropriate recognition for those involved in the actual case. More important, they recognize the participants who achieved the results, as well as the managers who allowed the participants to be involved in the project. The case study format has become one of the most effective ways to learn about consulting evaluation.

Communicating the Information

Perhaps the greatest challenge of communication is the actual delivery of the message. This can be accomplished in a variety of ways and settings based on the actual target audience and the media selected for the message. Three particular approaches deserve additional coverage. The first approach is providing insight into how to provide feedback throughout the consulting project to make sure information flows, so changes can be made. The second is presenting an impact study to a senior management team. This may be one of the most challenging tasks for the consultant. The third is communicating regularly and routinely with the executive management group. Each of these three approaches is explored in more detail.

Providing Early Feedback

One of the most important reasons for collecting reaction, satisfaction, and learning data is to provide feedback, so adjustments or changes can be made throughout the consulting project. In most consulting projects, data are routinely collected and quickly communicated to a variety of groups.

As the plan shows, data are collected during the project at four specific time intervals and communicated to at least four audiences—and sometimes six. Some of these feedback sessions result in identifying specific actions that need to be taken. This process becomes comprehensive and needs to be managed in a very proactive way. The following steps are recommended for providing feedback and managing the feedback process. Many of the steps and issues follow the recommendations of Peter Block in his successful consulting book *Flawless Consulting*.[1]

1. **Communicate quickly.** Whether it is good news or bad news, it is important to let individuals involved in the project have the information as soon as possible. The recommended time for providing feedback is usually a matter of days and certainly no longer than a week or two after the results are known.

2. **Simplify the data.** Condense data into a very understandable, concise presentation. This is not the format for detailed explanations and analysis.

3. **Examine the role of the consultants and the client in the feedback situation.** Sometimes the consultant is the judge, and sometimes the consultant is the jury, prosecutor, defendant, or witness. On the other hand, sometimes the client is the judge, jury, prosecutor, defendant, or witness. It is important to examine the respective roles in terms

of reactions to the data and the actions that need to be taken.

4. **Use negative data in a constructive way.** Some of the data will show that things are not going so well, and the fault may rest with the consulting team or the client. In either case, the story basically changes from "Let's look at the success we've achieved" to "Now we know which areas to change."

5. **Use positive data in a cautious way.** Positive data can be misleading and if they are communicated too enthusiastically, they may create expectations beyond what may materialize later. Positive data should be presented in a cautious way—almost in a discounting mode.

6. **Choose the language of the meeting and communication very carefully.** Use language that is descriptive, focused, specific, short, and simple. Avoid language that is too judgmental, macro, stereotypical, lengthy, or complex.

7. **Ask the client for reactions to the data.** After all, the client is the number one customer, and the client's reaction is critical since what is most important is that the client is pleased with the project.

8. **Ask the client for recommendations.** The client may have some very good recommendations of what needs to be changed to keep a project on track or put it back on track if it derails.

9. **Use support and confrontation carefully.** These two issues are not mutually exclusive. There may be

times when support and confrontation are needed for the same group. The client may need support and yet be confronted for lack of improvement or sponsorship. The consulting group may be confronted on the problem areas that are developed but may need support as well.

10. **React and act on the data**. Weigh the different alternatives and possibilities to arrive at the adjustments and changes that will be necessary.

11. **Secure agreement from all key stakeholders.** This is essential to make sure everyone is willing to make adjustments and changes that seem necessary.

12. **Keep the feedback process short**. Don't let it become bogged down in long, drawn-out meetings or lengthy documents. If this occurs, stakeholders will avoid the process instead of being willing to participate in the future.

Following these 12 steps will help move the project forward and provide important feedback, often ensuring that adjustments are supported and made.

Presenting Impact Study Data to Senior Management

Perhaps one of the most challenging and stressful communications is presenting an impact study to the senior management team, which also serves as the ultimate client in a consulting project (they fund the project). The challenge is convincing this highly skeptical and critical group that outstanding results have been achieved (assuming they have), in a very reasonable time frame, addressing the salient points, and making sure the managers understand the process. Two particular issues can create challenges. First, if the results are very impressive, it may be difficult to make the managers believe the data. On the other hand, if the data are negative, it will be a challenge to make sure managers don't overreact to the negative results and look for someone to blame. Following are guidelines that can help make sure this process is planned and executed properly:

- Plan a face-to-face meeting with senior team members for the first one or two major impact studies. If they are unfamiliar with the complete consulting ROI process, a face-to-face meeting is necessary to make sure they understand the process. The good news is that they will probably attend the meeting because they have not seen ROI data developed for this type of project. The bad news is that it takes a lot of time, usually one hour for this presentation.

- After a group has had a face-to-face meeting with a couple of presentations, an executive summary may suffice. At this point they understand the process, so a shortened version may be appropriate.

- After the target audience is familiar with the process, a brief version may be necessary, which will involve a one- to two-page summary with charts and graphs showing all six types of measures.

- When making the initial presentation, the results should not be distributed beforehand or even during the session but saved until the end of the session.

This will allow enough time to present the process and react to it before the target audience sees the actual ROI number.

- Present the process step by step, showing how the data were collected, when they were collected, who provided the data, how the data were isolated from other influences, and how they were converted to monetary values. The various assumptions, adjustments, and conservative approaches are presented along with the total cost of the project. The costs are fully loaded so that the target audience will begin to buy into the process of developing the actual ROI.

- When the data are actually presented, the results are presented step by step, starting with Level 1, moving through Level 5, and ending with the intangibles. This allows the audience to see the reaction and satisfaction, learning, application and implementation, business impact, and ROI. After some discussion on the meaning of the ROI, the intangible measures are presented. Allocate time to each level as appropriate for the audience. This helps overcome the potentially negative reactions to a very positive or negative ROI.

- Show the consequences of additional accuracy if it is an issue. The tradeoff for more accuracy and validity often means more expense. Address this issue whenever necessary, agreeing to add more data if required.

- Collect concerns, reactions, and issues for the process and make adjustments accordingly for the next presentation.

Purpose of the Meeting	Meeting Ground Rules
• Create awareness and understanding of ROI. • Build support for the ROI methodology. • Communicate results of study. • Drive improvement from results. • Cultivate effective use of the ROI methodology.	• Do not distribute the impact study until the end of the meeting. • Be precise and to the point. • Avoid jargon and unfamiliar terms. • Spend less time on the lower levels of evaluation data. • Present the data with a strategy in mind.

Presentation Sequence

1. Describe the program and explain why it is being evaluated.
2. Present the methodology process.
3. Present the input and indicators.
4. Present the reaction and learning data.
5. Present the application data.
6. List the barriers and enablers to success.
7. Address the business impact.
8. Show the costs.
9. Present the ROI.
10. Show the intangibles.
11. Review the credibility of the data.
12. Summarize the conclusions.
13. Present the recommendations.

FIGURE 15.1 Presenting the Impact Study to Executive Sponsors

Collectively, these steps will help prepare for and present one of the most critical meetings in the consulting ROI process. Figure 15.1 shows the details of this meeting.

Analyzing Reactions to Communications

The best indicator of how effectively the results of a consulting project have been communicated is the level of commitment and support from the management group. The allocation of requested resources and strong commitment from top management are tangible evidence of management's perception of the results. In addition to this macro-level reaction, there are a few techniques consultants can use to measure the effectiveness of their communication efforts.

Whenever results are communicated, the reaction of the target audiences can be monitored. These reactions may include nonverbal gestures, oral remarks, written comments, or indirect actions that reveal how the communication was received. Usually, when results are presented in a meeting, the presenter will have some indication of how the results were received by the group. The interest and attitudes of the audience can usually be quickly evaluated.

During the presentation, questions may be asked or, in some cases, the information is challenged. In addition, a tabulation of these challenges and questions can be useful in evaluating the type of information to include in future communications. Positive comments about the results are certainly desired and, when they are made—formally or informally—they should also be noted and tabulated.

Consulting staff meetings are an excellent arena for discussing the reaction to communicating results. Comments can come from many sources depending on the particular target audiences. Input from different members of the staff can be summarized to help judge the overall effectiveness.

When major project results are communicated, a feedback questionnaire may be used for an entire audience or a sample of the audience. The purpose of this questionnaire is to determine the extent to which the audience understood and/or believed the information presented. This is practical only when the effectiveness of the communication has a significant impact on the future actions of the consulting team.

Another approach is to survey the management group to determine its perceptions of the results. Specific questions should be asked about results. What does the management group know about the results? How believable are the results? What additional information is desired about the project? This type of survey can help provide guidance in communicating results.

The purpose of analyzing reactions is to make adjustments in the communication process—if adjustments are necessary. Although the reactions may involve intuitive assessments, a more sophisticated analysis will provide more accurate information to make these adjustments. The net result should be a more effective communication process.

Final Thoughts

This chapter presents the final step in the results-based approach to consulting accountability. Communicating results is a crucial step in the overall evaluation process. If this step is not taken seriously, the full impact of the results will not be realized. The chapter begins with general principles for communicating project results.

The various target audiences are discussed and, because of its importance, emphasis is placed on the executive group. A suggested format for a detailed evaluation report is also provided. Much of the remainder of the chapter includes a detailed presentation of the most commonly used media for communicating project results, including meetings, client publications, and electronic media. Numerous examples illustrate these concepts.

Call to Action

So there you have it, an entire book focusing on maximizing the value of consulting. To make it work for you, you have to take action. It's up to you. If you do nothing, consulting may lose support, influence, and funding, or it may not realize the full value of your consulting efforts—both at the overall organizational and project levels. Doing nothing is not an option. Waiting until the client forces this level of accountability can be disastrous. Waiting for the request for an accounting means that you are on a client or executive's time line, you're defensive, and you're on their agenda—not a good place to be. The challenge is to take the correct actions and, yes, you probably won't get there without a plan.

At the Organizational Level

As described in the initial chapters of this book, developing an effective consulting capability within both private and public sector organizations can be a major factor in improving their performance. To that end, this book has provided specific insights to help you shape a path forward, some of which may have already been taken, including the following five steps.

Step 1. Make the business case to either initiate or further develop the internal consulting capability in an organization and effectively integrate external consulting support to maximize impact on the enterprise (as outlined in Chapter 1).

Step 2. Organize the consulting function to deliver value, including business planning, project management, and business development (as summarized in Chapter 2).

Step 3. Manage the consulting practice to be more effective, including competency development and engaging clients (as indicated in Chapter 3).

Step 4. Implement guidelines for controlling costs and enhancing value, such as thoughtful budgeting and building supplier partnerships (as detailed in Chapter 4).

Step 5. Develop a comprehensive performance measurement and management system and demonstrate value (as discussed in Chapter 5).

At the Individual Project Level

For individual projects, here is a suggested nine-step action plan:

Step 1. Address the alignment issue. Review Chapter 8 and implement it. The steps outlined in the chapter will ensure that your projects are connected to the business and that your consulting content and process is the right solution for the problem or opportunity. This is critical to drive business value.

Step 2. Set objectives at the application and impact level. This is so fundamental, but often is missing. After alignment is achieved, it is easy to develop the objectives as indicated in Chapter 7. The objectives have value beyond the evaluation at those two levels. They place the proper focus on results for all individuals involved in the project. It keeps the business goal foremost in the minds of the entire team.

Step 3. Decide which projects would be the best candidates for Impact (Level 4) and ROI (Level 5) evaluation. Projects selected for evaluation at these levels are those that are very important to executives, connected to strategy, and very expensive.

Step 4. Select one project for Level 4 (and maybe even Level 5) evaluation. With that decision use the planning guidelines in Chapter 9.

Step 5. Using the data collection chapters (Chapters 10 and 11), decide which is the best method to use and make it part of the data collection plan. Decide on how the effects of the consulting project will be separated from other influences, and how the data will be converted to money. Also, indicate which costs will be included. These are all on the ROI analysis plan.

Step 6. Execute the plan. Collect the data along the way, according to plan, and conduct the analysis. It may be helpful to review some case studies to see some examples of how this is accomplished. As the process is followed and you complete the project, be sure to follow the guiding principles.

Step 7. When the project is complete, develop a full report explaining what you have accomplished, how the process worked, and the results at different levels, all the way through to ROI and including intangibles.

Step 8. Conduct a briefing with key clients and use this data to either drive improvement for this project or use it as learning for future projects. Remember, if the project is not successful, there probably is something the client did not do properly. This will usually be obvious with the data in hand.

Step 9. Repeat the process with another project. Continue until you have mastered this skill and built more results into your routine for your consulting projects.

Building Capability

Some individuals may be interested in developing capability. There is a special certification designed for this process, Certified Performance Consultant (CPC). This process, based on the material in this book (and others), focuses directly on ensuring your consulting process delivers the value needed at all levels, the results are credible, and are used to drive more projects in the future. For more information on this certification and process or to view the upcoming schedule, contact ROI Institute (www.roiinstitute.net) or the Association of Internal Management Consultants (www.aimc.org).

Notes

Acknowledgments

1. Trotter, *Internal Consulting Excellence*.

Preface

1. William D. Trotter, *Internal Consulting Excellence* (Marco Island, FL: AIMC Press, 2013).
2. Jack Phillips, *How to Build a Successful Consulting Practice* (New York: McGraw-Hill, 2006).
3. Trotter, *Internal Consulting Excellence*.

Chapter 1

1. William D. Trotter, *Internal Consulting Excellence* (Marco Island, FL: AIMC Press, 2013).
2. Ibid.

Chapter 2

1. Paul Mooney, *The Effective Consultant: How to Develop the High Performance Organisation* (Dublin: Oak Tree Press, 1999).

2. William D. Trotter, *Internal Consulting Excellence* (Marco Island, FL: AIMC Press, 2013).

3. Jack Phillips, *How to Build a Successful Consulting Practice* (New York: McGraw-Hill, 2006).

Chapter 3

1. William D. Trotter, *Internal Consulting Excellence* (Marco Island, FL: AIMC Press, 2013).

Chapter 4

1. William D. Trotter, *Internal Consulting Excellence* (Marco Island, FL: AIMC Press, 2013).

2. Jack J. Phillips and Patricia P. Phillips, *The Consultant's Guide to Results-Driven Business Proposals: How to Write Proposals That Forecast Impact and ROI* (New York: McGraw-Hill, 2010).

3. Jack Phillips and Patricia P. Phillips, *The Consultant's Scorecard: Tracking ROI and Bottom-Line Impact of Consulting Projects* (New York: McGraw-Hill, 2011).

4. Trotter, *Internal Consulting Excellence.*

5. Phillips and Phillips, *The Consultant's Guide to Results-Driven Business Proposals.*

Chapter 5

1. Robert S. Kaplan and David P. Norton, *The Balanced Scorecard: Translating Strategy into Action* (Boston: Harvard Business School Press, 1996).

2. William D. Trotter, *Internal Consulting Excellence* (Marco Island, FL: AIMC Press, 2013).

3. Jack J. Phillips and Patti P. Phillips, *The Consultant's Guide to Results-Driven Business Proposals: How to Write Proposals That Forecast Impact and ROI* (New York: McGraw-Hill, 2010).

Chapter 6

1. Kennedy Consulting Research and Advisory, "Consulting Research Portfolio." www.kennedyinfo.com/consulting/research/consulting-industry-research.

Chapter 12

1. Patricia P. Phillips and Jack J. Phillips, *Making Human Capital Analytics Work: Measuring the ROI of Human Capital Processes and Outcomes* (New York: McGraw-Hill, 2015).

2. James Surowiecki, *The Wisdom of Crowds* (New York: Anchor Books, 2004).

Chapter 13

1. Paul W. Farris, Neil T. Bendle, Phillip E. Pfeifer, and David J. Ribstein, *Marketing Metrics: 50+ Metrics Every Executive Should Master* (Upper Saddle River, NJ: Wharton School Publishing, 2006).

Chapter 15

1. Peter Block, *Flawless Consulting*, 3rd ed. (San Francisco: Pfeiffer, 2011).

Index

Page references followed by *fig* indicate an illustrated figure; followed by *t* indicate a table.